PATHWAYS TO
Thinking
SCHOOLS

PATHWAYS TO
Thinking
SCHOOLS

DAVID N. HYERLE | LARRY ALPER

EDITORS

FOREWORD BY YVETTE JACKSON

CORWIN
A SAGE Company

CORWIN
A SAGE Company

FOR INFORMATION:

Corwin
A SAGE Company
2455 Teller Road
Thousand Oaks, California 91320
(800) 233-9936
www.corwin.com

SAGE Publications Ltd.
1 Oliver's Yard
55 City Road
London EC1Y 1SP
United Kingdom

SAGE Publications India Pvt. Ltd.
B 1/I 1 Mohan Cooperative Industrial Area
Mathura Road, New Delhi 110 044
India

SAGE Publications Asia-Pacific Pte. Ltd.
3 Church Street
#10-04 Samsung Hub
Singapore 049483

Acquisitions Editor: Dan Alpert
Associate Editor: Kimberly Greenberg
Editorial Assistant: Cesar Reyes
Project Editor: Veronica Stapleton Hooper
Copy Editor: Deanna Noga
Typesetter: C&M Digitals (P) Ltd.
Proofreader: Annie Lubinsky
Indexer: Judy Hunt
Cover Designer: Gail Buschman
Marketing Manager: Lisa Lysne

Printed in the United States of America.

ISBN 9781412998697

This book is printed on acid-free paper.

SUSTAINABLE FORESTRY INITIATIVE
Certified Chain of Custody
Promoting Sustainable Forestry
www.sfiprogram.org
SFI-01268
SFI label applies to text stock

14 15 16 17 18 10 9 8 7 6 5 4 3 2 1

Contents

List of Figures

Foreword

Countries around the world are implementing educational standards they hope will guide their schools to produce the high performers needed to guarantee their vision of their ability to globally compete for the highest levels of productivity. Many school systems have shown that creation of programs to address the standards have resulted in increasing academic achievement scores for many; however, not only does a gap continue to exist between students labeled as achievers and those labeled "low achievers," but data from new assessments that focus on higher levels of thinking illustrate that the number of students on the lower end of the bell curve is increasing (Hernández & Gebeloff, 2013).

The most unfortunate collateral damage of the increasing pool of students labeled "low achievers" on these assessments is the interpretation of these results as indicative of these students' incapacity for high levels of thinking. The underestimated (or totally ignored) reality proven by the eminent psychologist Reuven Feuerstein (and substantiated by neuroscience) is that these students are *not* incapable of high levels of thinking and performance. Instead, it is the mental processes and "habits of mind" requisite for high levels of thinking and intellectual performances that are underdeveloped.

So what is a critical root cause of this problem and what is needed to ensure the development of thinking so the vast capacity of all students can be elicited, nurtured and guided for high performance?

I have dedicated my practice to these questions and proffer one significant recognition: The focus of education on academic scores and/or global competition has steered us away from the original purpose of education upon which the word is derived; that is, to draw out and encourage high levels of thinking for activating the vast potential of an individual. This purpose of education is the catalyst for a new vision for schools, a vision that transcends the narrow focus of instruction on high test scores indicative of school achievement (where a large portion of students continue to underperform), to a vision of stimulating high levels of students' thinking, enabling all students to the recognize and act on the vast capacity of their abilities for self-actualization and personal contribution to the world.

Thinking Schools presents us with explorations into schools where such a vision is a reality. In these schools, instruction becomes instead mediation of learning designed to address the intention that every student be a deliberate, reflective, critical, and creative thinker for personal achievement. With this as the intention, explicit attention is on developing thinking to critically analyze, engage in comparative behaviors, reflect, question, critique, evaluate, forecast, and innovate. This laser focus is delivered through cognitive tools that create the neural patterns that make learning more efficient and effective and practices that cultivate habits of mind that animate the self-determination needed for self-directed learning and high intellectual performance. The empirical evidence and neuroscience that substantiate these cognitive tools and practices are described along with guidance and insights from these Thinking Schools educators so this vision can be facilitated in every school for all students.

Paolo Freire once said the question we have to address is this: When we emancipate all students to be deliberate, reflective thinkers who question, critique, and want to take action, will educators, systems, and governments be ready for the power that will be unleashed? The answer to that question is clear: We are at a seminal point in the evolution of a global community. The paradigm of a global community negates competition among countries. In a global community, countries recognize reciprocal interests and the need and benefit of interdependence. Therefore, this new paradigm of a global community calls for Thinking Schools internationally, schools where students will be equipped to think dialectically, reflecting on the ramifications and possibilities of interdependence; schools where students will be cultivated to transform themselves to be self-actualized and make contributions to transform the world so this millennium is the one in which we achieve the global success of cooperation, high productivity globally, and innovation of efficient and effective use of our most promising and productive resource: our mind and the thinking it generates.

Yvette Jackson, Ed.D.

Author of The Pedagogy of Confidence

Chief Executive Officer of the National Urban Alliance

REFERENCE ■

Hernández, J. C., & Gebeloff, R. (2013, August 7). Test scores sink as New York adopts tougher benchmarks. *New York Times,* http://www.nytimes.com/2013/08/08/nyregion/under-new-standards-students-see-sharp-decline-in-test-scores.html?ref=robertgebeloff&_r=0

Preface

The title of this book represents a declaration of what many people inside and outside of education from around the world now believe should be the central focus of education. Presented within these chapters is documentation showing how the *explicit* focus on thinking may become a foundation for every school, from many different vantage points and from several different countries. In one sense, our schools need to "recharter" their vision of schooling. We know that our work as educators is no longer simply about delivering more content knowledge, better technology, or more complex testing regimens. We need to explicitly develop our students' thinking abilities so that they deepen content knowledge, build concepts, and filter the abundance of information flowing through virtual networks. The ultimate purpose of the Thinking Schools approach is to enable every student to become drivers of their own thinking and learning. We believe that for this to happen we must structure the school environment as a whole—not just in isolated classrooms and virtual mediums—so that students learn to engage interdependently and empathically with others, to become more reflective within their own, unique, ever-developing networking minds. We also believe, with our evolving understandings about the human brain, that every child needs to become more aware of—and take care of—the complex brain that hums unconsciously behind every thought, feeling, and action.

The ideal of schools teaching students *for, of, and about thinking* has been voiced, practiced in isolation, researched, and envisioned by many educators for decades, reaching back past the thinking skills movement in the United States and internationally during the late 20th century to John Dewey and, if you wish, back to Socrates. The educational community at large knows so much about language and cognitive development, facility with critical thinking, the independent and collaborative dimensions of learning, multiple and emotional intelligences, the neurosciences, and more recently, a bit about technologies and social media. Yet there have been few offerings of systematic, deep, and adaptable approaches supporting whole schools to make the systemic shift toward explicit teaching for what drives learning: thinking. There have been extensive research projects, theories, examples, and more convincing rhetoric about "changing mindsets" than real changes in classrooms around the world. Even the expanding use of technologies in the classroom is still primarily focused on delivering or accessing information rather than on how information can and should be processed and thought about. While this book does contain research of various forms, it is only presented in service of

Note: Before utilizing Thinking Maps™ as discussed herein, the educators highlighted in this professional book participated in required Thinking Maps™ training. Resources and training are provided by Thinking Maps™, Inc. (www.thinkingmaps.com). Thinking Maps™ is a registered trademark of Thinking Maps™, Inc.

the documented work surfacing from schools. The authors of this book are educators who are committed to systematically catalyzing, cocreating, and coaching "learning" communities that want to "thoughtfully" shift the paradigm over time toward becoming *thinking* communities.

Several abiding questions are boldly held up for your scrutiny and are met head-on throughout these writings: What are the similarities and unique differences between information and knowledge? Learning and thinking? Thought and language? Brain and mind? Please hold on to these challenging questions and your own educational background as frames of reference for considering what these authors are proposing.

The wider purpose of this book is to offer an introduction to the approach and adaptive implementation design developed by Thinking Schools International (TSI; www.thinkingschoolsinternational.com). Our work emerges from previous work, and there is nothing radically new here other than a group of people coming together to attempt to integrate what we have learned about the explicit development of thinking into a coherent, scalable, and sustainable approach for whole school change. Okay, maybe this is new!

There are eleven chapters ahead. The introductory chapter is the entry point description of the "what, why, and how" of Thinking Schools, a global initiative led by TSI. This is a group of educators who

- offer a broad *vision* of a Thinking School,
- model and train school faculty in practical *tools* for immediately beginning the shift toward a classroom and school-wide focus,
- support schools in planning a multi-year *implementation design* for making the shift, and
- work with the school to implement *student-centered models* for improving learning performance and long-term development of integrated thinking abilities, inquiry skills, and dispositions.

The TSI group is focused on working with a school faculty so that teachers, administrators, and the larger community creates and fully owns their own change processes. Key to this work is our commitment to documenting and networking schools from around the world so that they may share "best change models" as Thinking Schools. This book is one effort to document, communicate, and sustain this network.

The ten chapters following the introduction have a unique design, reflective of our interest in having multiple authors from different parts of the world, each with unique entry points for facilitating "thinking." As editors, we decided that we would write introductory comments for each chapter that would serve to introduce you to the authors, engage you in anticipatory thinking about the topic, and make thematic connections and transitions from one chapter to the next. After each chapter, we have offered reflective questions to further propel your own thinking and for use in book studies with colleagues.

We have also given each chapter a one word heading, each of which may be thought of as questions that are essential to educators as they consider this approach:

Chapter 1: How do we *catalyze* thinking across whole schools?

Chapter 2: Is there a moral *imperative* for thinking schools?

Chapter 3: How does our *brain, mind* and thus thinking develop over time?

Chapter 4: What are broad *criteria* for thinking schools?

Chapter 5: What has informed the *journey* of thinking schools?

Chapter 6: How does a thinking *school* keep moving forward?

Chapter 7: Can a school *system* make this shift toward thinking?

Chapter 8: Where is the common ground for *language* and thinking?

Chapter 9: How may we visually *coach* teachers' thinking?

Chapter 10: How does *leading* thinking develop across a school?

Chapter 11: Is a *country*-wide vision of educating for thinking possible?

As you will find across these chapters, the Thinking Schools approach has a structured yet adaptable design based on the central concern for developing every member of the school community as better thinkers for problem solving, decision making, and making productive changes needed around the world. This design was also created so that many schools within a region or country may be "scaled up" and be sustainable over time through face-to-face and virtual networking.

It is premature to announce that the Thinking Schools approach is an unequivocal "proven" success, but case studies, student- and school-wide performance results, and many other indicators of success presented in this book are strong indicators and are showing ways forward to improvements. A recent partnership is one proof of concept on a very large scale. The Malaysian education system is now in its second year of a five-year plan. It is a comprehensive, countrywide effort to transform *all* its 10,000 public schools from a lecture/rote learning format toward becoming Thinking Schools, using its own uniquely designed iTHINK approach. The Malaysian Ministry of Education, in conjunction with the Prime Minister's Office of Innovation, is creating a blended professional development model and an integrated layering of the three student-centered models offered with support from TSI that will be used by learners daily as they think more deeply and learn academic content.

A team of educators conducting follow-up visits in a school in Kuala Lumpur (one of 10 showcase schools geographically spread across the county) found promising results very soon and a structure for sustaining change. Eight months before, this team had seen in each of the 10 schools most teachers standing and lecturing in front of rows of students. Students were quietly working or boisterous but with very little deep academic interaction and minimal explicit engagement or improvement of their thinking. Mostly lower level questions were being asked, and verbal and written repetition was the norm for memorizing information linked to tests. These were content-driven, teacher-focused classrooms by an outdated design established long ago. Actually, this was the norm across Malaysia . . . *and much of the world.* What was observed during these return visits was a transformation: Students were in pairs and groups, actively mapping out the content together using visual tools (the Thinking Maps model in this case), with a very high level of engagement. There was a joy in learning that teachers and administrators expressed was a 180° shift. It was also obvious, as these visitations continued and further reporting and evidence was offered, that this was not a "showcase" in the sense of a mocked-up performance: When queried, it was clear that students had truly learned more about how to think better in order to learn better.

So does the Thinking Schools process work? The approach works only when each school plans its own the journey of transformation over time, not as an "outsider" quick fix for short-term performance pressures. Some schools have moved faster and deeper than others. Others will slowly shift, all finding their own pace of change.

Much of this book does describe in detail the positive outcomes and some of the pitfalls. The process and the "products" are found within case studies, assessments, surveys, and direct feedback from over 90 schools that have been accredited after creating their own design based on broad criteria for a Thinking School (see *Report on Thinking Schools* at www.thinkingschoolsinternational. com). It is important that, though many schools are focused on thinking for learning, this does not mean their unique character and public identity is solely determined by the term *thinking schools.*

The dramatic changes that can happen in some places such as in these Malaysian schools does tell us something we all intuitively know: The human qualities of thinking already exist in every person—students, teachers, administrators alike. The sculptor Michelangelo believed that carving from stone was a process of "releasing" from the rock the form that was already inherent within. Unlike other sculptors, he worked freehand, allowing the figures to be freed from the stone. Along the entry hallway to his carving *The David,* Michelangelo offers us a series of half-carved stones, jagged, uncertain figures seeming to emerge on their own as if they were held, as their title decrees, as *Prisoners* . . . all for us to view before looking up to his inspiring masterpiece of a human form.

Here is a metaphor for *growing thinking students from the inside out.* This is a vision held in this book for Thinking Schools: A range of ways of thinking, of abilities and dispositions in every child, are developed with care, artfully and with explicit, refined attention over time, as we give children the tools for unveiling their own forms of thinking evolving from their developing minds in dynamic interaction with the minds of others. In resonance with our time, here is a wonderful quote from Maxine Greene's (1995) *Releasing the Imagination:*

> In my view, the classroom situation most provocative of thoughtfulness and critical consciousness is the one in which teachers and learners find themselves conducting a kind of collaborative search, each from her or his own lived situation. (p. 23)

Acknowledgments

The distinct field of thinking development draws deep from the well of human experience across time and cultures, from Eastern and Western traditions, and with current ideas being dynamically shared across the continents. From Socrates to Laozi to John Dewey, we acknowledge that we, the authors and editors of this book, are indebted to reflective teachers, philosophers, and sages from over the ages. While there are many people who have dedicated themselves to the work at hand over the last few generations, one of our authors, Dr. Bob Burden, Professor Emeritus at Exeter University, long ago gave himself over to the vision of more thoughtful schools. Through his conversations and writings, Bob leaves us sturdy guideposts designed to bend to our needs, caring reflections, respectful skepticism, and cautionary signs along this transformational journey of evolving processes of thinking . . . a journey that has too often remained hidden within each of us over our lifetimes and that now is surfacing brilliantly from within every child and educator in schools around the world.

■ PUBLISHER'S ACKNOWLEDGMENTS

Corwin gratefully acknowledges the contributions of the following reviewers:

John Barell
Professor Emeritus, Montclair State University
Montclair, NJ

Sheryl L. Dwyer
Managing Director, Comprehensive Thinking Strategies LLC
Orange Park, FL

Rita Hagevik
Assistant Professor, University of North Carolina
Pembroke, NC

Steve Hutton
Superintendent, Beechwood Independent Schools
Ft. Mitchell, KY

Lynn Macan
Superintendent, Cobleskill-Richmondville Central Schools
Cobleskill, NY

Joy Rose
Retired Principal, Westerville City Schools
Westerville, OH

Rosie Young
Principal, Jefferson County Public Schools
Louisville, KY

Diane P. Zimmerman
Retired Superintendent
Fairfield, CA

About the Editors

**David N. Hyerle, Ed.D.,** is an independent researcher, author, and consultant focused on literacy, thinking-process instruction, and whole-school change. He is the developer of the Thinking Maps language and is presently codirector of Thinking Schools International, a consulting and research group based in New England. He is also founding director of the Thinking Foundation (www.thinkingfoundation .org), a nonprofit organization funding research and development on Thinking Schools and other approaches that make thinking a foundation for learning in schools for those with the greatest need.

**Larry Alper, M.S.Ed.,** is a former elementary school principal, codirector of Thinking Foundation and a Global Trainer for Thinking Schools International. Larry facilitates professional development seminars on leadership using Thinking Maps and is the lead author for the seminar guide *Thinking Maps: A Language for Leadership.* Larry is presently focused on research and development of the Thinking Schools web-based portfolio design used by schools from around the world and across cultures to reflect on and share their transformations as they continue to evolve.

For contacting the editors or contributors: David N. Hyerle, Ed.D., www .mapthemind.com.

About the Contributors

Elizabeth (Lisa) Dellamora, Ph.D., is a national educational consultant supporting teachers, principals, and other district leaders as they work to improve their practice. Previous to her full-time work as a consultant, Elizabeth worked as a primary teacher and reading specialist. She has successfully worked with students from pre-kindergarten through high school, as well as undergraduate and graduate students. Elizabeth's expertise is in primary and intermediate literacy, cognitive learning theory, visual tools for learning, classroom management, curriculum development, educational policy and supporting learning in urban school settings. Elizabeth has published on phonics, classroom management, and the impact of No Child Left Behind on the teaching and learning of urban students. In addition to her consulting work, Elizabeth is currently the Director of Thinking Maps in the northeast region of the country in New York, Connecticut, Rhode Island, Massachusetts, New Hampshire, Vermont, and Maine.

Kimberly Williams, Ph.D., is an independent consultant, author, and speaker and works as a teaching support specialist at Cornell University. She also teaches graduate education courses at Plymouth State University. She is the author of multiple books about education, most recently *Healthy Children, Healthy Minds* with Marcel Lebrun (Rowman Littlefield, 2014). Her author page can be found at http://www.amazon.com/Kimberly-M.-Williams/e/B001KMD25C

Robert (Bob) Burden is Emeritus Professor of Applied Educational Psychology at the University of Exeter, UK, where he founded the Cognitive Education Development Unit on his retirement as Director of the Graduate School of Education. The development of his interest and expertise in cognitive education was inspired in the 1980s by the mentorship of Reuven Feuerstein, whose theories have provided the foundation for much of Bob's subsequent research in introducing cognitive education to various aspects of the school curriculum as well as to teaching English as a second or other language (TESOL) and the training of school psychologists. He is a longstanding Fellow of the British Psychological Society and former President of the International School Psychology Association, from whom he has received several awards for his contribution to school psychology research and practice.

Gill Hubble, M.A., LTCL, Dip Tchng, is an international consultant on teaching thinking strategies, the design of whole-school thinking and learning programs, and organizational change. Associate Principal of St. Cuthbert's College for 16 years, she now supports the development of Thinking Maps in many schools, school districts, and countries.

Richard Coe, B.A., is currently Vice Principal at the Federation of Glenmoor and Winton Arts & Media College, UK. Over several years, Richard led his previous school, Rochester Grammar, to become one of the first to gain Advanced Thinking School Accreditation status from Exeter University. He is now enjoying the challenge of facilitating the journey of Thinking Schools within his new school community on the South Coast of England. Richard is also a National Director/Global Trainer for Thinking Schools International and was one of the lead trainers for the TSI Malaysia project.

Donna J. DeSiato, Ed.D.,, a respected leader in the field of public education, proudly serves as superintendent of the East Syracuse Minoa Central School District (ESM). During her tenure as Superintendent of ESM since 2005, the District has realized significant gains in student achievement, experienced a continual increase in the graduation rate, and developed innovative educational models with business partnerships. Most recently ESM was recognized nationally by the College Board on their 2011 AP Achievement list and by *Newsweek* for their Best 2000 High Schools in the nation. Dr. DeSiato is highly regarded in education and in the business community for her expertise and leadership in 21st century learning and preparing graduates for our global society.

Judy Morgan, M.S., is a former Executive Director of Curriculum, Instruction and Accountability and principal with over 25 years of experience in schools. She is currently an educational consultant working with school districts on strategic planning and the implementation of research-based instructional strategies. She also serves as president of New York State ASCD.

Estrella (Estee) Lopez, Ed.D., is a professor and the Assistant Director for the Center of Teaching Learning and Leadership at the College of New Rochelle, NY. She is also a Director/Global Trainer with Thinking Schools International. Estee is a former teacher and school district administrator with over 40 years' experience leading schools, engaging in state education policy and standards development, and ensuring equity and high-quality teaching and learning experiences through professional learning communities. The essential focus of her work is on the integration of language, literacy, and cognition with an emphasis on the most challenged and underserved student populations: struggling learners and second language learners. Estee is the author of two educator's resources guides, *CCSS and ELLs: Common Core State Standards and English Language Learners* (2012) and *ELLs: Thinking Skills and CCSS Focus on the Six Shifts* (2013). Her dissertation, *The Effect of a Cognitive Model, Thinking Maps, on the Academic Language Development of English Language Learners* (2011), provides empirical evidence to support a "Model for Full Access for High Achievement." She is a national and international presenter since 1990, most recently presenting at the International Thinking Skills Conference in the UK, State Association for Bilingual Education, Puerto Rico TESOL Conference, Bank Street College of Education Language Series, and NYTESOL Conference on Early Child.

Kathy Ernst currently serves as senior advisor to Thinking Foundation. She has served in various roles in education, including co-founder of an alternative elementary school, teacher of grades Pre-K–8, developer and teacher of gifted programs, adjunct professor, mathematics coach and professional developer, and consultant for the Vermont and U.S. Departments of Education. For over thirty years she has been a change agent, providing school-embedded support to schools throughout the United States to improve mathematics teaching and learning. She has used Thinking Maps Register to develop collaborative, efficient, and explicit processes of lesson study, professional learning, coaching, and supervision. Kathy is co-author of *Success From the Start: Your First Years Teaching Elementary Mathematics* (NCTM, 2014). She holds a M.S.Ed. in Educational Leadership from Bank Street College of Education.

Robert Seth Price is an independent international consultant on teaching thinking strategies, the design of whole school thinking and learning programs, and organizational change. He has recently co-authored *Growing Thinking Schools from the Inside Out* and the accompanying "MoM Handbook" for the documentary film *Minds of Mississippi* (2010) produced by Thinking Foundation. He has developed and written the *Structuring Thinking Environments* guide, which has been used as a professional development model. His work with "student voice" includes developing and implementing a model for National Urban Alliance that the organization continues to use as part of its professional development. Robert has also produced, directed, and edited many short films and developed and created other multimedia models with students, educators, and NGOs. His website is www.eggplant.org.

Bereket Aweke lives in Addis Ababa, Ethiopia, and has over seven years of experience in the education and training sectors. Having graduated from Addis Ababa University in Applied Biology, he has worked with several educational institutions as a teacher, coordinator, and director. Bereket has passion and commitment for teaching and children. He believes it is through quality education that sustainable, long-term change could come to Africa. While teaching in a private school in Ethiopia, he was introduced to the Thinking Schools Ethiopia program. He became lead facilitator, certified trainer, and later Director of the program with Eminence Social Entrepreneurs. The program, under his leadership, achieved public recognition from government ministries, private schools, and NGOs while training over 2,000 teachers and school leaders. Bereket had been involved with the initial pilot of Thinking Schools Ethiopia since its inception in August 2009 including all professional development in Addis Ababa and Hossana Ethiopia. This includes professional development in Thinking Schools, leadership, visual tools, and other sessions that were attended by educators and representatives from NGOs committed to these change processes.

Catalyst

Thinking Schools as a Catalyst for Transformational Change

David N. Hyerle

WHY THINKING? ■

In the past dozen years—the first decades of the 21st century—I have journeyed hundreds of thousands of miles around the globe to collaborate with and learn from fellow educators. My recent travels to such places as Malaysia, Thailand, Japan, South Africa, Ethiopia, Mexico, Brazil, New Zealand, Australia, the United Kingdom, and here within the United States have filled me with a renewed sense of optimism. In the course of these travels, I frequently encounter a recurrent question from seatmates, taxi drivers, and others with whom I cross paths: "What are you doing *here*?" When I offer my typical response, "I'm here to help build thinking schools," my new acquaintances usually smile politely. Some even laugh and say, "Isn't that what every school is supposed to do . . . teach children to think?" I tell them that many organizations and individuals have helped build actual school buildings in underserved regions, and then ask them to consider what happens inside the walls: What happens between teachers and students? And then, in a millisecond of insight, they answer their own question: "Not really, I guess. Schools don't teach you how to think. I wish I had learned how to think better. We've got to teach students how to think."

These informal conversations reflect a rapidly shifting awareness of the need for changing all levels and dimensions of education—from pre-K through college and workplace training—in response to increasingly complex problems. Across continents, I am aware of the tension between unbridled optimism and the hard realism of the challenges to change. I read about a renewed effort to focus on developing students' thinking, collaborative problem solving, decision making, emotional intelligence, and an entrepreneurial drive for social change as a central focus of education. But at the same time, I continue to encounter policies and practices that seem antithetical to these goals. Some say, "Why change?"

Because the world doesn't just *seem* to be more complex. It *is*.

Dynamic new tools and technologies, social media, access to information, and globalization have led many to question whether we have adequately prepared our children for the challenges of higher education and a rapidly changing workplace. Of course, our minds and brains have also been opened to (and assaulted by) a daunting, sometimes overwhelming, new level of cognitive load. Students now have whole libraries and dynamically changing Wikipedia in their palms as well as powerful software for immediate communication and knowledge creation. This information overload is also a common point of conversation in the public square and global media network, and not just about educating, but the day-to-day experiences of our children. Too much information, too much entertainment, not enough time to think, and not enough quality thinking occurring in classrooms. Yet, with access to unlimited information at our fingertips, why are so many schools fixated on multiple-choice, one-answer responses and rote memorization of testable knowledge bits?

There is an unstated fear—and sometimes a hardened polemic argument—that if educators actually refocus their efforts on teaching for thinking they will somehow need to abandon teaching content. Some leaders across different fields and many educators believe that the direct facilitation of thinking draws the focus away from "hard" content learning into an unmanageable (read "untestable") morass of "soft" learning-to-learn processes.

A central premise of this book, as evidenced by the work of the gifted educators who have contributed chapters, is that we have proven that we can, in fact, accomplish both goals simultaneously. The recurring themes throughout this book crystallize to these three key points:

1. The dramatically changing world requires changing the educational paradigm toward a focus on applied thinking, problem solving, and collaborative decision making by students in classrooms, not after they leave schools.

2. New technologies and access to information not only have had many benefits, but also have a downside by overwhelming students and teachers without offering them the requisite tools for dealing with the overload.

3. Teaching for, of, and about thinking—and teaching for content—are not antithetical but are deeply complementary when unified in classroom practice.

One reason for the misperception that thinking process approaches are "soft" is that traditionally, such skills have been ill-defined and not explicitly and rigorously integrated into daily content learning in the classroom. Additionally, cognitive development and critical reflection is not systematically developed over time in schools to a point where students, as independent learners, become metacognitive and thus aware of their own thinking processes. We have often promoted the idea of "aligning" the curriculum so there is continuity within each content area. There is now a dramatic need for aligning the development of thinking for every student from preschool to the workplace.

Framing "content" and "thinking" within a polarity construct is no longer relevant and an antiquated point of view for understanding the purpose of education given what we now know about the brain, the mind, learning, and thinking. Delivering evermore challenging and conceptually complex content knowledge—without the direct facilitation of higher orders of thinking, and then testing for the "expected" outcomes in schools—may be challenging but certainly not scaffolding and thus supporting our diverse student population in meeting these lofty goals. More provocatively stated, this model of change is actually replicating an educational achievement gap linked directly to the growing disparities in income across many countries around the world. Of course, educational attainment and income levels *are* tied together. So is the wealth and well-being of nations.

In sum, using multiple-choice formats along a statistically formed bell curve grading system is no longer viable as a feedback mechanism to accomplish the needs of an information glutted, global society. Moving the goal posts by making tests more complex every few years only increases the separation between the underserved and the privileged few in societies (who can afford test-prep courses and private schools), while weakening the adaptability of the broad range of people within a country. More specifically, we must have a clear break and alternative to the disproven "IQ" bell curve mindset that tests children to a certain growth point compared to others on the some finite *curve of memorized content knowledge* rather than toward their own arc of brain-mind development as learners, as adaptable thinkers.

Our profession continues to be driven by an endlessly scattered range of isolated solutions for improving education (all "proven" in isolated studies), and it is often much ado about adding and subtracting, and using carrots and sticks: teaching *more* content, more time in school, and more homework for students (and teachers), more and/or better technology for virtual learning, decreasing or increasing class or school size, monetizing teacher performance based on questionable year-to-year statistical growth in student test scores, creating competition via magnet or charter schools, or just privatizing schools completely. Perhaps, most notably, we have endured an ever-growing push to *increase* the complexity and frequency of multiple-choice tests that are reported, but from which *students* learn very little. The idea of teachers continuously "disaggregating the data," while of importance on one level, has now become the mantra of "high-quality" teaching. Within our education industrial complex, "content providers" market packaged content information, often tethered to test publishers, as if delivering more engaging individualized content at greater speed of access across multiple platforms will bring about improved learning and decision making. However, these approaches do not go to the source of learning—the human mind and brain—and thus do not directly draw from the animating source of knowledge: thinking.

This book offers a reframing of the work of education without throwing out much high-quality work in schools. Thinking Schools is an evolutionary, transformational vision and pragmatic design for education and a distinct redefinition of the phrase *academic rigor* in the 21st century: *Rigor is grounded in thinking as the foundation for content learning*:

Academic rigor is the *simultaneous* teaching of content deep learning within and across disciplines *with* the explicit, systematic and continuous development of thinking processes, dispositions and inquiry methods for thinking across whole schools.

We now need a defined, continuous, sustained "thinking" approach and models as much, or more as some would argue, as we need an "academic" vocabulary in each content area. In this chapter, and throughout the book, the vision, framework, and professional development design for Thinking Schools is described. However, rather than simply offering another "vision piece," the book introduces readers to a school-wide approach and classroom models for *explicitly* teaching cognitive processes via visual tools, explicitly teaching dispositions via habits of mind, and explicitly teaching the processes of inquiry via questioning. The expected outcomes are that students are able to independently orchestrate these processes in an integrated way and consciously transfer these tools in novel ways to content learning at every educational level, in the workplace, and in their personal lives.

Why should we focus on something called "thinking" in the 21st century? In a "back to the future" way, Albert Einstein long ago framed our present dilemma by suggesting that *the significant problems we face today cannot be solved at the same level of thinking we were at when we created them*.

What did Einstein mean by suggesting that we need to *think* at a different level? In a similar vein, what is the meaning of Apple Computer's popular advertising campaign that was built on the phrase *think different*? Both suggest that the *ways* in which we think—not "what" we think—needs to shift dramatically with the demands of our changing times.

■ CAN WE DEFINE THINKING?

This brings us to the ancient, seemingly unanswerable question: What is thinking? The oft-told Sufi parable of the six blind men and the elephant offers us a metaphor: Each of the men touches a different part of an elephant, yet none are able to define the whole. Let's update the parable and tell a story of a group of six people sitting around a table trying to define "thinking" for a parent whose child is entering school: a philosopher, a kindergarten teacher, a college professor, an artist, a CEO, and a social entrepreneur trying to make change in the world. They might become as disoriented in their dialogue as the six blind men touching the elephant, yet over time they would find agreement about common dimensions of thinking and even practical approaches, if they focused on how to support students as adaptive problem-solvers over their lifetimes. If our group of six had access to the behavioral cognitive sciences, research and practice in classrooms, and the new neurosciences, they would find distinct pathways for giving definition to the term *thinking*. We do know how to improve every child's ability to think, as cognitive psychologists and researchers have shown for decades.

One entry point is the well-documented thinking skills movement of the last decades of the 20th century. The history, research, applications, and range within the field of thinking-based education may be found in a comprehensive text *Developing Minds* edited by Art Costa (2001). This primer for offering different definitions for thinking and showing how different approaches and models are integrated into classroom practice is a precursor to what we call *Thinking Schools*. During the thinking skills movement, Drs. Art Costa and Ron Brandt offered three broad categories for engaging schools in bringing thinking to the center of the school. Costa (2008) uses the metaphor of a "Schools as a Home for the Mind." The school house is a place wherein all who live there focus on these areas:

Teaching FOR Thinking: Creating school-wide and classroom conditions that support thinking development.

Teaching OF Thinking: Instructing students in the skills and strategies of thinking directly and/or implementing thinking programs.

Teaching ABOUT Thinking: Helping students become aware of their own and others' thinking processes, brain research, and use in real-life situations and problem solving.

From present times, our group of six could also draw theory, research, and concrete applications derived from leaders in the field of education who have directly influenced existing practice in some schools with now well-known models and approaches: Howard Gardner (multiple intelligences), Art Costa (Habits of Mind), David Perkins ("Smart Schools"), Matthew Lipman (Philosophy for Children), Daniel Goleman (emotional intelligence), and Edward de Bono (Lateral Thinking and "Six Hats Thinking"). Over the course of this book, you will be introduced to these models within the context of Thinking Schools designs.

Collectively, from cognitive-neurosciences and learning theory backed up by research-based practices and proven classroom *models* for applied thinking, effective and efficient ways of developing *all* students' thinking is the grounding for Thinking Schools. The animating concern of each school taking this journey is *how* to refine and synthesize these definitions and models so that they are practical *and* scalable *and* sustainable across their learning community. There is a need to catalyze whole learning communities toward improving thinking abilities and in practice developing new models for engaging the human mind and emotional "intelligence." Brain sciences and artificial intelligence studies will add significant insights along the way.

The missing link is that while there may be a unified understanding of the need to teach students to think "better," there have been no reliable *approaches* for whole schools to use for changing the processes to support this shift. There are calls by leaders across all fields for isolated "techniques" to develop thinking, or turns to new technologies as "the" answer, and/or a scattered array of seemingly disconnected lists of "21st century" skill sets and umbrella approaches that ultimately don't put forward an integrated design.

There is no one way forward or cookie cutter design, but here is an offering: In this book we are sharing

- a clear and adaptable definition for thinking schools,
- a sustainable approach for transforming schools over time,
- five broad dimensions for a school to use to consider a range of models,
- six practical "starting points" for student use immediately, and
- three "student centered" models (what we call *pathways*) for implementation over 3 years that are integrated and used together by students.

The definition, approach, dimensions, practical starting points, and three major models for long-term implementation are presented in summary below and surfaced throughout the chapters of this book. (In addition, in Chapter 4, 14 criteria for guiding the implementation, assessment, and optional accreditation as a Thinking School from Exeter University are described by Bob Burden.) The fundamentals of this framework are excerpted in part from the awareness and planning guide, *Growing Thinking Schools from the Inside Out* (Hyerle, 2010). This Growing Thinking Schools (GTS) guide is used by facilitators who are working with school faculties in one- or two-day workshops as they begin investigating the needs of their school, plan a multiyear design for systematic change, and engage in a dialogue about how to move forward, and why.

I. The Thinking Schools Definition

The overall approach of Thinking Schools was developed through the collaborative efforts of U.K. and U.S. educators who over many years worked to refine the resources for Thinking Schools that could be translated into different languages and adapted for use in different countries. The Thinking Schools International network formally began 6 years ago and is a synthesis of a rich history of educational approaches to improving thinking abilities. Its vision is to *catalyze* and support schools using an organic structure that is adaptable by design yet systematic in focusing on development of students' thinking in a school and across networks of schools.

Our development group, after working across whole schools in pilot approaches, knew we needed a formative definition of a thinking school, and fortunately one of our colleagues, Professor Bob Burden (2006), offered a thoughtful description that has been revised several times, and that almost every school has used and adapted for their own community:

A "thinking school" is an educational community in which all members share a common commitment to giving regular, careful thought to everything that takes place. This will involve learning how to think reflectively, critically and creatively, and to employ these skills and techniques in the co-construction of a meaningful curriculum and associated activities. Successful outcomes will be reflected in students across a wide range of abilities demonstrating independent and co-operative learning skills, high levels of achievement, and both enjoyment and satisfaction in learning. Benefits will also be shown in the ways in which all members of the community interact with and show consideration for each other and in the positive psychological well-being of both students and staff. (para. 1)

In order to achieve this goal, a whole school approach will be necessary whereby all stakeholders (including parents and school board members/ governors) are fully committed to the school's aims and how they can best be achieved. Staff will need to be specially trained and methods will need to be introduced into the curriculum for teaching the skills of thinking and associated cognitive and meta-cognitive strategies. The widest possible application of these skills and strategies should underpin all other aspects of the curriculum and should guide behavior policies and expectations about human interactions at every level and care for the environment. (para. 8)

This definition is purposefully broad to support school faculties and their wider learning community as they establish their own principles. At the same time, it is clear that by definition this undertaking is not about simply implementing a single thinking skills "program" or seeking to create a parallel curriculum based on developing thinking. It is a whole school approach that focuses on the development of every student's range of abilities to consciously learn to apply integrated models for thinking content learning in collaboration with other students, teachers, and administrators beyond the walls of the classrooms, down the halls, and into the community.

A renewed ethos across the learning community of Thinking Schools that draws from multiple meanings of the word "thoughtful" has been documented over the years. It is in this term through which we may find a useful definition for thinking: The mental and emotional skill and behaviors of the individual to skillfully reflect on their own perceptions and processes of making sense of the world by engaging with empathy and care with others, thereby improving their ability to learn and the infinite capacities for thinking.

2. An Approach for Developing Thinking Schools Over Time

A near universal metaphor of "life is a journey" (Lakoff, 1980) is explicitly used as the guiding concept for the Thinking Schools approach. The "journey" described in the GTS text is much like one you might take to a foreign country. Imagine yourself holding a guidebook, describing possible options, and accompanied by an actual local guide who can provide deeper background information about the sights around you as well as recommend additional options for exploration based on *your* interests. GTS facilitators "guide" whole school faculties in reflecting on the context of their learning community, framed by their culture, for planning the itinerary for their own change and development. Each school faculty begins drawing its own ideas together for what will work in their school environment—with their students—while not depending on western frameworks and definitions for thinking as the sole source for creating a plan of action and implementation.

Within the initial workshop, it is stated unequivocally that the development of thinking schools will not be effective if it is episodic; it must be *planned* by the school that will be making the change in the short term and for years ahead. Such a shift needs to be well-structured, sustainable, and adaptive to every school. Most important, it must be fully owned by the school community. The process of change, the explicit shift toward a new paradigm for schools, also needs to be congruent with the vision of open-minded, more democratic thinking, again not solely defined by one absolute definition of "democracy." Obviously, this shift is about thinking, and not "thought control." To be authentic rather than prescriptive in our "thinking" requires a process that is not about imposing a template—a Western model—on each school. Rather it involves *catalyzing* and thus empowering local stakeholders to take ownership of the change process as a community, committed to a sustained focus on developing thinking. This is not easy, because many "change" processes are often forced down from the top or implemented somewhat randomly across schools with very little professional development support on the front end nor sustained over time. Though demands to "make" thinking a foundation from learning may often come in many countries from the top down and tied to funding, ultimately a sustained focus on the development of thinking in a school community must come *from the inside out*.

GTS facilitators are *catalysts* for *third-order change*. Organizational change is often characterized as having different *levels* or *orders* of development. One practical model, identified by Baruntek and Mock (1987) describes first, second, and third-order change. Consider as you read that each of these orders of change may happen in a school simultaneously.

First-Order Change is the most common path for schools as they focus on improving existing practices and patterns. This is especially problematic when deeper changes are needed. This may be good for less complex problems, troubleshooting, and meeting short-term needs (such as raising test scores), but not for long-term shifts in the school as a whole. It rarely, if ever, brings about significant shifts in student performance.

Second-Order Change occurs when school members believe that significant change is needed to meet new challenges—such as we have now with schools needing to adapt to the "flat world" global economy. Schools may bring in new programs, new technologies, expert consultants, and aligned curriculum to help them respond to the new challenges. Though big picture ideas like becoming a "21st century school" may loosely frame the change, and the change may be significant, it often does not shift the school into renewal and the self-guided transformation that is possible. Many of the changes may not be integrated together: There may be more technology, more hands-on learning, more cooperative problem-based learning, and even the deep and systematic use of a single "thinking skills" program, but ultimately the outcomes in real terms of student learning may not shift the school forward to a new vision of education given all the positive efforts and financial investments that are made.

Third-Order Change happens when school members decide that they want to shift the organizational vision into practice. Taking on this level of change cannot be sustained from the outside, but must be driven from the inside, by the school at large. The school must take control of the change process. It is not about a single program or a "heroic," charismatic principal who single-handedly changes the course of a school, though focused, collaborative leadership is essential. Third-order change requires articulating a new direction or paradigm by creating a dynamic and flexible plan that all educators attend to regularly (not a stale "strategic plan"). It also includes nurturing differentiated teaching approaches and the existing practices and programs that are working. It does not mean just throwing high-quality programs and processes out the door!

At the same time, it means that teachers agree to ensuring that as new students come into the classroom the thinking process models are reinforced with each year so that there is alignment in practice, just as there is alignment with scope and sequence in content learning, and flexibility in how each teacher engages students in the content.

For Thinking Schools, third-order change thus encapsulates improving existing best practices (first-order change) and bringing in outside expertise and programs (second-order change) while projecting a new vision for school change over time. Important to note, this order of change envisions that all members in the school community are actively and skillfully engaged in the process of shifting and shaping the ethos and culture of the school. It is within the context of third-order change that Thinking Schools work. The third-order processes of Thinking Schools, embodied in the school-wide development and GTS guide, offers an approach that engages the balancing act of offering structure and adaptability, providing clarity and guidance without prescribing a singular direction that every school should take on the journey of becoming a thinking school.

The broad dimensions of thinking, "starting points" for initiating the work, and three pathways for implementation offer teachers and whole schools a synthesis of the field of possible ways forward and a high degree of flexibility for each learning community to make this paradigm shift in their own way.

3. Five Broad Dimensions of Thinking

In the early stage of the introductory GTS workshop with faculty, the question that is on everyone's mind has surfaced: *So . . . what is thinking?* As discussed above, this is not so simple. Given a few thousand years of recorded history, it seems plausible to at least have a general sense of the categories, or dimensions, of thinking. There are so many ways of framing and categorizing different types of thinking, so these five dimensions are offered as a summary and not as a definitive, exclusive view:

1. *Cognitive Processes,* which are sometimes called "mental operations," are generative as well as logical in form.

2. *Inquiry Processes* focus on questioning, philosophical dialogue, cooperative learning, and collaborative problem solving.

3. *Dispositions* include facilitating characteristics of a high-quality thinker, instilling habits of mind, and development of emotional "intelligence."

4. *Learning Modalities* as represented through visual, auditory, and kinesthetic modes of processing information and the theory of multiple intelligences.

5. *Creativity* or what may be called "generative" thinking is being able to search for unique or novel alternatives during problem-solving processes.

Facilitators ask participants in the workshop to question, critique, and add to this model and engage with each other in discussion about what is missing and how these dimensions interact and overlap. It is less important to get a definitive taxonomy of thinking "right" than to become aware that the ongoing questions (What is thinking? or How do we think?) will be an engaging part of the journey of discovery over many years, no doubt without end! Just as travel guides are helpful, no guide can replace the experience of being there and seeing the subtleties of people and places. The journey toward a thinking school is exciting, year after year, as these questions become one of the animating centers of students' classroom interactions.

Here are the brief descriptions of the five dimensions offered participants:

1. *Cognitive Processes.* There are many different models of cognition, starting long ago with Jean Piaget's identification of mental operations such as comparison, categorization, and cause-effect reasoning. In the past, these have been defined as logical operations, but this severely constrains our understanding of these skills. Benjamin Bloom's *Taxonomy of Cognitive Objectives* (revised) includes six types of cognitive processes (from knowledge to creative) and four types of knowledge (from procedural to metacognitive). (Anderson, et al., 2001)

2. *Inquiry Methods.* Methods of enquiry often engage deep questioning techniques, problem-based learning, decision making, cooperative learning, and use of the scientific method. Matthew Lipman's *Philosophy for Children* program is one example of how to integrate critical thinking, questioning, and Socratic processes applied to important issues. Another area more recently developed is the field of conflict resolution.

3. *Dispositions.* The development and mediation of the "character" of thinkers is a focus of Reuven Feuerstein's *Instrumental Enrichment* program. Art Costa's *Habits of Mind* model includes dispositions such as persistence, flexibility, and metacognition that are used by students to understand how they

approach problems where solutions are not immediately apparent. Many schools also focus on development of emotional intelligence or social-emotional learning.

4. *Learning Modalities*. Learning modalities commonly focus on visual, auditory, and kinesthetic learning. Howard Gardner's *Multiple Intelligences* does not offer an IQ or measure for each type of intelligence, but a range of how knowledge is represented. Visual tools and the language of *Thinking Maps* is a model of how the visual processing and organizational capacities of the human brain and mind support learners at any age. This model (Hyerle, 2010) draws deeply from the cognitive processing dimension.

5. *Creativity*. Directly facilitating creativity engages students' open-ended, innovative, and expressive thinking. Many techniques for focusing on flexible, creative thinking have been developed. Some models are Edward de Bono's *Lateral Thinking* and *Six Hats Thinking* for problem solving within and across disciplines. Here are the "hats":

White hat thinking identifies the facts and details of a topic

Yellow hat thinking focuses on the positive aspects of a topic

Black hat thinking examines the problems associated with a topic

Red hat thinking looks at a topic from the point of view of emotions and feelings

Green hat thinking requires creativity, imagination, and lateral thinking

Blue hat thinking focuses on reflection, metacognition

As with the other three models taught to students across the whole school as described in the sections below, students learn to independently put on one or several "thinking hats" when they are learning content, problem solving, and decision making.

The five dimensions of thinking are overlapping, unified in our daily thinking, and certainly not exclusive of other definitions, approaches, and models, and ways of thinking that may surface inside and outside schools. Even more important to realize is that most richly developed models for implementation cross many if not all these categories.

4. Starting Point Classroom Strategies

The five dimensions described above initiate a rich discussion of broad types of thinking. The next step in the GTS workshop is to introduce teachers to "starting point" thinking strategies that may be used immediately on returning to classrooms and for use in faculty meetings. This is essential as teachers see in concrete terms how the five broad, abstract "dimensions" may inform fundamental, pragmatic, everyday strategies in classrooms—some they may already use as regular tools of the trade.

Figure 1.1 Six Starting Points for Thinking

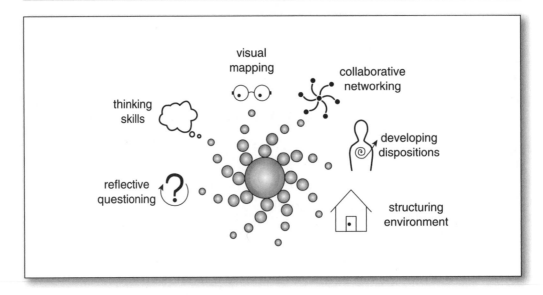

The six starting points for thinking that are modeled and used during the work include

1. Visual tools for mapping content using concept mapping, inductive towers, and Thinking Maps.

2. Thinking (cognitive) skills such as comparison, cause-effect reasoning, categorization, sequencing, and metaphor (also supported by visual tools).

3. Reflective questioning that engages upper levels of Bloom's taxonomy and metacognition.

4. Habits of Mind such as persistence and open-mindedness.

5. Collaborative networking through well-designed cooperative learning techniques and questioning techniques via an inquiry cycle.

6. Designing a classroom habitat that supports a "thinking" environment.

There is often a range in degrees to which teachers who attend the initial seminar already use some of these "best practices" strategies. Many teachers often feel that they do use best practices, yet we also surface two essential questions during the workshop:

1. *To what degree are your students practiced and fluent in these processes so they can integrate these models of thinking together while independently and interdependently using these models without your continuous guidance and direction?*

2. *To what degree do your students have continuous follow-up use and improvement of their thinking that is developmentally appropriate from year*

to year across disciplines, whether at the elementary, secondary, or college level?

These two questions together are the fulcrum for propelling a school forward toward the long-term, consistent development of students' fluency in thinking. Simply stated: How does a school move from *best practices* to *best models* for developing students' thinking over time across the entire school so that students are *fluent* with integrated *models* for thinking?

5. Implementation of Three Pathways and Best Models

The five dimensions of thinking are broad brushstrokes on an evolving tapestry that help establish an Understanding that a Thinking School is not simply about using a few starting-point best practices that create a more open classroom for thinking across the schools. On the other extreme, taking on a highly generalized school-wide theory such as "interdisciplinary" learning or asking more "philosophical" questions may be useful ways to begin, but then what?

This is why during and after the initial GTS workshop a select few research-based models are introduced to faculty as exemplars that have been shown in practice to support a school through more systematic implementation. These models are purposefully **student-centered**. There are many worthy and strong theories, models, and programs for thinking that have been developed with a primary focus on improving teacher quality and engaging students in their thinking. Most of the other models, on close analysis, may promote student-centered *instruction*, but not necessarily student-centered fluency and automaticity with the approach. There are very few models that have at their core the intent—built into their implementation design—for students to become fluent with explicitly using the model independently and in cooperative groups to learn and improve their thinking.

Let's look at a very common situation in many schools in the United States. Bloom's Taxonomy of Cognitive Objectives (even in revised form) is primarily used as a teacher-centered model. But it doesn't have to remain that way and may be used by students during the inquiry process, for their own development of questions, and to see different types of cognitive areas. The taxonomy has been used thoughtfully, but almost *exclusively* by teachers for structuring and designing curriculum, for improving teachers' range of questioning skills, and even for school-wide curriculum alignment. Some teachers may hang a poster of Bloom's taxonomy on their walls and consistently reference the vocabulary *for* students and say, "Let's analyze this and then we will evaluate what we have learned." There are some students who are relatively fluent with the vocabulary of the taxonomy, *but rarely as an independent model for their own use.* This is crucial: If you ask students what they know about Bloom's taxonomy, or better yet, if they can apply Bloom to their own learning, they will sit in stunned silence. The transition from a primary focus on teacher quality of instruction to student quality of thinking is an essential discovery on the path to a Thinking School.

There are three pathways for systematic focus and implementation that have been used across most Thinking Schools and described in more practical detail in this book. Within each pathway a school normally chooses one research-based model that drives to the heart of the pathway and has proven, practical applications and success in other Thinking Schools. Here is a summary of the three "pathways" that are suggested:

Visual Tools for Thinking, which focuses on students applying thinking skills (cognitive processes) using a consistent set of nonlinguistic tools (visual, spatial, and often verbal) such as the Thinking Maps model.

Dispositions for Mindfulness, which gives students access to and a language for improving their intellectual-emotional behaviors as they learn, such as Costa and Kallick's Habits of Mind model.

Questioning for Inquiry, focusing on improving *student-centered* abilities to ask questions in the context of developing a Community of Inquiry, integrating high-quality questioning models, Bloom's revised taxonomy, Six Hats Thinking model, and norms for using cooperative learning.

Of course, there are many other models or programs that a school may decide on implementing and GTS facilitators support schools in creating their own approach. Schools normally implement only one new model each year or even longer so that students (and teachers and administrators) can learn these models deeply, focus on how to integrate the models together for improved thinking and performance, and not be overwhelmed by too many new tools at a time. Each of these models has unique characteristics. The models need to be accessible and practical for teachers *and* students to use in everyday classroom activities and transferrable across grade levels and content areas. The models are also "tool-based," meaning that students can learn to use the processes without buying extensive written "programmatic" materials or a separate "thinking" curriculum that becomes an "add-on" program in the school.

There are few approaches that actually have these characteristics. Important to note, as described in several chapters, these models approach thinking from different pathways yet work together as a coherent framework when used by students year after year. After a school is satisfied with basic student fluency in one model, they begin layering in second and third models within the broad pathways for thinking, creating a differentiated approach unique to that school over several years. Here are brief descriptions of select models within each pathway. Remember that this is not about learning a simple "skill set" but rather that students are learning about how they think and how to weave together visual thinking tools, develop dispositions for thinking, and deep processes of inquiry and questioning.

The Visual Tools for Thinking Pathway and the Thinking Maps Model

Visual tools, or "nonlinguistic" symbols systems, include three basic categories, each with a specific purpose for supporting learners in creating visual patterns from information, ideas, and experiences. Visual tools reflect the brain's capacity to construct patterns from information and construct relationships between and among ideas and concepts.

As shown in the tree map, there are three general, overlapping categories of visual tools that are now seen across many schools, but often in scattered fashion.

The research behind this pathway may be reviewed in *Visual Tools for Transforming Information into Knowledge*, along with a synthesis model, Thinking Maps (Hyerle, 2009). One type of visual tool is "brainstorming webs," used for fostering creativity and open-mindedness and often called webbing, clustering, semantic mapping, and Mind Mapping. A second type of tool is now common in schools: graphic organizers for fostering analytical content and process specific learning. These tools are often "preformed" visual displays for guiding students to systematically organize information or to follow a specific task. A third type of visual tool is "conceptual mapping," supporting students in building interconnected, nonlinear conceptual understandings. Concept maps, inductive towers, and systems thinking modeling are all conceptual visual tools with different theories and practice driving classroom use. All these visual tools, in unique ways, facilitate students in deep patterning of connected information or "factual" content into organized, dynamic, connected knowledge.

A synthesis model of visual tools, Thinking Maps, was developed in the early 1990s and is often used in Thinking Schools. This "language" or model has a common visual grammar and in practice by students integrates the creative dynamism of webs, the analytical structures of content-specific learning, and the conceptual model building fostered by concept mapping.

Students become fluent with the eight Thinking Maps by creating them from blank paper, white boards, or computer screens, linking information across multiple maps. A rectangular frame may be drawn around each map as needed, within which students jot down and reflect on the "references" that influenced

Figure 1.2 Types of Visual Tools

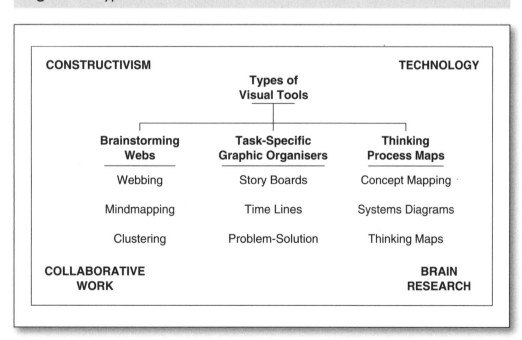

Figure 1.3 Introducing the Thinking Maps Language

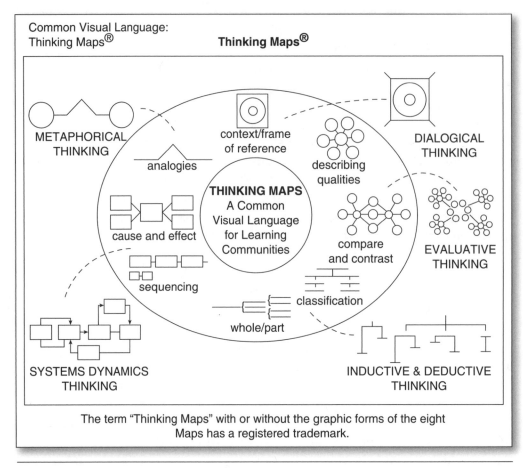

The term "Thinking Maps" with or without the graphic forms of the eight Maps has a registered trademark.

Source: Hyerle and Alper (2011).

or "framed" their ideas, how they patterned the ideas, and even their decisions about what cognitive processes and multiple patterns of "thinking" they decided on using to build their understanding and make meaning. This "frame of reference" is also defined as a *metacognitive frame* so that students begin to see where their ideas are coming from, to critically reflect on who and what media may be influencing how they think, as well as engaging empathically with their peers and their teacher by concretely *seeing* each other's thinking in maps.

The use of each Thinking Map (Hyerle and Yeager, 2007) also reflects a range of essential questions, each based respectively in a cognitive process (shown in bold below) and used during inquiry processes. Here are a select few questions fostered through the use of each map as a thinking process:

- Circle Map: *How are you **defining** this (concept) and in what context?*
- Bubble Map: *How would you **describe** the sensory, logical, and aesthetic/ emotional attributes?*
- Double-Bubble Map: *How are these similar and different, and how would you **compare** these things?*
- Tree Map: *How are these grouped together or **classified**?*
- Brace Map: *What are the **parts** and subparts of a physical, whole object?*

- Flow Map: *What was the **sequence** or cyclical steps of events?*
- Multi-Flow Map: *What were the **causes and effects** and feedbacks?*
- Bridge Map: *Is there an **analogy** or metaphor that is guiding these ideas?*

In many Thinking Schools, and as described within chapters in this book, students have significantly improved their capacities to learn academic language, think through information, read and write with greater depth and organization, and become more metacognitive about their thinking. They also see how their different thinking processes may be orchestrated as they comprehend text, write essays, understand complex concepts, and work collaboratively to solve problems with peers. As with the other approaches used in a Thinking School, Thinking Maps are introduced, modeled, and used by students so they internalize the maps as a language for learning and their long-term fluency with fundamental processes of thinking is fully developed.

The Dispositions for Mindfulness Pathway and Habits of Mind Model

There is a long history of theory, research, and practical means for giving students a clear model for the often-elusive and ill-defined area of thinking: how to develop the qualities of mind that support thinking, or what are called *dispositions*. This is not to be construed as "character education" driven by a dominant cultural value system. This field of thinking is explicitly framed by the cognitive psychology research on how we as human beings, in general, approach and solve problems. Teachers in classrooms, as well as parents at home, are concerned about how children may develop dispositions for engaging confidently and openly with any problem, content learning, complex cross-disciplinary concepts, challenges of college and the workplace, or life decisions they grapple with every day. Here is a definition of *dispositions*, or Habits of Mind, developed by Art Costa and Bena Kallick (2000), who have over the past 40 years done the most systemic and well-documented work in this area:

> By definition, a problem is any stimulus, question, task, phenomenon, or discrepancy, the explanation for which is not immediately known. Thus, we are interested in focusing on student performance under those challenging conditions that demand strategic reasoning, insightfulness, perseverance, creativity, and craftsmanship to resolve a complex problem. Not only are we interested in how many answers students know, but also in knowing how they behave when they DON'T know. Habits of Mind are performed in response to those questions and problems the answers to which are NOT immediately known. We are interested in observing how students produce knowledge rather than how they merely reproduce knowledge. The critical attribute of intelligent human beings is not only having information, but also knowing how to act on it. (p. 3)

Yvette Jackson (2011), in *Pedagogy of Confidence*, describes how the direct mediation of cognitive processes and dispositions, such as those framed by the Habits of Mind model, directly influences students who are underachieving. This highlights the need to focus on emotional intelligence as well as direct instruction in content learning for all students, but especially those who do not *feel* confident and have not yet developed the resilient character of a high-quality thinker.

A unifying theme across these descriptions is that the essence of thinking does not simply lie at the foot of pure reason and logic, or "information processing," but in a wide array of interdependent social-emotional-intellectual traits and attitudes that grow over time within each person. How each of us responds independently, internally, as we think in the relative quiet of our own minds also happens as we interact with others, interdependently, as we solve problems and make decisions with others. The more effective we are in supporting mindful, reflective thinking, the greater opportunities there are for learners to master the cognitive load of information in the world and not get overwhelmed while being able to bend, mold, and create knowledge, innovate, and make better decisions.

Every day in classrooms teachers observe, often with exasperation, that so many students don't persist and persevere when confronted with a problem; they don't think openly and creatively about alternative solutions, and they do not draw on the innate powers of their mind to systematically check or reflect on their work. In the daily practice of teaching and learning, many teachers and students move on to the next set of exercises and activities, rarely pausing to mindfully step back and think about *how* they are thinking. Benjamin Bloom long ago named this problem: one-shot thinking. While intuitive leaps are key to insight and novel breakthroughs in thinking, many learners (of every age) jump to conclusions regularly as they go with "whatever comes to mind."

So how does a school develop more reflective students in explicit ways? Students need to be systematically introduced to more than single "dispositions," or told repeatedly to "pay more attention," or use a few problem-solving strategies out of context. The Habits of Mind model for students is introduced in the classroom slowly, systematically, and explicitly over time, enabling students to grow to a more sophisticated awareness of how each disposition has a direct influence on their thinking and their classroom performance.

Here is a brief summary of the 16 Habits of Mind (Figure 1.4):

Costa and Kallick believe that these dispositions may be understood as fundamental outcomes, or goals for education. Within the vision of a Thinking Schools approach, when students explicitly begin the lifelong development of these dispositions as a *habitual* dimension of their approach to learning, they have these habits reinforced within each classroom. At every grade level they are challenged by more complex problems requiring persistence, flexibility, and an openness with others as they work interdependently. Thus, a sustained attention to these dispositions is important over time and not perceived and defined as a "soft" skill, rather as an essential array of interdependent traits of effective learners and lifelong thinkers.

The Questioning for Inquiry Pathway and Cycle of Inquiry Model

The pathways described above, Visual Tools for Thinking and Dispositions for Mindfulness, are just two possible first steps for a school, and there is no "correct" order of implementation. Thinking Maps and Habits of Mind, as

Figure 1.4 16 Habits of Mind

Persisting—Persevering in a task through to completion; remaining focused. Looking for ways to reach your goal when stuck. Not giving up.

Managing impulsivity—Thinking before acting; remaining calm, thoughtful, and deliberative.

Listening with understanding and empathy—Devoting mental energy to another person's thoughts and ideas; making an effort to perceive another's point of view and emotions.

Thinking flexibly—Being able to change perspectives, generate alternatives, and consider options.

Thinking about your thinking (metacognition)—Being aware of your own thoughts, strategies, feelings, and actions and their effects on others.

Striving for accuracy—Always doing your best. Setting high standards. Checking and finding ways to improve constantly.

Question and problem posing—Having a questioning attitude; knowing what data are needed and developing questioning strategies to produce those data. Finding problems to solve.

Applying past knowledge to new situations—Accessing prior knowledge; transferring knowledge beyond the situation in which it was learned.

Thinking and communicating with clarity and precision—Striving for accurate communication in both written and oral form; avoiding overgeneralizations, distortions, deletions and exaggerations.

Gathering data through all senses—Paying attention to the world around you. Gathering data through all the senses: taste, touch, smell, hearing, and sight.

Creating, imagining, innovating—Generating new and novel ideas; striving for fluency and originality.

Responding with wonderment and awe—Finding the world awesome and mysterious and being intrigued with phenomena and beauty.

Taking responsible risks—Being adventuresome; living on the edge of one's competence. Trying new things constantly.

Finding humor—Finding the whimsical, incongruous, and unexpected. Being able to laugh at oneself.

Thinking interdependently—Being able to work and learn from others in reciprocal situations. Engaging in teamwork.

Remaining open to continuous learning—Having humility and pride when admitting you don't know; resisting complacency.

Source: Adapted from Costa and Kallick (2011, p. 37).

student-centered models, both draw on questioning techniques for facilitating thinking. This brings us to a third pathway that may be an important first step for a school that has not had exposure to questioning processes, or for a school that uses high-quality questioning and has yet to help students internalize these skills within a cycle of inquiry process or problem-based learning. The capacity to confidently pose thoughtful and challenging questions in a more systematic way is essential to learning, lifelong, and critical thinking when engaged in complex problems requiring attention to value-driven solutions with "moral" or ethical contexts. Supporting *student-centered* questioning, embedded within a more comprehensive focus on inquiry, is a third pathway along the journey toward becoming a Thinking School.

We use questions every day. As educators, how many of us in classrooms, in professional development contexts or in faculty meetings hear ourselves, in a pro forma way, ask this question and then *very* quickly move on: "Do you have any questions?" We may (or may not) want to know if our students or colleagues understand something we have said or if they *really* have questions. But most of time—and often because of time constraints or force of habit—we don't even give our audience time to think before we move on. Many schools have used different models for questioning and often with sophistication at higher orders of thinking. Frequently, though, these questions have a glass ceiling: They are initiated by and scaffolded by teachers alone. Students remain receivers and responders. Developing student-centered questioning and collaborative learning approaches within the processes of inquiry takes questioning beyond these artificial ceilings of use.

Questions are powerful, and they can be deadening as well as provocative. Professional development for improving teacher questioning over the past decades has brought a welcome focus on the importance of questioning, mostly through the use of Bloom's taxonomy as a framework for "higher-order" thinking. Additionally, isolated techniques such as "wait time" to give students time to reflect and grounding curriculum unit development in "essential questions" have been useful additions to the field. Unfortunately, Bloom's model has been misconstrued as being a *sequential* model, one that moves up step by step, much like being on a ladder. This means, in practice, many teachers have been trained for making sure that students can thoroughly answer lower-level questions before asking higher-order questions. Because of the sheer amount of content "to cover," content mastery questions then hold sway in classrooms.

Curriculum designers, publishers, and test makers who are key drivers of teacher quality performance create teacher resources with this hardened view that students must show that they have acquired lower-order "factual" basic knowledge in a subject before higher-order questions that involve synthesis, reflection, creativity, and evaluation may be asked. A teacher who is asking questions every day is *implicitly* modeling for students how they may become better at using questions to improve their own learning and thinking. When the questions year after year focused on low-level responses, students came to see learning as fundamentally about "right" and "wrong" answers to close-ended questions *from someone else* rather than generating a questioning mind-set from within.

Much of the research and practice of questioning techniques in education have been on teachers' use of questions to promote student understanding of content and concepts and very little about developing students' fluency within more comprehensive processes of inquiry. Evident in schools across the United States and around the world is that questioning in classrooms remains relatively low level, focused on rote responses and testable items, and often disconnected from meaning making. Additionally, teachers may structure their classrooms for cooperative learning and even set clear roles and norms for "group work," yet these essential parts of the inquiry processes are also left to the service of content specific learning alone. Cooperative learning groups are the perfect venue for students to develop questions on their own rather than as places were "work" is done in groups.

Asking questions has been perceived as *the* key tool set for teaching since Socrates. During the aforementioned "thinking skills" movement of the 1980s and early 1990s, Matthew Lipman (2008) developed the *Philosophy for Children* approach that still is used based on his guiding vision, embedding questioning in a wider vision of a community of inquiry:

> The approach that I have created in *Philosophy for Children* is not about prescribing any one philosophy to children, but about encouraging them to develop their own philosophy, their own way of thinking about the world. It is about giving the youngest of minds the opportunity to express ideas with confidence and in an environment where they feel safe to do so. (p. 32)

Roger Sutcliff and Larry Alper have developed a focused, school-wide pathway called *Questioning for Inquiry*, drawing from a select few proven models

Figure 1.5 The Cycle of Enquiry

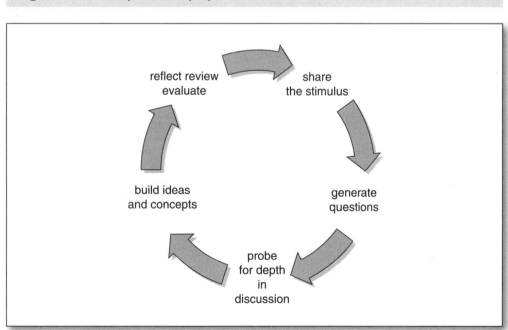

that have been used in Thinking Schools. An overarching design that students learn is the cycle of inquiry.

Embedded in this cycle over time are the use of Bloom's revised taxonomy (Anderson, et al., 2001), techniques from *Questioning for Reflective Thinking* (Walsh & Sattes, 2011), and the "What, Where/When, Which, Who, and Why" dimensions in a questioning matrix, or "Q-Matrix."

The larger vision of developing a classroom community, or culture of inquiry, is essential to Questioning for Inquiry. Here are outcomes of the *Questioning for Inquiry* design developed by Alper and Sutcliffe, for students:

1. Explore and develop their own views and the beliefs and values of others.

2. Learn to be clear in their thinking and make responsible judgments.

3. Learn to be more thoughtful by basing decisions and actions on reasons.

4. Make links between matters of personal concern (friendship, fairness, growing up, love, and more general philosophical issues), change, personal identity, free will, and truth.

5. Learn to listen and respect each other, developing self-esteem and self-confidence.

How teachers scaffold questions so that students' thinking is engaged and supported as they learn is a key to high quality education. There has been a shift in the field toward student-centered questioning. Consider, as an example, the following outcomes *for students* from teachers' use of quality questioning articulated by Jackie Acree Walsh and Beth Dankert Sattes (2011):

- Focus their thinking on specified content knowledge
- Use cognitive processing strategies to develop deep understandings and long-term retention of content
- Ask academic questions to clarify or extend understandings
- Monitor progress toward learning targets through self-assessment and use of formative feedback
- Develop personal response ability by using structural supports for thinking
- Contribute positively to the creation of a classroom learning community in which thinking is valued (p. 3)

Notice that at the core of these desired outcomes is the ability of each student to develop as an agent of his or her own learning in the context of a school focused on student thinking. The specificity of the work by Walsh and Sattes is part of the larger purpose teachers have in mind for this approach as students are engulfed in the tsunami of information they are accessing and the complexity of living in the 21st century.

It is a rare learning community that explicitly and systematically develops questioning *students* and *their abilities* to question in skillful and intentional ways. It is even rarer that teachers across a whole school develop students' questioning within the more encompassing processes of inquiry over many years. Questioning—within the overall vision of developing inquiry as foundation for Thinking Schools—invites students to ask their own questions, gives students "wait time" or time to think in response to questions, asks students questions that support them in thinking through their reasoning, engages students in questioning how their own lives are concretely related to abstract ideas, and most important, gives students time to practice asking high-quality questions and listening with openness. These specific techniques, along with the introduction and ongoing use *by students* of Bloom's Taxonomy, the Q-matrix, and the Walsh-Sattes techniques noted above, are used in the service of developing a classroom culture within a community of inquiry: a Thinking School.

Questioning for Inquiry also offers a broad and deep pathway for the *Visual Tools for Thinking* path as well as crucial to the successful integration of dispositions, or Habits of Mind, into classrooms. As a matter of design, the *Growing Thinking Schools* process, as described above, reaches maturity when, after 3 or 4 years, students and teachers have fluency across these models and see their thinking as a boundless integration of possibilities, not dictated or tightly framed by one model or another. It is the integration of using these student-centered models together along with other unique aspects of each school that shows the sum as being greater than each part or pathway.

SUMMARY VIEW: DIALOGUE AT A NEW DEPTH ■

Reaching out beyond borders, networking between Thinking Schools, and making change from student to student, school to school, and country to country, is a grounding for the idea of transforming education globally. To this end, Thinking Schools is initiating a video web-based network so that people can share quality classroom practice using a similar constellation of approaches that will ensure "thinking" is not defined by one cultural frame of reference. This reflects the work of Thinking Schools International: to *catalyze* a network of educators from around the world that is evolving from a synthesis of proven practices, documentation, research, and the development of new designs in different contexts.

A catalyst is an agent that is added to two or more ingredients in a process that activates cascading change. As described in this chapter and across the following chapters, this catalyst metaphor for Thinking Schools represents

- a big picture vision of broad dimensions and definition for thinking to begin the journey toward a focus on thinking "school wide" for every student,
- the professional development with the school community so that the school creates its own systematic plan for third-order change, and
- training across several pathways with specific "best models" for student-centered use and for improving teaching across the whole school.

There is no one solution for different countries, cultures, or, really, even one classroom, one student. But we must catalyze the thinking abilities of every student. We now face the reality that students live: They are increasingly deluged by the overweighted and overtested "tree of knowledge." The branches are breaking. Education has become for many students a burden and a wall of frustration from which they mentally and emotionally retreat. Many students who have access to computers and handheld devices sit in classrooms knowing that after school they can easily access the "information" that teachers, textbooks, and closed computers offer in tidbits hour by hour. This *must* be frustrating, especially when students are tested on "the facts" that they could easily find in an instant using Google. This dissonance harkens back to the times when students at the high school level were not allowed to use readily available calculators and had to do basic but time-consuming calculations on paper.

Too often students drop out of school, with so little time offered to them to think and no clear way through the forest of information to an opening of their own minds. We must honor their abilities to think and offer them the tools and time to build their capacities. Many people in the business world repeat the mantra that the jobs of the future have not even been created yet, thus students need to know how to think, adapt, work together, and communicate. At the same time, we cannot reduce the idea of *thinking* as skill sets for workers in the reductionist fashion of the 20th century. We face systemic, global problems that will require our children to *think* differently, not perform within walled cubicles of tested performance at every turn. There is no crystal ball, and this is the lesson of the moment: We must now prepare our students to do what humans have done best—adapt.

The Council of Chief State School Officers, in partnership with the Asia Society, recently published a document outlining the need for "Educating for Global Competence: Preparing our Youth to Engage the World." They state that "global competence is the capacity and disposition to understand and act on issues of global significance" (Asia Society, 2011, p. xiii).

The world needs to develop competence and, as Paulo Freire offered, a *critical consciousness* within our children from the inside out. *Growing Thinking Schools*, as described by the authors of this book, broadens our view of what is needed while refining the focus to the pragmatics for making change in schools. We all saw this need coming, but we have not responded to the degree we need to in order to make the shift. We now can offer *every* student open windows into their own unique ways of perceiving and pathways to competence drawn from practical tools for their own internal dialogue and thinking, and for the collaboration that is absolutely required across cultures around the world for dialogue at a new depth.

■ REFERENCES AND FURTHER READINGS

Anderson, L. W., Krathwohl, D. R., Cruishank, K. A., Mayer, R. E., et al. (Eds). (2001). *A taxonomy for learning, teaching, and assessing: A revision of Bloom's taxonomy of educational objectives.* New York, NY: Longman.

Asia Society. (2011). *Educating for global competence: Preparing our youth to engage the world.* Retrieved from http://www.edsteps.org/CCSSO/SampleWorks/Educating forGlobalCompetence.pdf

Baruntek, J. M., & Mock, M. K. (1987). First-order, second-order, and third-order change and organizational development interventions: A cognitive approach. *Journal of Applied Behavioral Science, 23*(4), 483–500.

Burden, B. (2006). *What is a Thinking School?* Retrieved from http://www.thinking schoolsinternational.com/the-tsi-approach-and-training/what-is-a-thinking-school/

Costa, A. L. (2008). *The school as a home for the mind* (2nd ed.). Thousand Oaks, CA: Corwin.

Costa, A. L. (Ed.). (2001). *Developing minds: A resource book for teaching thinking* (3rd ed.). Alexandria, VA: Association for Supervision and Curriculum Development.

Costa, A., & Kallick, B. (2000). Describing 16 habits of mind. Adapted from *Habits of Mind: A Developmental Series*. Alexandria, VA: Association for Supervision and Curriculum Development.

Hyerle, D. (2009). *Visual tools for transforming information into knowledge*. Thousand Oaks, CA: Corwin.

Hyerle, D. (2010). *Growing thinking schools from the inside out*. Swindon, UK: Thinking Schools International.

Hyerle, D., & Alper, L. (Eds.). (2011). *Student successes with thinking maps* (2nd ed.). Thousand Oaks, CA: Corwin.

Hyerle, D., & Yeager, C. (2007). *Thinking Maps, a language for learning*. Cary, NC: Thinking Maps.

Jackson, Y. (2011). *Pedagogy of confidence. Inspiring high intellectual performance in urban schools*. New York, NY: Teacher's College Press.

Lakoff, G. (1980). *Metaphors we live by*. Chicago, IL: University of Chicago Press.

Lipman, M. (2008). *A life teaching thinking*. Montclair, NJ: Institute for the Advancement of Philosophy for Children.

Walsh, J. A., & Sattes, B. D. (2011). *Thinking through quality questioning: Deepening student engagement*. Thousand Oaks, CA: Corwin.

2

Imperative

Editors' Introduction

Imagine yourself standing outside looking into Nelson Mandela's former cell block on Robbin Island, Cape Town, and reflecting on how his near two decades there ultimately led to later years as president of a post-apartheid South Africa. In the same moment, consider that second-term president of the United States, Barack Obama, was born amidst the era of the Brown v. Board of Education Supreme Court finding that "separate but equal" laws were unconstitutional, and only a handful of generations away from Jim Crow laws and back to slavery times. One of the key tools of oppression by any one group over another has often been laws preventing literacy and basic education. Apartheid and slavery, as forms of oppression, were no different. The process for societies to transition from oppressed states to more democratic representation and to equal access is a long haul. And even when political leaders attempt to make shifts, their best intentions may have consequences that actually delay change.

After leaving classroom teaching on the West Side of Chicago, Elizabeth (Lisa) Dellamora spent time in South Africa studying the impact of the post-apartheid government policy option given to every school to select one of 11 state approved languages. A few years later, she also conducted research in a school in New York City on the impact of the No Child Left Behind legislation. This act of law mandated strict testing requirements that had the stated intention of improving success rates for all students, including those with the greatest needs and challenges. In this chapter, Lisa draws from these two unique research experiences to challenge us to consider the implications for policy decisions here in the 21st century. This chapter heightens our awareness that this time is a turning point in education, and the direction we take will ripple like a tsunami across our schools for generations to come. Lisa guides us through what she calls the "unintended consequences" of the policy directions these two countries mandated as they attempted to bring equal access and higher achievement to students of color in underresourced schools, in communities of high unemployment and generational poverty. Both the multilingual options set into law by South Africa and the No Child Left Behind act, as Lisa describes in this chapter, have taken these two countries down a path toward stasis and with few major benefits, and even some backtracking, for children of color. In South Africa, it has meant a confusion of language choices across schools, leading to limited performance. In the United States, it has meant that many children of color, those children in poverty, and those students in low-performing schools are often being taught with a focus on lower-order testing regimens rather than higher-order thinking. The results have been mixed at best at a time when high-quality education is key to success.

The question of equality of access is now centered on the quality of teaching in schools around the world, but for what purpose? It is quite possible to have "high-quality" teachers in schools that are focused on the purpose of improving students' scores on lower-order assessments.

Starting in 2001, Lisa spent several years studying a school in the Bedford-Stuyvesant area of Brooklyn, New York City, observing, interviewing, and engaging teachers and administrators in longer conversations about the impact of No Child Left Behind on their teaching and the impact on students of color. This chapter opens our minds to larger questions: How can we simultaneously teach for 21st-century thinking and learning while engaging fundamental literacy development? Can we teach to a lower order and expect high-quality results? These questions resonate across this whole book as our authors enter these concerns from different points along the same pathway to a common theme. We can and must engage every student at higher orders of thinking, with meaningful questions within the context of inquiry, while also facilitating dispositions for mindfulness. If we don't, we will be sustaining an "intellectual apartheid" as we offer equal access to the school house door with new computers, textbooks, and better teaching—but staying at ground level rather than rising to the rooftop.

WORKING TO AVOID INTELLECTUAL APARTHEID

A Synthesis View of Thinking Schools for Merging Core Academic Knowledge With 21st-Century Skills

Elizabeth Dellamora

INTRODUCTION ■

Schools are now dynamic places nested in complicated communities that are part of a broader world of infinite complexity. Given this complexity, at its core, education is not and simply cannot be about preparing students to take a test and move on to the next grade or school as current policy in the United States may lead some people to believe. The work of Thinking Schools (Thinking Schools International, 2011) explored in this book is focused on preparing students for a life of meaningful and purposeful self-fulfillment and citizenship outside and beyond their years of schooling. It requires a blend of core, academic content knowledge balanced by the skills and abilities necessary to thrive in the 21st century.

At no time in history have the framework, pragmatic approach, and vision of Thinking Schools been more important. There is a distinct need for a shift from the current prevailing focus of most schools to an explicit focus on thinking as a foundation for improving achievement, promoting more dynamic classroom interactions, and creating innovators who will change the world, as Tony Wagner (2012) states is the necessary outcome of education today. As a result of technology, people of our world today are interconnected with greater ease, frequency, intimacy, and purpose. This rate of change is growing exponentially. Necessarily, this not only brings opportunity for some, but also the clear possibility of confusion and conflict. Providing an education that nurtures innovation, creativity, and thinking is more important now than at any other time in our history. As we enter the 21st century, we are responsible for preparing students for a future world that we have not yet even begun to fully imagine.

Herein lies the argument for Thinking Schools that target the development of students who will need to navigate the landscape that lies before them: Students need more than core academic knowledge. Success in their future requires that their thoughts and actions are driven by active, inquiring, questioning minds that consistently seek to engage deeply with content learning and demonstrate the dispositions that will allow them to experience success. Such success needs to be framed by what is necessary within the actual or virtual walls of schools of tomorrow and also in the world beyond that is changing more rapidly than we could ever prepare them for through conventional schooling principles.

The importance of developing schools focused on thinking as a foundation cannot be underestimated. There is now clarity across the field that there is a need to prepare students for a society that already and increasingly demands high levels of thinking and technology use, the ability to generate and innovate, and the capacity to collaborate and communicate with a focus on solving open-ended problems with many possible solutions. This is a moral imperative, an obligation we have to all students, but even more so to those who have been historically marginalized. The current focus on shared standards across most of the United States with the onset of the Common Core lays out higher standards for all students than those expected at any time in U.S. history. But far too many students never even graduate, much less achieve the high levels of school performance that set them up for success in college and career post–high school. A very high percentage of Latinos and African Americans in the United States—and other similar "minority" groups and impoverished members of our diverse society—perform far below their more privileged peers and could be considered educationally, as well as economically, impoverished. And it isn't because we are not trying, but rather trying with a misguided perception of the problem that impacts all students, most significantly poor and minority students, as we work to prepare them for life and work in the 21st century.

The broad context of the global achievement gap between the United States and other countries, and the internal gap between minority and impoverished students and their more privileged peers has long attracted my attention as an educator and citizen. Over time, I have become increasingly aware of these gaps and of the unintended consequences of well-intentioned education policies that can make situations worse—attempting to address a problem at one level but creating additional problems in the process.

Much of my 20-year career in the field of education has been drawn to the disparities I have observed both within and outside school settings that ultimately help or hinder a child's potential for success in their years during and beyond public education. As I reflect on these decades of experience in schools across the United States and the world, two stand out to me as being significantly relevant to the conversation within the pages of this book dedicated to exploring preparation of our youth for meaningful citizenship in the 21st century.

The first experience was my journey to South Africa in the summer of 2004. My intent for this trip was to learn about the educational opportunities available to the once-oppressed majority of the South Africa population in a post-apartheid society. The site visits, research, and interviews revealed an education system that, with all good intentions, had led to some unforeseen challenges and unintended consequences. The newly liberated South Africa, in its efforts to bring equity and empowerment to diverse schools across the country, enacted legislation that instituted a "choice" policy that provided every school community the opportunity to select one of the 11 "official" languages of post-apartheid South Africa. With the best of intentions toward equity and opportunity, this policy unintentionally led to a new set of problems and challenges.

A second experience that surfaced across many years was my in-depth doctoral research conducted in the Bedford Stuyvesant area of Brooklyn, New York. My doctoral work was partially driven by my early teaching on the West Side of Chicago, where I found myself working as a first-year teacher in a school that was underresourced in comparison to my own education and teacher-preparation opportunities. Through my doctoral research, I looked at one school deeply, investigating how the No Child Left Behind (NCLB) act impacted leadership, teaching, and learning of the poor and minority students who made up the population of this school. I found, once again, that a policy with the best intentions did not ultimately have the outcome it planned, because unforeseen consequences surfaced as a result of adherence to the policy. In this case, NCLB was intended to improve teaching and close the achievement gap. But one of the major effects is that teachers and administrators in this school were driven, instead, to test the gap rather than close it.

Both in South Africa and in the United States, educational and political responses to obvious, deeply systemic problems seem to have led educators spiraling away from schooling efforts being focused on well-developed literacy and higher orders of thinking. In fact, they have done the opposite. I found in both situations and within different contexts that despite intentions toward good and opportunity for all, the policies and related practices have remarkably created a stasis that may take several generations to change. In this chapter, we first journey to South Africa before returning to the United States to investigate the parallels and how the Thinking Schools approach offers a practical pathway forward.

UNINTENDED CONSEQUENCES ■

In 1992, the end of the apartheid "experiment" was announced by the President of the National Party, then leader of South Africa, F. W. de Klerk. Simultaneously, citizens, "black" and "white" and "colored," found themselves in a new world characterized by both hope and fear. Previous to that world, people of South Africa found themselves in one of two not-so-rough categories: The minority white citizens were the privileged, and the majority population of black and colored residents of the country were not recognized as rightful citizens. During the years of apartheid, although over 90% of the population could not claim either English or Afrikaans as their native tongue, the languages of the minority, the white South African population, were given rank over the other indigenous languages. The educational system was designed to keep the Afrikaners in their place of privileged opportunity. Once the spell of the separate and unequal design of apartheid was broken, one among many daunting and immediate problems to solve was how to educate all children in preparation for equal citizenship in this new world.

Many looked to the educational system as an important element in moving the country on to its reincarnated status as the "New South Africa." Previous to the end of the apartheid era, schools had been used as "tools for underdevelopment" (Abel, 2003, p. 129) for the black population. Throughout the apartheid regime, families and communities had been broken, separated, and spread throughout townships across the country—an intentional mixing of the African tribes and native communities—with the intent to diminish the possibility of the different tribes rising up against their oppressors. Children found themselves in schools filled with peers and teachers who spoke any one of the nine native languages, most often not their own first language. Using the Afrikaans language as a medium for instruction in black schools provided a constant reminder to teachers and students of who dominated their world. Language, culture, and power are so inherently tied to one another that one of the fundamental conditions of the new South African Constitution of 1996, intended to provide opportunity to *all* citizens of the country, guaranteed the privileging of the languages represented across the nation, in all areas, including education. Rather than select one single language to unify the country, all groups were recognized equally and, in total, 11 languages were ultimately designated as official languages of the country, two of them being English and Afrikaans, the remaining nine being those of indigenous black African peoples (Smith, 1993). Literally, "multilingualism is enshrined in the post-apartheid Constitution of South Africa" (Abel, 2003, p. 128).

Following the construction of a new constitution, countless other laws and policies were designed and implemented across all walks of South African life. One of the most profound and closely linked to the constitution was the Language in Education Policy of 1997. This policy encourages the cognitive development in learners' home languages while at the same time developing competency in another language (Abel, 2003). *Curriculum 2005*, the nation's educational curriculum, went one step further, guaranteeing every student the right to learn in an academic setting in the language of his or her choice (Abel, 2003; Buthelezi, 2002; Republic of South Africa, 2002). The decision on the language of instruction for each school falls into the hands of the school community it serves.

In the wake of so many years of oppression, the power of choice was an important one for black South Africans. Many students are now learning from a curriculum that is free of the blatant racism that it was once characterized by, and the choice of language for instruction was an additional provided opportunity. These decisions about the language for instruction came with challenges, though, as within any one school community the student populations had a wide range of the nine official languages. Any decision about the language for instruction in any school community, therefore, *automatically* advantaged some learners over others. As a result, "significant and increasing numbers of South African schools were characterized by large numbers of students experiencing learning in a language that is not their home language" (Abel, 2003, p. 130).

Policies may be engineered with the best intentions, and the Language in Education Policy that is now encompassed by Curriculum 2005 is a premier example of the efforts made by well-meaning policymakers. One of the unfortunate, unforeseen consequences of the Language in Education Policy that sought to privilege such communities with their choice of language for instruction in schools is that most of the schools chose English as the language for instruction over any of the other 10 national languages, even though many languages were represented at each school.

This choice was typically made for one or both of two reasons: (1) an opportunity to register formal displeasure with the history of oppression by shunning Afrikaans (the language of white, European South Africans), and (2) English was seen as the language of power, opportunity. The school communities that selected English as the language of instruction with the greatest of intentions quickly found themselves in difficult situations that I witnessed during my school and classroom visits: a lack of materials in English, teachers who struggled with the English language, classrooms full of students whose native language was quite likely different from that of their teacher and many of their classmates, and a general lack of proficiency across staff and students in the English language.

The notion of the impact of the unintended consequences of policy decisions captured my interest in South Africa and surfaced repeatedly throughout my doctoral studies and now confronts our schools here in the United States as we work to prepare our students for citizenry in the 21st century.

INTELLECTUAL APARTHEID IN THE UNITED STATES ■

While there is certainly not a point-by-point parallel, there are interesting comparisons between the revolutionary overthrow of apartheid in South Africa and the educational impacts of the civil rights movement over 50 years ago and other efforts toward equity in the United States. It is clear that the attempt to move beyond these past injustices evidenced in social and political contexts is bound by a need to "equalize" opportunity and thus achievement by all members of society. The idea of "separate and equal" did not survive logical argument or the outcomes in either country. The continued attempt to provide equal access to high-quality resources and educational opportunity for "minority" students and those in low socioeconomic communities resonates and overlaps with South Africa's focus on the same. One similarity is the failure of educational and political leaders in both the countries to change the situation, even when they set out to do so with the best intentions. Larson's warning (personal communication, June 15, 2004) holds true on this continent as well as in South Africa: "Policy plays out in practice with intended and unintended consequences."

There have been a number of pivotal moments in the history of public schooling in the United States where we can see the effects of policies on practice. In the 1800s, the American common school arose with a formal focus on providing a basic academic foundation for students with the interest of preparing citizens (largely white) for participation in society. In the 1900s, the definition of *student* evolved with a "commitment to educate all Americans regardless of race, gender, social class, or ethnicity" (Gardner, 2010, p. 9) and there were decades of change in the access and quality of education granted to students of all demographics.

In the 21st century, we currently face another significant, pivotal moment: how to equip students with the skills they need to thrive in this century while not compromising the academic foundation of the 19th and 20th centuries. Currently, there is a significant chasm between educators and political policy makers: those insisting on a "core knowledge and academic skills" approach systemically tied to strict accountability through test scores, and others who believe that a new road must be taken, a journey toward what is now based on the need for a systemic paradigm shift toward developing 21st century skills. There are also those in between these polarities who call for both, yet finding that middle ground has thus far proven to be elusive. It is becoming increasingly clear that the focus on high-stakes standardized testing directly linked to funding has not proven to lead to widespread improvement in teaching and learning. Instead, the results show that, like the South Africa experience, our country has created a new, more ominous problem at a time in history when our education system needs to move dynamically away from "teaching to the test" with the intent of closing the achievement gap to a focus on what are called *21st-century skills*. More children across *all* demographics are now being left behind children from other countries around the world because teachers and administrative leaders are threatened by the "big stick" of poor test scores. In a nutshell, higher-order thinking and innovation in schools has been pushed to the side by lower-order testing regimens.

Students who are subjected to curricula developed with a heavy focus on core academic knowledge as measured by standardized tests to the exclusion of intentional development of 21st-century skills such as those offered as a foundation for Thinking Schools might very well fall victim to some sort of unintentional intellectual apartheid. These students do not benefit from the development of applied cognitive and critical thinking approaches, dispositions, and rich questioning enquiry. The victims in this case are those who are educated with a narrow and limited curricular focus on content knowledge development bolstered by the big stick of high-stakes testing. These content-rich, 21st-century-skills-poor students stand in contrast to their privileged peers, both in this country and across the world, who are being prepared for life in the 21st century. The privileged students are those with the opportunity of learning through a curriculum that honors core academic knowledge, but that is simultaneously and intentionally designed to develop applied cognitive and critical thinking processes and dispositions that will adequately prepare them for productive life in the 21st century.

There are many who argue the importance of explicit instruction in what have come to be defined as essential skills for successful citizenry in the 21st century (Bellanca & Brandt, 2010; Johnson, 2009; Lemke & Coughlin, 2009; Partnership for 21st Century Skills, 2006; Trilling & Fadel, 2009). Considering again this pivotal moment in U.S. schooling, Kay (2010) asserts that:

> The new social contract is different: only people who have the knowledge and skills to negotiate constant change and reinvent themselves for new situations will succeed . . . without 21st century skills, people are relegated to low-wage, low-skill jobs. Proficiency in 21st century skills is the new civil right for our times. (p. xvii)

My studies in South Africa surfaced an injustice that was the unintended outcome of the Language in Education policy put into place with the best of intentions. This research was nested in the middle of more extensive research I was doing between 2002 and 2009 on educational opportunity in the United States. In 2002, I began my doctoral studies with a focus on tracking the impact of how NCLB (U.S. Department of Education, 2002) would influence educational opportunity and achievement in urban schools serving poor students of color.

Similar to the Language in Education policy enacted with the best of intentions in South Africa, NCLB was enacted with the highly publicized intent of supporting low-achieving students and closing "the achievement gap," most often in reference to statistics detailing how African American and Hispanic populations, especially in low socioeconomic contexts, were not achieving at high levels. Like the policies in South Africa, unintended consequences of federal education policy have surfaced in the United States and appear to be, at best, maintaining the existing gap between poor students of color and their more privileged, white peers. Although National Assessment of Educational Progress (NAEP) results show improvement in subgroup scores since the first administration of the test as reported in 1975, a significant gap continues to exist across racial and social class subgroups. Analysis of the 1975, 2004, and 2008 NAEP results of the reading and mathematics tests show no significant change in the gap between black or Hispanic and white students (National Center for Education Statistics, 2008). It is becoming clear that the fundamental intentions of NCLB have not been realized from the enactment of this legislation. The law has not resulted in the closing of the achievement gap. Educational opportunity for historically poor-performing students has not been enhanced. Any instructional and curricular shifts for these students have moved even further away from those of their advantaged peers.

Chester Finn and Diane Ravitch (2007), early advocates of NCLB, now express concern for how testing has taken over classrooms and curriculum as a result of NCLB. They write:

> We're already at risk of turning U.S. schools into test prepping-skill factories where nothing matters except exam scores on basic subjects. That's not what America needs, nor is it a sufficient conception of educational accountability. We need schools that prepare our children to excel and compete not only in the global workforce, but also as full participants in our society, our culture, and our economy. (sec. 3, para. 3)

Mirroring Paolo Freire's (1970) concern that different sectors of the population are exposed to different educational models, Finn and Ravitch (2007) identify the widening social divide and deepening of preexisting inequities that will result as schools respond to NCLB's demands for increased performance on standardized tests, noting that ". . . rich kids will study philosophy and art, music and history; their poor peers will fill in bubbles on test sheets" (sec. 3, para. 3).

The guiding question for my study was this: How does the emphasis on achievement under the umbrella of NCLB play out in teachers' practices and in the experiences of both students and their teachers? I used three primary methods for gathering data—observations in the school and in classrooms; interviews with urban students, teachers, and administrators; and document analysis of relevant school materials—to gain insight into how NCLB is impacting the teaching and learning of poor students of color. In seeking a school for the purposes of my case study, I sought out an urban public elementary school in New York City with a significant number of poor students of color. The School of Academic Excellence (names of the school, principal, and teachers have been altered for privacy reasons), is an exemplar of an urban school struggling to support the achievement and success of its students and teachers. The majority of the students are poor and of color, and the teaching staff has a broad range of experience and come from varied backgrounds, paralleling the reality of the majority of public schools in urban settings. At the time of my study, the enrollment was 298 students. The school is located within the boundaries of a well-known area of Brooklyn called Bedford-Stuyvesant, which is locally known as Bed-Stuy. Bed-Stuy is not famous for its landmarks, bridges, or museums like many parts of New York City. Bed-Stuy's fame is more closely aligned with Barry Stein's portrayal of the community as "the largest ghetto in the country" (1975, p. 1).

Standardized test results show that the school had made Adequate Yearly Progress (AYP) at all grades and all subgroups for the previous three years, but the "students with disabilities" subgroup has made AYP only through the Safe Harbor provision of the law. The "Safe Harbor" designation indicates that if a subgroup did not make AYP, but at least 10% of the students who were "not proficient" the previous year moved into the "proficient" range, the subgroup could make AYP under the Safe Harbor provision (U.S. Department of Education, 2002). The staff was quite proud of their accomplishment because they had increased student achievement in all areas and had recently moved off the city's "Schools in Need of Improvement" list. This change in status related to test scores was cause for celebration. It, unfortunately, also resulted in diminished funding for the school, bringing about fewer resources for the school.

Lorena, the principal, committed herself to serving the needs of her students in ways that extend far beyond preparing them for the tests they will be taking throughout their intermediate school years, but as she conveyed, it is impossible to escape their influence:

> It's important for the kids to do well on the tests because this is basically how every school is being rated. That's a statement that really does bother me because I don't want anyone to look at our school and say, "Okay. They're all about test scores." (Dellamora, 2009)

NCLB is grounded in the assumption that all children can achieve, the achievement gap can be closed, and can best be achieved and measured by holding schools accountable via standardized testing. Locally imposed initiatives resulting from the national NCLB policy have also forced Lorena to operate under a "politics of universalism" (Larson & Ovando, 2001) that dictates that all students in all schools and all subgroups will take and be judged by tests that will determine the fate of students, staff, and school.

Through extensive interviews with many teachers, it became clear that, though there was an agreement with the need for some testing, the overwhelming focus on the test itself has driven teachers away from attending to the core needs of students in the context of generational poverty, second language concerns, and a large population of special-needs students. This has been called "the diversity penalty" because schools with a highly diverse, high-need student population have intangible needs that require resources and attention that are not reflected in a test-centered paradigm. One teacher, Jason, offered insights into the range of learning needs of his students that are not honored and valued by NCLB and therefore not measured by the all-important tests. NCLB requires that all students achieve proficiency on standardized tests and use this as the primary indicator of successful schooling. Although second grade is not a mandatory year for standardized testing, Jason was required to test his children *every week* under the Reading First program as mandated under NCLB. Jason comments on what matters to him as a teacher that is not measured by the tests:

> It's a lot of intangible stuff. Like with one of my students, Pedro. I noticed that when he makes mistakes or when he gets into a fight or something like that, he always tells me the truth. He always tells me how he's feeling about it. He's always willing to take risks or to look silly or to make mistakes. Telling the truth is important. And knowing it's okay to be wrong. I think it's really important to see which kids are willing to make mistakes because there's something creative that's attached to making mistakes. With all these tests, somehow we're not looking at what kids are gifted at. We're not looking at the way kids are creative and the way kids are gifted. We're expecting them to fit in a very rigid box. Tests don't measure the important things. How can a test measure honesty? Creativity? Taking risks? Making mistakes? Not with a test. You can't. (Dellamora, 2009)

Jason has tried to find value in these tests but asserts that testing time takes away from "what we're supposed to be doing in reading." When speaking of the tests, he says several times that "they're not useful" and adds, "I don't feel that they're really that relevant." Jason believes that his role as a teacher is to expand educational opportunity for his students and to teach important character skill (*dispositions* in the Thinking Schools model) in addition to essential skills in the content areas. Rather than continue to repeatedly test his students, Jason would prefer to spend more time developing social skills and providing the "serious intervention" that his students need based on the observations he makes as they read and write. Again, in the Thinking Schools design, the focus on deep processing and higher-order thinking is key to reading comprehension and writing skills. He feels that his own observations are of greater value than the data he receives in the form of printouts and testing sheets. Frustrated by this external imposition of content that often does not match the needs of his students, Jason is overwhelmed by the significant volume of testing that he feels has little value. Jason finds himself in an uncomfortable position and says, "I do the tests because I have to do them." The bulk of time in his classroom is dedicated to preparing for and taking tests while he tries to fit in time for what he believes his students need to learn in the minutes and seconds that he is able to carve away from his mandated curriculum that is required in order to prepare students for the tests to come. Jason qualifies these negative statements about the tests by pointing out his concerns for the overemphasis on the finite areas measured by the test and the reduced value of his own professional judgment:

> I want to make it very clear that I don't think that there is no value in the tests. I really don't think that, but they are just so incomplete. They are dangerously incomplete in my view because we're talking about raising a child here. (Dellamora, 2009)

In the era of high-stakes testing and under the shadow of NCLB, the numbers produced by a weekly computer printout are of greater importance to the Department of Education than what Jason has to say about his students.

Go up the grade levels a bit, and we find a fifth-grade teacher, Kara. She and her students are subjected to the imposition of standardized tests three to four times a year. All students must take the social studies, English Language Arts, and mathematics tests. All English Language Learners are required to take an additional test, the New York State English as a Second Language Achievement Test (NYSESLAT). Never more than 2 months pass in Kara's classroom when a test is not on the immediate horizon.

> I hate test prep. It doesn't help. It's a waste of time and I wish I could take it away. More than it just being a waste of time. More than it being nonproductive. It literally saps away the time where you could be productive. (Dellamora, 2009)

Kara was never hesitant to express her frustration about the tests, which force her to dedicate a significant amount of teaching time to a process that is disconnected from deep learning, the facilitation of thinking, and the contextualization of teaching and learning in our society. Previous to the emphasis on high-stakes tests, Kara received national awards for the amazing technology projects that she and her students were working on. Hearing of Kara's success, other teachers would come to her school to learn from Kara and her students. Unfortunately, there is no longer room for such opportunities in her curriculum. The previous school principal and administration felt that the visitors from other schools who came to observe the success in Kara's classroom had become a distraction to teaching and learning and no longer permitted such cross-fertilization within the teaching profession. Not only were Kara's students becoming isolated within the box of testing, but also her life as a teacher was being boxed in.

NCLB set out to measure student learning and teacher effectiveness through its systematic use of standardized tests. Yet, in Kara's classroom, much of her innovative teaching has been replaced by lessons engineered to prepare them for performance on standardized tests, and the learning that is taking place is most often in service of the tests. Kara does find time to sneak her innovative methods in, as she did with an impromptu lesson on the hazards of filling our bodies with the chemicals that are found in soft drinks. Her students listened with rapt attention as Kara taught, digging deeply into an analysis of the label on a soda bottle, identifying the effects many of the ingredients would have on the body of a young child. This area of inquiry is essential to the Thinking Schools design and engages students in questioning about important issues in their lives. Several times she looked at me with a look of confused guilt on her face, conflicted between the stack of test prep packets on the table by the door and her intuition to continue with the lesson that had the potential to change the lives of her students through its impact on their health. This internal conflict, from my experiences in working in schools around the country, continues to be a source of anxiety in 2014.

Given the increase in test preparation and its increasing role in driving classroom instruction, the validity of these tests ought to be questioned. If the purpose of tests is to measure the academic learning of students and the effectiveness of teaching, how can performance resulting from overt and explicit test preparation be helpful in assessing curriculum mastery? Standardized tests at The School of Academic Excellence and thousands of others like it no longer measure student learning in various subject areas. Instead, they are a measure of the quality of test prep programs, and are, unfortunately, leading to instances or the temptation of cheating by students, teachers, and school and district leaders.

Consequently, test preparation programs and practice tests take time away from valuable learning within and across the content areas and negate the underlying purpose of such tests, which is to measure student learning. As a result of the high stakes attached to tests, teachers in this school found that there is increasingly less time for teaching the content, skills, and strategies that students actually need to learn. Instead, they feel pressured into using prepared tests that no longer measure what they were originally intended to measure. While the expansion of the new Common Core State Standards heralds the possibility of a shift in emphasis toward thinking and not simply superficial content learning, it has brought with it a renewed emphasis on testing. Although schools are being encouraged to include alternative measures of assessment in their determination of student progress, schools and teachers are still largely being judged by the results of a single measure. Such pressure has the danger of focusing attention on improving test-taking abilities and test scores but diverting attention away from the educational opportunities the Common Core State Standards are *intended* to promote.

NCLB is based on the assumptions that all students can learn at the same level, based on age, and that the achievement gap can be closed by focusing on academic achievement. A secondary set of assumptions underpinning this policy is that greater equity in achievement can be attained by establishing high standards, hiring highly qualified teachers, and holding schools and students accountable for learning on standardized tests (U.S. Department of Education, 2005; U.S. Department of Education, National Center for Education Statistics, 2003). The findings of my study reveal that there is a serious disconnect between what is assumed and mandated by NCLB and the lived realities and actual needs of the students this policy purports to serve. As a result, the teachers at The School of Academic Excellence struggle to make sense of and balance the demands of this achievement-only policy and the needs of their students. The principal and teachers at The School of Academic Excellence simply did not have the luxury of focusing on academic achievement only because the forces of poverty directly impacted their abilities to do so.

Racially and economically diverse schools with greater numbers of sub-groups simply have more opportunities to fail. In Philadelphia, for example, many of the district's larger and more diverse schools failed to make AYP, while 24 of the 25 more homogenous and smaller schools managed to do so with ease (Socolar, 2004). While some view this "diversity penalty" as a necessary compo-nent of the Act that will bring attention to the achievement gap and result in improved instruction, resources, opportunities, and achievement for those within more diverse schools, others see the situation differently. According to Socolar (2004), "critics of the NCLB 'diversity penalty' say that it creates incen-tives for schools and districts to segregate their students to minimize the num-bers of subgroups represented in individual schools. It may also create an incentive to underreport or reclassify students and avoid having to count the data for a subgroup" (p. 3).

Research on the actual activities within classrooms demonstrates growing differences in the practices and pressures of teachers in high- versus low-poverty school settings. According to a study by Moon, Callahan, and Tomlinson (2003), teachers working to increase student achievement in high-poverty settings spend 75% more time on test preparation, feel more pressured to bring up their students' test scores, and feel more threatened professionally. If the aim of the law is to increase overall student achievement and to close the achievement gap, attention must be given to how *achievement* is being defined. According to NCLB, achievement is best measured by test scores. Many researchers would argue that achievement cannot and should not solely be defined by test performance, yet this is the foundation that NCLB stands on. Through its emphasis on testing, NCLB is influencing education in many ways. Limiting an evaluation of its effectiveness to exclusively data-driven student achievement on close-ended test items limits the expectations of all students. If the Act is intended to improve opportunities for all students, especially poor students of color, we need better insight into how this policy and the perception of achievement are being interpreted by educators and how these interpreta-tions are impacting the education of the children NCLB aims to serve.

Further complicating the growing body of literature related to the achieve-ment gap are the arguments of the late Asa Hilliard, Gloria Ladson-Billings, and other researchers who contend that the achievement gap has been inappropri-ately labeled. Hilliard (2003) suggests that differences in achievement are best described as "opportunity gaps" that exist between poor children of color and their more privileged peers. Hilliard states that efforts to improve student achievement need to be directed toward addressing the differences in students' life opportunities, which limit their real opportunities to achieve, asserting that "some critics of public education obscure the work of public education in order to divert attention from the larger matters of income inequality and inequality and inadequacy in the provision of resources for schools" (p. 141). According to Hilliard, unless inequalities in opportunity are addressed, there is little hope for improved achievement for children living in impoverished communities.

Similarly, Ladson-Billings (2006) disagrees with the label of "achievement gap," arguing that the "all-out focus on the 'Achievement Gap' moves us toward short-term solutions that are unlikely to address the long-term underlying problem" (p. 4). According to Ladson-Billings, the achievement gap would be better labeled as a long-term "education debt" that has accrued over time as a result of America's long history of unequal treatment of minority and impoverished citizens.

Not only does the achievement gap continue to exist between racial and socioeconomic class groups, but also the overwhelming focus on tests is negatively impacting teaching and learning for *all* students. This overemphasis on testing and data is not only seen at the local level. It is replicated both at the school and classroom level and at the federal level as well. The art of teaching children seems to have been lost in this drive for accountability and achievement—a frightening indicator of the ways in which federal policy has turned schools into factories dedicated to test preparation and performance. Somewhere in all this, the children have, in fact, been left behind.

THE LARGER GAP: BETWEEN THE 20TH- AND ■ 21ST-CENTURY DEFINITIONS OF KNOWLEDGE

When thinking toward preparing 21st-century learners, we must focus on what policies will be put in place in this century *and* consider how those policies will ultimately play out in practice. Howard Gardner (2010), Professor at Harvard School of Education and well-known for his theory of multiple intelligences, reflects on such pivotal times in the history of U.S. schooling: "At such times, we can no longer just carry on as before: we must consider whether fundamental changes may be in order" (p. 9). Although there are many who continue to argue that the primary importance of public schooling is to develop academic content knowledge, there is a rapidly growing force of leaders in business, education, and government, in addition to parents and communities, who argue for an explicit focus on the development of 21st-century skills in public school curriculum. Trilling and Fadel (2009) argue, "The world has changed so fundamentally in the last few decades that the roles of learning and education in day-to-day living have also changed forever" (p. xxiii). They quote from Jared Diamond's (2005) book, *Collapse*, "The crux of success or failure is to know which core values to hold on to, and which to discard and replace when times change" (p. 433).

Students in U.S. schools, like those around the world, are at a critical threshold at this time. It is the responsibility of public school systems from here in the United States to adequately prepare students for an immediate context as active and productive citizens, because these students are now entering into a world far different from the one even of our most recent past. The future is now. At this current pivotal moment in the history of public schooling in the United States, "educators are faced once again with a daunting challenge: this time, it is to equip students with 21st-century skills. Critics oppose the idea on the grounds that emphasizing skills such as critical thinking and problem solving will erode the teaching of important content, including history and literature" (Brandt, 2010, p. ix).

If the ideas of such critics prevail, U.S. students are at risk of falling victim to the limits of academic curriculum if core content knowledge is to take precedence over or exclude deliberate efforts toward 21st-century skill development. The results for the 2006 Programme for International Student Assessment (PISA) revealed startling data about U.S. student performance—out of 40 countries, U.S. students ranked 35th in mathematics and 31st in science. Compared only to themselves, U.S. students showed a significant decline from the 2003 PISA results. U.S. students were also found to have the lowest scores on the problem-solving items in all categories (Darling-Hammond & McCloskey, 2007). Graduates of U.S. public schools are simply not on par with their peers internationally and the typical outdated, traditional curriculum in the United States is simply not sufficient for future citizens of the 21st century.

Kay (2010) poses an argument for the integration of content knowledge and 21st-century skills, focusing particularly on a counterargument for those who claim that developing 21st-century skills would replace or compromise the acquisition of content knowledge:

Rigor traditionally is equated with mastery of content (core subjects) alone, and that's simply not good enough anymore. Knowledge and information change constantly. Students need *both* content knowledge *and* skills to apply and transform their knowledge for useful and creative purposes and to keep learning as content and circumstances change. (p. xxiii)

Kay continues with the clear difference between 20th- and 21st-century learning demands:

In the United States, we tell students the same thing a hundred times. On the 101st time, we ask them if they remember what we told them the first hundred times. However, in the 21st century, the true test of rigor is for students to be able to look at material they've never seen before and know what to do with it. (p. xxiii)

The argument continues to surface again and again, yet there seems to be an obvious pathway if our intent is to truly prepare students for productive life in the 21st century. Perhaps Lemke and Coughlin (2009) frame it best when they put forth two possible options for the future of our schools and the young learners within them:

> We can either leverage the democratization of knowledge and the power of participatory, authentic, and multimodal learning in the service of our students, or . . . we can continue with current practice and careen down a path to irrelevancy. (p. 59)

The second option would most certainly qualify as educational malpractice. It is simply unacceptable that we might consider subjecting learners in the 21st century to an education that would so inadequately prepare them for life. It is the responsibility of parents, educators, and policy makers to ensure that the students of today are the citizens of tomorrow. They simply need the knowledge and tools to do so.

The following sections of the chapter define the "knowledge" we need to arm students with by clarifying what is meant by 21st-century skills and by suggesting one powerful "tool" easily implemented in schools that operates efficiently and effectively to privilege learners with rigorous, balanced development of both content knowledge and 21st-century skills.

WHAT IS 21ST-CENTURY LEARNING? ■

To prepare students for productive life in the 21st century, we must first define what demands will be placed on the citizens of an increasingly global world that has technology and global human interaction at its core. NCLB directed attention to the importance of technology literacy, but does not address the full range of capacities that are essential for success in life and learning in the 21st century.

Several prominent groups have surfaced frameworks for 21st-century skills. These groups include the North Central Regional Laboratory (NCREL) and the Metiri Group, the Organization for Economic Co-Operation and Development (OECD), the National Leadership Council for Liberal Education and Promise (LEAP), and the Partnership for 21st Century Skills (Dede, 2010).

Of all these groups, the framework put forward by the Partnership for 21st Century Skills is the most detailed and is widely accepted as a leading voice in this work and, therefore, is the framework that is detailed here.

The Partnership's Framework (2006) targets four broad categories and the support structure that are identified as critical to the development of 21st-century skills: Core Subjects and 21st Century Themes; Learning and Innovation Skills; Information, Media, and Technology Skills, including Information, Communications, and Technology (ICT) Literacy; Life and Career Skills; and the 21st Century Support System that is necessary to support students to master the skills and abilities required of them for productive life in the 21st century. All these outcomes can only be realized if our schools evolve in a way that leaves behind old paradigms and move operationally, pedagogically, and philosophically to embrace the foundations that underlie the new paradigm of schools that prepare students for the 21st century: Thinking Schools.

Figure 2.1 Tree Map of Partnership for 21st-Century Skills Framework

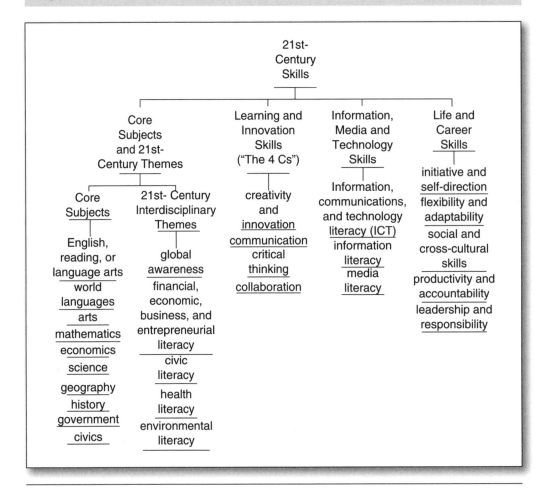

Source: Adapted from *Framework for 21st Century Learning.* (n.d.). Washington, DC: Partnership for 21st Century Skills, Author, http://www.p21.org.

■ THINKING SCHOOLS INTEGRATED PATHWAYS

Visual Tools for Thinking, Dispositions for Mindfulness, Questioning for Enquiry

Thinking Schools deliberately and intentionally work to develop in students a problem-solving disposition that honors deeper and more reflective knowledge. Thinking Schools provide a unique balance, merging the importance of core academic knowledge and the dispositions for learning required for success in navigating challenges of the 21st century. Models for thinking, such as Thinking Maps, used throughout the chapters of this book, can facilitate the shift from the current, narrow focus of many schools on content knowledge to a more inclusive focus that includes development of the 21st-century skills that will allow us to avoid falling victim to intellectual apartheid and work to meaningfully eliminate the achievement gap. Imagine how different the schools of post-apartheid South Africa would have been had they had a common visual language for thinking and learning that could have transcended the 11 national languages that diluted classroom instruction as teachers and students worked to make meaning? More so, this tool set has the potential to transcend the kinds of barriers put in place by apartheid that did not disappear with deKlerk's decree of the end of apartheid in South Africa in 1992. According to Hyerle (2009),

> Visual tools are also used across cultures and languages and may become keys to new levels of more democratic participation in human systems. Across traditional cultures and new "virtual" cultures, visual languages ultimately may be used for uniting diverse and distant learning communities as people in schools, communities, and businesses and in different countries *seek to understand* each other through *seeing* each other' thinking and perceptions through multiple frames of reference. (p. xix)

A teacher cited by Trilling and Fadel (2009) helps us see this more clearly as she made the shift from a content-based instructional model to one that focused on developing thinking skills: "I had to unlearn the idea that teaching was about my content; I had to learn that it was about their thinking and their skills" (p. 39).

Further, Brandt (2010) argues, "Effective teaching involves students *using* skills to acquire knowledge" (p. ix). Visual tools, in general, and Thinking Maps, in particular, can do just that—"visual tools escalate the speed and efficiency with which an individual can identify new knowledge and connect it to what is already known" (Marzano, 2009, p. viii). It is time to "move beyond an antiquated view of isolated information and knowledge and realize, in the research and classrooms, that we are working with a very different mindset and set of student expectations than what existed 50 years ago" (Hyerle, 2009, p. 9).

Thinking Maps, along with the simultaneous development of Habits of Mind (Costa & Kallick, 2000), inherently foster the development of 21st-century skills. Competence in each of the five categories of the Partnership for 21st Century Skills' Framework is rapidly elevated to a high level of proficiency within schools and classrooms led by adults who are committed to developing a system for language, learning, and thinking. Each of the following sections illustrates examples of ways in which Thinking Maps can be used as a tool to both develop and assess 21st-century skills.

Even before 21st-century skills were formally named and prior to the Common Core State Standards explicitly identifying cognitive skills as being essential additions to current school curriculum, students fluent in the use of Thinking Maps were already demonstrating aptitude in these areas. Through even the most basic applications of Thinking Maps, the nature of the model itself requires the kind of sophisticated thinking inherent in 21st-century skills. More complex uses of the maps for collaboration, questioning, and inquiry round out the full complement of 21st-century skills that Thinking Maps support. Each of the following sections includes a range of examples from across elementary, middle, and high school classrooms.

1. Core Subjects and 21st-Century Themes

Our world grows increasingly smaller and, at the same time, more complex as a result of the interconnectedness resulting from new technologies.

Consequently, 21st-century knowledge is also inclusive of content that has not historically been represented in the traditional school curriculum. Our world is also changing at an alarming rate, and a new set of content knowledge is required to successfully navigate life on our ever-changing planet. Today and into the future, students need a solid foundation in 21st-century core subjects that will promote understanding in areas such as global issues, financial literacy, health issues, and environmental awareness. These are areas that are becoming increasingly important for individuals to be aware of as our lives become more complicated and interconnected with others.

The core subjects recognized by the Partnership are identical to those identified in NCLB: "English, reading or language arts; mathematics; science; foreign languages; civics; government; economics; arts; history; and geography" (www .p21.org). If the focus of teaching and learning were to remain just here, students would be victimized by the aforementioned intellectual apartheid. The Partnership, like other similar groups putting forth frameworks for 21st-century learning asserts that there is far more learning required for success in this new millennium. These emerging content areas that have been previously overlooked, or deemed unnecessary, include global awareness; financial, economic, business, and entrepreneurial literacy; civic literacy; health and wellness awareness; and environmental literacy. Understanding of these areas is critical to success for college, career, and independent life once students leave home and take on their expected adult roles of contributory citizens to this democracy we live in. These are content areas that are currently not emphasized in schools.

This category of skills in the Partnership's framework focuses on the fundamental content knowledge essential for students in the 21st century. The core subjects listed in the previous section on 21st-century skills are currently emphasized heavily in schools today, sometimes to the exclusion of other 21st-century skills. In addition to adding to the current repertoire of core subjects, 21st-century schools need to consider the ways in which students will be expected to use this broader base on core subject knowledge. Twenty-first-century learners will no longer be responsible for solely learning the content of the core subjects; they will need the skills to be able to think *about* that content in sophisticated ways. The use of Thinking Maps is designed to help students meaningfully access, retain, and recall content knowledge and move fluidly between and among, for example, the complex range of thought framed by Bloom's Taxonomy (Anderson, et al., 2001). Since the maps store information the way the brain does (Wolfe, 2011, xiii), learners are able to dedicate more thoughtful energy toward the information being learned. Because the use of Thinking Maps requires that students represent their thinking visually, they automatically engage with the content in deeply rigorous ways that extend far beyond basic recall. In 21st-century learning, the objective is no longer simply about acquiring the content knowledge but about having the ability to use that knowledge.

Students quickly come to realize the value of these tools and self select to use them as resources to support their own learning. Perhaps the most powerful self-directed use of the maps is seen in a student's use of the maps to study for her Advanced Placement Biology exam. Fluent in the use of the maps after years of use in her public school experiences at Adlai Stevenson High School, near Chicago, the student took it upon herself to create hundreds of maps representing the content of her entire high school biology textbook. Her maps not

Figure 2.2 Student Note-Taking: High School AP Biology Textbook Tree Map

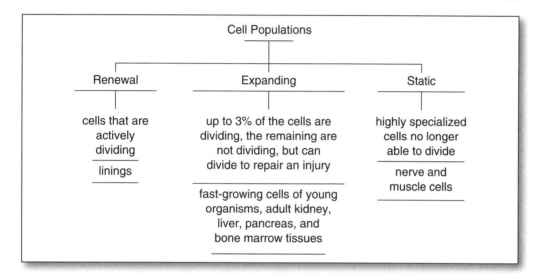

Figure 2.3 Student Note-Taking: High School AP Biology Textbook Double-Bubble Map

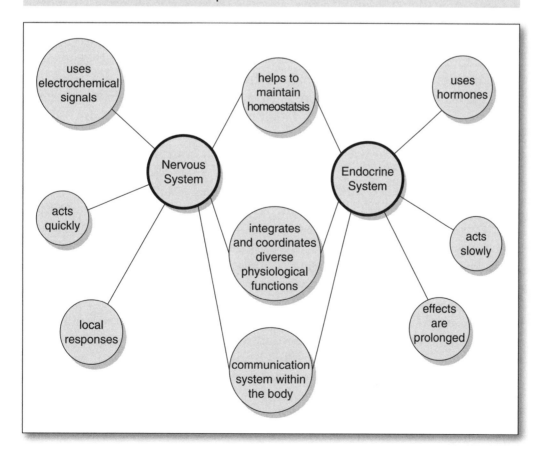

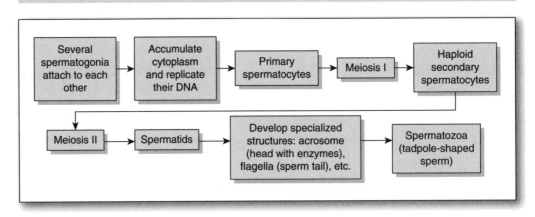

Figure 2.4 Student Note-Taking: High School AP Biology Textbook Flow Map

only helped her recall important information, but representing the information with visual cognitive patterns also immediately engaged her in processing the information on a more analytical level.

Another brilliant example of student application of the maps comes from the sophisticated thinking around health awareness that was brought to my attention by a high school physical education teacher at the Bronx Academy High School in New York City. This school is a last resort of sorts for high school students who have dropped out of or been removed from other high schools in the city. Many of the students are over-aged, and all have faced significant challenges both in their academic history and in their lives outside school that have resulted in their registration at this site. Thinking Maps have been used as a tool to support this community of learners who are typically in attendance only long enough to recover the credits they need to graduate.

During one of my visits, the main hallway was decorated with dozens of large presentation boards that were filled with the research students had done in connection to the final projects for their health class. As I walked through the gallery, one caught my eye more than the others. The map that was featured at the center of the board was a Tree Map with one branch that extended three times farther down the paper than all the others. As I looked at the awkward-looking tree that looked more like a cross, the teacher approached me. As we discussed the map, she called the student over to explain his logic in not breaking the overly long category down into multiple, smaller categories. It turns out that the design of this Tree Map was very intentional. The student had conducted research on a variety of drugs commonly used in the local community—alcohol, tobacco, marijuana, cocaine, and heroin were all included in the map. The branches that stretched down the paper laid out for the viewer all the serious outcomes related to each of the various drugs. The branch representing the effects of heroin use stretched far beyond the length of the others. Explaining his reasoning for not breaking each branch of outcomes for use of each drug into subcategories, the student explained passionately, "But, Miss! That sh—'s baaaaaaaaaad! Heroin is bad sh—, man. People gots to know, Miss! People gots to know!" Not only did his use of the Tree Map allow him to make better sense of his research, his use of the visual tool allowed him to clearly and emphatically communicate his message to others, a clear demonstration of 21st-century skills thinking. The student was not content to simply regurgitate the information he learned; he was able to do something with that information and present it in a way that showed his deep thinking *about* the information.

2. Learning and Innovation Skills

In addition to massive revision to the content of school curriculum, the Partnership (2006) emphasizes in its framework that learning and innovation, or thinking, skills must also be redefined. Not only must students of the 21st century be able to learn academic content, but they also need to know how to keep learning new information, unlearn what becomes discredited, and use what they have learned in innovative and effective ways. Trilling and Fadel (2009) quote Alvin Toffler, who asserts that "the illiterate in the 21st Century are not those that cannot read or write, but those that cannot learn, unlearn, and relearn" (p. xxxiii). Rote knowledge of core subjects is no longer enough. Students today need to have the skills and abilities to "transform information into knowledge" (Hyerle, 2009).

The new-generation learning and thinking skills not currently taught in schools include critical thinking and problem solving, communication, creativity and innovation, collaboration, information and media literacy skills, and contextual learning. Such Habits of Mind (Costa & Kallick, 2000) depart significantly from those that follow traditional trends of schooling. "Conventional, 20th century K–12 instruction emphasizes manipulating predigested information to build fluency in routine problem solving rather than filtering data derived from experiences in complex settings to develop skills in sophisticated problem finding" (Dede, 2010, p. 53). Among the dispositions of a learner that today's Common Core State Standards require is that students be equally adept in *asking* questions as they are in answering them.

Central to success in the 21st century is the ability to move beyond content knowledge. Learners need not only to master the content, but also to be able to use the content and to keep learning. The 21st century brings forth a new set of demands on individuals for communication, collaboration, thinking, and problem solving. Students who are fluent in the use of Thinking Maps learn very quickly how to take content "off the map" both orally and in written format, making it easier for students to share their thinking. The basic design of each map facilitates the sharing of content with ease—the oral or written presentation simply aligns with the structure of the map.

In Chapter 7, DeSiato and Morgan share an example of how maps become tools for higher-level thinking. In their district, the use of Thinking Maps evolved from "What *map* do we need to use?" to "What **thinking** do we need to solve this problem, deepen our collective understanding or to develop shared understanding and create new knowledge?" This shift demonstrates how metacognition—thinking about our thinking—plays a significant role in the use of Thinking Maps. Such metacognition is essential for the critical-thinking and problem-solving demands of the 21st century. It is expected that this will soon be reflected in standardized tests used to measure student achievement. In the near future, with the onset of the Common Core State

Standards being adopted by nearly all the states, traditional, multiple-choice-oriented standardized tests are expected to be replaced with tests that largely call on students to demonstrate their knowledge through performance tasks that require critical thinking and creative problem solving (www.parcconline .org; http://www.k12.wa.us/SMARTER/). These performance tasks will require students to explain the process of their thinking as they develop a solution to a problem and not simply present the solution to the problem, independent from the context of the problem-solving process.

3. Information, Media, and Technology

Collaboration and communication skills are also markedly different in the 21st century. The Internet has connected people who would otherwise never interact with one another. Suddenly, the distance across states, countries, and even around the globe has been reduced to a series of simple keystrokes. This global interconnectedness places new demands on socialization and communication. Suddenly, we need to understand and get along with people who might look or hold beliefs quite different from ourselves. Johnson and Johnson (2010) go so far in their argument for the importance of explicitly teaching students how to collaborate to say that "any teacher who does *not* use cooperative learning or relies solely on telling students to 'collaborate' may be considered not fully competent" (p. 237).

The learning environment in which such skills can be nurtured differs radically from most classrooms today. McTighe and Seif (2010) refer to a large-scale study by Pianta et al. (2007). According to the study, in which 1,000 5th graders in 737 science classrooms were observed, it was found that much elementary instruction is around learning discrete skills taught through specific lessons or worksheets. Ninety-one percent of student time was spent listening to the teacher or working alone, usually on low-level worksheets. In the study, "three out of four classrooms were described as 'dull, bleak' places, devoid of any emphasis on critical reasoning or problem-solving skills" (McTighe and Seif, pp. 154–155). Such classrooms are inexcusable if the intent is to prepare students for life in the 21st century.

Perspective taking—the ability to consider ideas from multiple points of view—is another critical dimension of communicating effectively in today's interdependent world, perhaps even more important than in the past given the exponentially increasing numbers of people with whom others interact in the 21st century as a result of the Internet and other communication technologies. Shifting, again, from a narrow focus on the content itself to considering how that same content might be viewed differently by some, is essential to making meaning in an interconnected world. The deliberate and intentional use of the Frame of Reference in the work with Thinking Maps gives concrete expression to this otherwise abstract, elusive idea. By literally drawing a frame around each Thinking Map and considering how the content might be altered or kept the same from different points of view, learners are challenged to move beyond their own mental maps and the set of assumptions they might have already formulated, which often, unknowingly, influences their thoughts and dictates their actions.

4. Information, Communications, and Technology Literacy

A subcategory from the Partnership's Framework (2006) is information, communications, and technology literacy (ICT). Students of the 21st century need to have the precise and evolving literacy required for success in a world that is increasingly driven by technology. Not only does technology hardware evolve at an alarming rate, but also the skills required to successfully navigate the information made available are radically different from those skills and abilities applied in other, pre-21st-century acts of literate behavior. Dede (2010) emphasizes these demands:

> Due to the prevalence of ICTs, people are, for the first time in human history, inundated by enormous amounts of data they must access, manage, integrate, and evaluate . . . many of these resources are off-target, incomplete, inconsistent, and perhaps even biased. The ability to separate signal from noise in a potentially overwhelming flood of incoming data is a suite of 21st century skills not in *degree,* as with collaboration, but in *type.* (p. 53)

Hyerle (2009) reinforces the importance of developing abilities to navigate the magnificent volume of content now available almost instantaneously via massive search engines. He asserts that "one of the greatest needs we now all recognize students must have is the ability to filter vast amounts of information from the Internet" (p. 51). Unfortunately, according to Lemke and Coughlin (2009) "most children and youth don't know how to use technology as informed consumers, intelligent learners, creative producers, and effective communicators" (p. 59). It is our due diligence to respond to this 21st-century phenomenon. If we choose not to do so, we are "doing a disservice to our students" by "not supporting their development as global citizens who understood the power and responsibility that [comes] with technology" (Fisher & Frey, 2010, p. 227).

This category represents one of the fastest growing new paradigms of the 21st century. Technology becomes outdated almost as quickly as it makes its way off the shelf and into consumers' hands. Twenty-first-century skills in this realm range far beyond simply being able to utilize technology skillfully, but knowing how to use technology and filter media responsibly. I am reminded here of a lesson I taught early in 2009 at a middle school in the Bronx, New York. The students were just being introduced to the maps, and I observed the teacher struggling with a lesson during a walkthrough I was on with the assistant principal. I offered to conduct an impromptu lesson and chose a map and topic I thought would be easy for the students—a Circle Map defining what the students knew about Barack Obama. I thought this would be an easy task for two reasons: 1) Circle Maps are tools for brainstorming, so it would be an easy lesson for me to conduct without the intensive planning I usually engage in before demonstration lessons; and 2) this was a school with a predominate African American student population, and I reckoned that the students would easily be able to provide me with content to fill the map given the recent election and considerable number of Barack Obama posters throughout the school.

The lesson proceeded smoothly, but students started to quickly share facts about Barack Obama that were quite popular media hype at the time, but largely unsubstantiated, unsourced claims. The students were confident in the content knowledge they offered up. The social studies teacher and assistant principal appeared mortified by the facts being lifted up by their students because much of the information was contradictory to those stated in the posters around the school and shared by the staff present for the lesson. I continued to fill in the map with the information the students offered and then moved to the Frame of Reference with the assumption that the students would then surface the sources for their information that would provide more insight into the development of the students' thinking around the topic. Their "sources" included generic statements like "TV," "everyone knows that," and "he just is." At this time, it became clear to the teacher that there was a need to dedicate instructional time to recognizing varied sources, points of view, and the influence of media on information retrieved on screen and online. This ability to be a savvy consumer and to develop the habits of responsible enquiry as a critical consumer of media is an essential skill in the realm of content literacy. Explicitly identifying sources of information and critically analyzing those sources to determine relevancy, accuracy, and bias are other examples of the essential shift that has been discussed in this chapter. No longer is it enough to access information from multiple sources. With so many purveyors of content on the Internet and other media sources with no governing body to substantiate claims made, it is irresponsible to accept information without critically examining the source.

5. Life Skills

The final category of 21st-century skills identified in the Partnership's Framework are those essential life skills that have always been incorporated in pedagogy, but within this Framework, they are explicitly called out with the charge made to strategically and deliberately infuse the development of these essential skills into school curriculum. These fundamental life skills include leadership, ethics, accountability, adaptability, personal productivity, personal responsibility, people skills, self-direction, and social responsibility.

The Life Skills category of the Partnership's Framework targets the skills and knowledge that are necessary "to navigate the complex life and work environments in the globally competitive information age" (www.p21.org). These skills represent the collective behaviors that allow individuals to self-select personal actions and behaviors that will allow for both individual success and successful participation in group settings. In many schools, Multi-Flow Maps have been used for the unique task of inviting learners to reflect on the causes and effects of their behaviors in social contexts, particularly in the school setting. I share with you two examples of the Multi-Flow Map being used to assist students in learning to self-regulate their behavior in the classroom.

In a bilingual, special education classroom at PS 169 in Brooklyn, New York, a kindergarten teacher moved ahead of the typical introduction cycle of maps and introduced the sophisticated Multi-Flow Map during the first week of school. Given the behavioral challenges she anticipated from her students, she created three Multi-Flow Maps that hung next to her door. Each showed the causes and effects of different student behaviors. The events at the center of each of the three cause-and-effect maps were: "I have good behavior" (paired with a large green smiley face), "I need to fix it" (paired with a large yellow passive face), and "I need to behave" (paired with a large red frowning face). The charts are stacked on top of each other right next to the classroom door like a stoplight, and each has a small pocket underneath it. At the beginning of each day, all children's name cards are in the pocket of the "I have good behavior" Multi-Flow Map. If students misbehave during the day, the teacher simply walks to the chart and helps the child understand how their behavior has shifted into the yellow or red zone by explaining the causes and effects of that behavior.

I have also observed a similar technique used with more mature learners in a middle school setting where much more responsibility for identifying causes and effects (consequences) of an inappropriate behavior is placed on the students. At I.S. 330, the School for the Urban Environment, Assistant Principal Terry Swords uses a series of maps as a tool to help students reflect on their behavior. Students who are sent to the office are required to use a Flow Map to show the sequence of events that led them to the office and then create a Multi-Flow Map identifying multiple causes and effects of their behavior. Students are required to step outside their viewpoint and to include in their Map at least two causes and effects that are from their teacher's and classmates' points of view. Following the completion of the map, the students reflect on their choices and then create a new Flow Map showing an alternate sequence of events that would not have resulted in their being sent to the office.

Figure 2.5 Multi-Flow Maps of Kindergarten Classroom Management

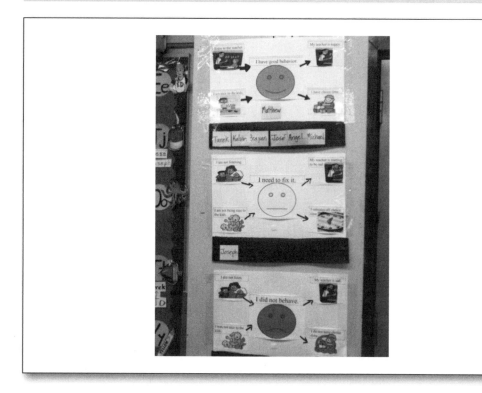

Figure 2.6 Student Disciplinary Referral Form Flow Map

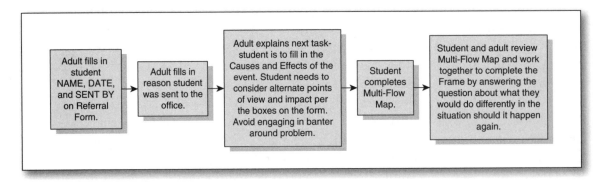

Figure 2.7 Middle School Student Disciplinary Referral Form Multi-Flow Map

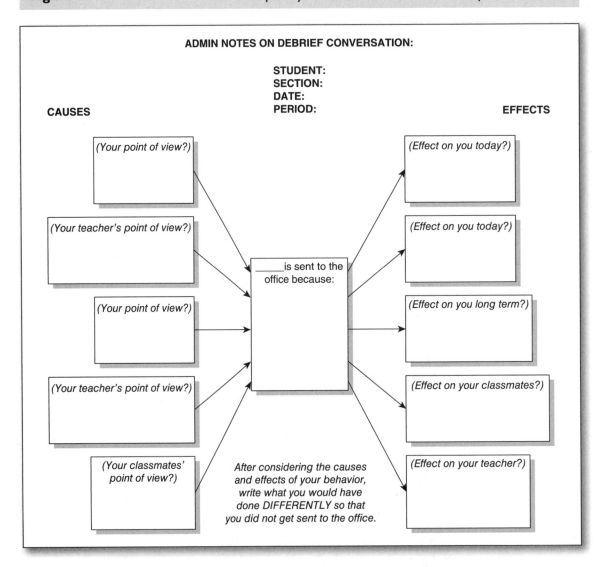

The examples in both Figure 2.6 and Figure 2.7 promote the kind of self-reflective thinking required of students so that they are able to engage appropriately in social contexts with people who may be similar but are increasingly more likely to be far different from themselves. Here again, the explicit use of the

Frame of Reference associated with Thinking Maps helps learners thoughtfully and deliberately reflect on experiences from multiple perspectives, increasing the likelihood that insight of greater significance will develop from them.

CONCLUSION ■

It is clear that our schools are at a pivotal moment in their history. Our history. At this point, our students have already raced ahead of many of us into the 21st century as they instant message, text, and Twitter their way through their school years. We now need to catch up with them and work diligently to provide them with the skills they need to thrive responsibly in this millennium. It is our responsibility to use the knowledge of 21st-century skills and the tools at our disposal to reconsider the fundamental charter of each one of our public schools as we prepare our students for life outside and beyond their education.

Avoiding the insidious slide toward intellectual apartheid in education throughout the world and closing, no, abolishing the achievement gap that persists for far too many students requires a seismic shift in our educational mindset. In rethinking the charter of each one of our unique and dynamic schools, it may be that we may need to recharter the very foundation on which every school is built as a school fundamentally based on the long-term development of *every* child's thinking . . . and, thus, to courageously welcome the challenges and opportunities this century has to offer us and our young citizens.

QUESTIONS FOR ENQUIRY

In Chapter 8, retired New Rochelle elementary principal Yigal Joseph observes, "Always remember, a child is not a test score. A literate citizenry is just a citizenry that can read. It is not a citizenry that can think." Michael Fullan (2003) has stated that "premature clarity is a dangerous thing." Dellamora raises serious issues with No Child Left Behind and other policy decisions that fail to look beyond their perhaps worthy intentions to see the potential, unintended problems such decisions will create. Articulating core values and beliefs is a necessary first step to creating a fully aligned system. Consider the decisions you make on a daily basis or that your school makes over the course of a year. What might be the values and beliefs those decisions reflect? How aligned are those decisions with the values and beliefs you or your school espouse?

How are current, prevailing ideas about what is required of a person to succeed in the 21st century aligned, or not, with some local, state, and national policy decisions influencing your educational practice?

Dellamora states that the rate of change in the world is "growing exponentially." It would be hard to argue with that statement if we only consider the items we have come to rely on for everyday use such as cellphones. In fact, to refer to them as *phones* is already antiquated. They are *mobile devices*, a nebulous enough term that anticipates they will be continually evolving and for purposes yet to be identified. All around us, everything is being reconceptualized, sometimes simply because it can, and not necessarily for the better. Conventional schooling principles, she proposes, are inadequate for preparing students for a world that is constantly changing. If the future is now unmoored, how does that require us to reconceptualize education? In what ways? What policy decisions are needed that might truly propel education forward and ensure that all students will have the opportunity to succeed in the 21st century and beyond?

■ REFERENCES AND FURTHER READINGS

Abel, L. (2003). Challenges to reading teachers in multilingual settings in South Africa. In E. Arua, (Ed.), *Reading for all in Africa* (pp. 123–127). Newark, DE: International Reading Association.

Anderson, L. W., Krathwohl, D. R., Airasian, P. W., Cruikshank, K. A., Mayer, R. E., Pintrich, P. R., . . . Wittrock, M. C. (2001). *A taxonomy for learning, teaching, and assessing: A revision of Bloom's taxonomy of educational objectives.* New York, NY: Longman.

Bellanca, J., & Brandt, R. (Eds.). (2010). *21st century skills: Rethinking how students learn.* Bloomington, IN: Solution Tree.

Brandt, R. (2010). Preface. In J. Bellanca & R. Brandt (Eds.), *21st century skills: Rethinking how students learn* (pp. ix–x). Bloomington, IN: Solution Tree.

Buthelezi, Z. (2002, July). *Researchers, beware of your assumptions! The unique case of South African education.* Paper presented at the IRA Multilanguage Symposium, Edinburgh, Scotland.

Costa, A. L., & Kallick, B. (2000). *Discovering and exploring habits of mind.* Alexandria, VA: Association for Supervision and Curriculum Development.

Darling-Hammond, L., & McCloskey, L. (2007). Assessment for learning around the world: What would it mean to be internationally competitive? *Phi Delta Kappan, 90*(4), 263–272.

Dede, C. (2010). Comparing frameworks for 21st century skills. In J. Bellanca & R. Brandt (Eds.), *21st century skills: Rethinking how students learn* (pp. 51–75). Bloomington, IN: Solution Tree.

Dellamora, E. (2009). *Who cares about these kids anyway? A case study of the impact of No Child Left Behind on educational opportunity for impoverished youth* (Doctoral Dissertation, New York University).

Diamond, J. (2005). *Collapse: How societies choose to fail or succeed.* New York, NY: Viking Books.

Finn, C. E., & Ravitch, D. (2007, August 8). Seeds of competitiveness. *Wall Street Journal.* Retrieved from http://www.hoover.org/publications/digest/13870387.html

Fisher, D., & Frey, N. (2010). Preparing students for mastery of 21st century skills. In J. Bellanca & R. Brandt (Eds.), *21st century skills: Rethinking how students learn* (pp. 221–241). Bloomington, IN: Solution Tree.

Freire, P. (1970). *Pedagogy of the oppressed.* New York, NY: Herder and Herder.

Fullan, M. (2003). *Change forces with a vengeance.* London, UK: Routledge.

Gardner, H. (2010). Five minds for the future. In J. Bellanca & R. Brandt (Eds.), *21st century skills: Rethinking how students learn* (pp. 9–31). Bloomington, IN: Solution Tree.

Hilliard, A. G. (2003). No mystery: Closing the achievement gap between Africans and excellence. In T. Perry, C. Steele, & A. Hilliard (Eds.), *Young, gifted and black: Promoting high achievement among African-American students* (pp. 131–165). Boston, MA: Beacon.

Hyerle, D. (2009). *Visual tools for transforming information into knowledge* (2nd ed.). Thousand Oaks, CA: Corwin.

Hyerle, D., Executive Producer. *Minds of Mississippi.* (2010), www.thinkingfoundation.org

Johnson, D., & Johnson, R. (2010). Cooperative learning and conflict resolution: Essential 21st century learning skills. In J. Bellanca & R. Brandt (Eds.), *21st century skills: Rethinking how students learn* (pp. 201–219). Bloomington, IN: Solution Tree.

Johnson, P. (2009). The 21st century skills movement. *Educational Leadership, 67*(1), 11.

Kay, K. (2010). Foreword. In J. Bellanca & R. Brandt (Eds.), *21st century skills: Rethinking how students learn* (pp. xiii–xxxi). Bloomington, IN: Solution Tree.

Ladson-Billings, G. (2006). From the achievement gap to the education debt: Understanding achievement in U.S. schools. *Educational Researcher, 35*(7), 3–12.

Larson, C. L., & Ovando, C. J. (2001). *The color of bureaucracy: The politics of equity in multicultural school communities.* Belmont, CA: Wadsworth.

Lemke, C., & Coughlin, E. (2009). The change agents. *Educational Leadership, 67*(1), 54–59.

Marzano, R. (2009). Foreword. In D. Hyerle (2009). *Visual tools for transforming information into knowledge* (2nd ed., pp. viii–ix). Thousand Oaks, CA: Corwin.

McTighe, J., & Seif, E. (2010). An implementation framework to support 21st century skills. In J. Bellanca & R. Brandt (Eds.), *21st century skills: Rethinking how students learn* (pp. 149–173). Bloomington, IN: Solution Tree.

Moon, T. R., Callahan, C. M., & Tomlinson, C. A. (2003). Effects of state testing programs on elementary schools with high concentrations of student poverty—good news or bad news? *Current Issues in Education, 6*(8). Retrieved from http://cie.ed.asu.edu/volume6/number8/

National Center for Education Statistics. (2008). *The Nation's Report Card: Long Term Trend 2008.* Retrieved from http://nces.ed.gov/pubsearch/pubsinfo.asp?pubid=2009479

Partnership for 21st century skills. (2006). *Framework for 21st century learning.* Retrieved from http://www.p21.org

Pianta, R. C., Belsky, J., Houts, R., Morrison, F., & the National Institute of Child Health and Human Development. (2007, March). Teaching: Opportunities to learn in America's elementary classrooms. *Science, 315.*

Republic of South Africa. (2002). *South Africa year book 2001–2002.* Retrieved from http://www.gcis.gov.za/resource_centre/sa_info/yearbook/2001-02.htm

Smith, F. (1993). *Whose language? What power?* New York, NY: Teachers College Press.

Socolar, P. (2004, Winter). Education law is tougher on diverse schools. *Public School Notebook.* Retrieved from www.thenotebook.org

Stein, B. (1975). *Rebuilding Bedford-Stuyvesant: Community economic development in the ghetto.* Cambridge, MA: Center for Community Economic Development.

Thinking Schools International. (2011). *Growing Thinking Schools from the inside out.* Retrieved from www.thinkingschoolsinternational.com

Trilling, B., & Fadel, C. (2009). *21st century skills: Learning for life in our times.* San Francisco, CA: Jossey Bass.

U.S. Department of Education. (2002). *No Child Left Behind Act of 2001.* Washington, DC: U.S. Department of Education.

U.S. Department of Education. (2005). *No Child Left Behind.* Washington, DC: U.S. Department of Education. Retrieved from www.ed.gov/nclb/accountability/achieve/edpicks.jhtml?src=ln

U.S. Department of Education, National Center for Education Statistics. (2003). *Digest of education statistics, 2003.* Washington, DC: U.S. Department of Education. Retrieved February from http://nces.ed.gov/programs/digest/d03/index.asp

Wagner, T. (2012). *Creating innovators: The making of young people who will change the world.* New York, NY: Scribner.

Wolfe, P. (2011). Foreword. In D. Hyerle & L. Alper (Eds.), *Student successes with Thinking Maps: School-based research, results, and models for achievement using visual tools* (p. xiii). Thousand Oaks, CA: Corwin.

3

Brain-Mind

Editors' Introduction

As Lisa Dellamora gave us a global view of the political and personal need for shifting toward schools based on the development of student thinking, Kim Williams in this chapter zooms in to a view a smaller, complex globe: the brain. Given our rapidly expanding understanding about brain development through the neuroscience research of the past decades and linked to our longer history of behavioral cognitive sciences, we now know, unequivocally, that the human brain has a dynamic plasticity, evolving and adapting in ways we never imagined. We interact through our minds and bodies in the world, patterned by our quietly humming brain, in a dance of complexity and beauty. The chapter before you is an attempt to give a small measure of insight into this dynamism across the lifetime of each of us, with particular attention to the idea of directly facilitating thinking in schools that nurtures the seemingly infinite capacity of each of our brains, in mind.

We humans do have unique capacities in this wide world—not just to think *but also to* think about *our thinking and feelings—as we mature over a lifetime. Kim Williams draws on brain research with an understanding that by the time this book is in print new research will have already outdated some references, inferences, and assumptions. Nowadays, old news is pruned and discarded as quickly on the Internet as the human brain does when its neural nets are not used, remnants lost in the recesses of our minds.*

It is amazing to see how far down the line we have come in the past few decades. At this moment, President Obama has put forth a challenge resonant with President Kennedy's vision of putting a man on the moon: Map the human brain. This is beyond even many neuroscientists' present beliefs of what is possible because brain science itself is in its infancy. Other than the universe itself, the human brain is the most complex organism we know, and really don't know yet.

Kim, as an educator who works across fields, not only guides us through the lifetime of our brain's development, stopping short of simple anecdotes and immediate answers, but also engaging us in considering how we may directly facilitate thinking in our homes, schools, and workplaces. Important to note, she links the actual networking brain with the conscious cognitive patterns of the mind that ultimately drive learning. She keenly observes that neuroscientists have revealed that the two basic structures of the brain—hierarchical structure and sequential processing—are reflected in the cognitive processes of hierarchical, "tree like" categorization and sequencing "flows." She then links these brain-mind patterns to the underlying designs grounding Thinking Maps. Kim also makes the link to emotional drivers in the human brain, mind, and body, influencing and framing our intellectual behaviors, the dispositions and Habits of Mind that affect learning. Of course, cognition and emotion twine together when we have whole schools that are focused on developing inquiring minds. The naturally inquisitive brain is grounded in an infant's thinking as he or she is tracking a moving mobile often found floating above in the crib. (Many mobiles, of course, are hierarchical in structure and rotate in sequential, rotating, repeating patterns.) We now know we do not have blank slates awaiting our instructions, but rather "scientists in the crib."

If there is a collective calling out for supporting "thinking" children whose brains are learning every single moment, then shouldn't we focus on how to directly nurture this natural capacity in our daily interactions in school? Shouldn't our students be fully aware of their fundamental thinking patterns? Do we enable them to problem solve and make life-changing decisions for themselves for the betterment of free societies in a complex "flat" world webbed together by the Internet? Kim offers us a constellation of starting points for reflecting on our whole lifetimes, embodying schools as a place for this practice of thinking in brain and mind.

BRAIN MAPPING AND MAPPING MINDS

Kimberly Williams

THINKING IN SCHOOLS ◼

As members of a larger society, parents, educators, researchers, business leaders, and most recently politicians and media opinion outlets say that we want and need to teach our children how to think for themselves as they reach into adulthood and leave school. This is analogous to a young bird being able to fly once leaving the nest: Today's students are stepping off into a world of work that offers access to an abundance of information keyed at our fingertips. There is a high demand for those being able to organize, analyze, synthesize, and evaluate information so that they can innovate and generate solutions. It is no longer about remembering vast stores of information in the brain since we have instant access to "information"; it is about how to effectively work with information to create new knowledge.

However, do we explicitly and purposefully teach children thinking strategies at home or at school? Do we develop thinking as a foundation for schools, systematically through to adulthood? How might we teach thinking even more explicitly and purposefully? Of course, while there is a growing demand for students who can think through problems, defining the term *thinking* is like a Rorschach test for us all, especially when we bring emerging neuroscience research into the picture. The paradigm has now shifted. The combination of information technology, globalization, the need for innovative entrepreneurs, and fascinating brain research is captivating the general public.

Yet, in today's era of standards-based assessment, school personnel are being evaluated and thus captivated by making sure that students learn the content outlined in the state standards (and now in the "common core"). For decades, perhaps even centuries since the beginning of schooling in America, the focus has been on the alliterative (and misspelled) phrasing that so easily spills off the tongue: the "3 Rs" of reading, 'riting and 'rithmetic. These have been called "the basics," and those educators who attempt to step outside this box for whatever reason know that in the past the odds of falling flat are high in public discourse. Schools seem to carry the blame. Nonetheless, as a society, throughout the history of public schools, there has been an accepted truth and little true debate about these three areas providing the focal point of education. Call it the 3 Rs' paradigm. When schools in America were formed, dating back to the very first law in Massachusetts in 1647, the established goals were simple: learn enough to be able read the Bible and know enough arithmetic to be able to compute and pay taxes.

In addition, schools in America have also been about building and developing character, studying democracy, and engendering the next generation of democratic citizens who can make *educated* decisions that allow them to keep democracy functioning. This is how Social Studies (which has come to encompass U.S. History and Democratic character building) came to be included as a core subject area. In addition to the social studies, our public schools added additional core content areas—although these additional content areas have been embraced relatively recently. When the former Soviet Union launched Sputnik, the United States countered with a federal initiative, The National Defense Education Act (NDEA) in 1958, to provide federal funding to improve mathematics, science, foreign language, and technical and vocational education in the schools. These different content areas began to develop more formalized curricula and were taken more seriously throughout the school years.

For all the attention to "21st-century learning," most of today's schools in the United States and around the world still focus most of their attention and evaluation on developing student "content" knowledge in the following areas: English Language Arts (ELA—including reading and writing), Mathematics, Science, Social Studies/History, and maybe a bit of foreign language, physical education, and the arts (including music). Assessment has focused on the "core content" areas of reading, writing, math, science, and to lesser degree, social studies. Yet most of the accountability standards focus on the standards of reading, writing, and mathematics.

Letting go of our history for a moment, let's consider our time and place in the world. While most schools and districts have a mission statement that includes the development of intellectual and/or cognitive growth, as well as the social, emotional, and physical foundations, each of these areas is filtered and watered down through a compliance-driven system attending to teaching and testing content knowledge and the skills within each content area (such as reading, writing, and arithmetic). The guiding assumption has been that by giving students content information and concepts at increasing levels of complexity over time there will be a direct impact on their abilities to think and problem solve. The dominant belief system is that if educators stay focused on "the basics" in every content area, then reflective, higher-order thinking will develop *naturally*. This is incorrect and an antiquated view. Of course, cognitive development (as well as social, emotional, and physical changes) do occur "naturally." Every child around the world matures to a certain degree (as they have for thousands of years) within or outside formal schooling through personal, interpersonal, family, and societal interactions. All people mature naturally within a wide array of what may be called the *learning networks* of family ties, peer interaction, formal schools, workplace engagement, and religious/ spiritual places of worship.

WRITING ON THE BLANK SLATE ■

The brain is always learning—it can't help it. The brain learns like the heart beats—it is what it does—all the time, even when we are sleeping. When we are sleeping, the brain is consolidating memories from the time of the day when we are awake. These patterns in brain activity have a direct link to cognitive patterns that may be unconscious and seemingly inaccessible, yet become clearer when unveiled as conscious patterns of thinking for all learners. As learners are introduced to the fundamental cognitive skills as visual patterns through Thinking Maps, or intellectual dispositions such as persistence, perseverance, open-mindedness, and empathy, the often unconscious mental processing students do rises to the surface and can be improved. When these processes remain hidden by the focus on content-specific learning of isolated "facts" and are tested as such, learners rarely rise to a point of metacognition, or becoming actively and continuously engaged in "learning how to learn." They merely "learn" content with fewer opportunities to uncover their own thinking patterns in mind, veiled in the networks of patterns in their brain. We need to make this shift from the "having of content knowledge" to include "reflection on how to learn new knowledge." John Dewey (1933) offered long ago that people don't learn from experience, but from reflecting on the experiences they have.

The awareness of brain processes also informs how our minds work, and tells us much about how in a range of different forms of Thinking Schools, the focus on explicitly teaching students how to become aware of and consciously apply and transfer their own cognitive patterning, dispositions for mindfulness, and questioning for inquiry processes across content areas and in different phases of their lives are keys to the wide-open door of lifelong learning. At the same time, the cognitive science studies over hundreds of years offer a rich tapestry from which we can draw insights, as offered by Alison Gopnik, Andrew Meltzoff, and Patricia Kuhl (2001) in an in-depth synthesis of brain and mind research called *The Scientist in the Crib:*

> We actually know much more about how the mind develops than we do about the brain. There is a tendency to think that changes in the brain must somehow cause changes in our knowledge, that there is, say, some physical change that causes babies to understand things in a new way at eighteen months. But it would be just as accurate to put this another way around. Babies' brains change as a result of the new things they learn about the world. (p. 266)

Consider how a preschool child, a student, and adult learners (teachers and administrators) "learn how to learn" and improve their thinking—the cognitive processes, their dispositions, their acts of inquiry—and how this has a direct impact for more significant future learning, and how brain functioning will be enriched. Each of us has our own unique, integrated combination of cognitive strengths that build and emerge as the brain-mind changes with age. However, just as we have a range of cognitive strengths, we also have areas that are less strong, and these can be improved.

For the past century, psychologists and educators with formal training held firm to the paradigm of a static blank-slate vision: a view of singular and static definition of intelligence, or what is commonly called *smart*. It is as if we each are born with a blank Etch A Sketch for a brain just waiting for someone else from the outside to etch networks onto our brains. This has changed. Neurosciences have opened up the mind from the once "black box" of unknowns because now we can see the new brain at work in utero. Now we *know* differently.

■ THE BRAIN IN MIND

Before we take a pathway through brain developments and implications for learning and the direct facilitation of thinking, let's take a brief detour to make some distinctions between "brain" and "mind" that are key to our discussion. For our discussion here, the *brain* refers to the physical and tangible network of neurons, neurotransmitters, and brain matter (white and grey) contained within our skulls. The *mind* is what we experience as the brain works—that is, the conscious and unconscious experiences we have because the brain is engaging in the work of developing new neuronal patterns, increasing blood flow to stimulate different brain areas, and so on. In teaching and learning, we primarily focus on the prefrontal cortex (described as the seat of reason) and the limbic system (the seat of emotion).

Jeff Hawkins (2004), in his book *On Intelligence* proposed a unifying model of the brain based on what we know about how the cortex works. He argued that all areas of the cortex function largely the same way—they take signals from our senses and translate these into a series of electrical impulses that are stored in a series of sequential patterns. He wrote:

> By design, every cortical region attempts to store and recall sequences. But this is still too simple a description of the brain. The bottom up inputs to a region of cortex are input patterns carried on thousands or millions of axons. These axons come from different regions and contain all sorts of patterns. The number of possible patterns that can exist on even one thousand axons is larger than the number of molecules in the universe. A region will only see a tiny fraction of these possible patterns in a lifetime. (p. 133)

The brain sequences information from our experiences into patterns. Patterns are stored and retrieved. He argues that the cortex functions hierarchically and functions to classify information and passes information both up and down the hierarchy depending on its complexity and novelty (there are six layers/levels). For example, if lower levels of cortex receive new information through the senses (let's say the eyes), and do not recognize a given pattern, it will send the pattern up the hierarchy until it reaches a level that does. Once the cortex recognizes a pattern it sends signals back down the hierarchy. If it receives a pattern it doesn't recognize, it goes to the hippocampus where it is either stored and remembered as a new pattern—or forgotten if it is viewed as insignificant (i.e., no emotional connection is made).

As he admits, Hawkins's theory falls short in the area of understanding how we create new memories from patterns. He states that his theory of the brain and neural networks focused exclusively on the cortex—ignoring the limbic system (older, emotional brain)—because his goal is to build intelligent machines that operate like the human cortex, without the emotional component. Yet, as human learners, choosing what we attend to, what we learn, is determined very much by the limbic/emotional system of the brain. That is, many researchers have shown that for a memory to be retained it must have some kind of emotional connection—what Anthony Damasio termed a "somatic marker."

Of course, there is more to learning than the sequencing and categorizing of neuronal networks developing in the brain, yet these two brain processes surface as conscious processes of the mind, or cognitive processes, as patterns. The study of how people categorize is one of the defining touchstones of behavioral, linguistic, biological, and philosophical research and inquiry. Interestingly, categorization is a central operating principle in the human brain *and the mind*. A second touchstone is sequential reasoning. What we experience from these brain and mind processes is represented in two of the eight Thinking Maps that have been used systematically across Thinking Schools: the Tree Map for categorization, the Flow Map for sequencing. A third Thinking Map, the Multi-Flow Map for predictive, cause and effect reasoning, supports us in conducting causal reasoning generated from our perception of simple sequences. Developmental psychologists from before Jean Piaget through to today have shown the direct linkage of these three cognitive processes to the capacities for defining things in context, describing using our senses, comparing/contrasting, part-to-whole (spatial) reasoning, and thinking by way of analogies and metaphor—which in turn form the basis, respectively, for each Thinking Map. Each of these processes, identified by Piaget (1969/2000) as "mental operations," are interdependent and central to learning. Piaget also stated that these fundamental processes only grow in use toward greater complexity in the context of learning, because they are orchestrated in an endless symphony of thinking and problem solving over a lifetime. Psychologists, such as Piaget, did not have access to the new neuroscience research, but their behavioral/cognitive research nonetheless unveiled fundamental patterns of thinking both in mind and brain. Of course, other theorists such as Sigmund Freud and B. F. Skinner didn't have access either, yet came up with theories that in many ways are still nested within our "old" understandings of human development. In *The Scientist in The Crib*, the authors note as a counterpoint to what we are now finding out about brain, mind, and learning that

Freud and Skinner got the developmental story wrong . . . Freud saw children as the apotheosis of passion, creatures so driven by lusts and hungers that their most basic perceptions of the world were deeply distorted fantasies. Skinner's view was that children were the ultimate blank tablets, passively waiting to be inscribed by reinforcement schedules. (p. 44)

Instead, they state that

The new developmental research shows that this historical consensus about children was just plain wrong. Children are not blank tablets or unbridled appetites or even intuitive seers. Babies and young children think, observe, and reason. They consider evidence, draw conclusions, do experiments, solve problems, and search for truth. Of course, they don't do this in the self-conscious way that scientists do. (p. 35)

Our minds and brains, as we are "processing" incoming information through a very complex matrix of hierarchies and sequences, are forming memories, learning. The way the brain and mind function throughout the human lifespan changes slightly, but the sequential and hierarchical functioning of the neurons as well as the brain areas enlisted for certain cognitive tasks remain the same (although depending on development or aging may change in effectiveness). Researchers are still examining the implications of the developing brain for learning. Understanding our own cognitive portraits in relation to others with whom we are learning and working can be quite useful. In formal learning environments we want students to engage their minds purposefully— reflecting on what their minds are doing both cognitively (processes) and behaviorally (metacognition). The following sections examine what researchers have found out about the developing brain and the implications for the mind and learning in home, school, work, and beyond. But let's remember that it is the *union* of brain, mind, and body within our different environments, languages, cultures, and schools that is essential for the shift in learning for every child.

■ DEVELOPMENTAL JOURNEY OF THE BRAIN

Implications for Developing Purposeful Thinkers

The brain is fascinating, elegant, and complex. We have only begun to scratch the surface in understanding its complexities. However, the evidence we have from the fairly new field of cognitive neuroscience and decades of education and psychological research can help us create a new path in educating ourselves and others to become better users of our brains. Let's take a brief journey through brain development and its implications for thinking from in utero through infancy into early childhood, adolescence, adulthood, and late adulthood. Our first steps begin in the place we first learn how to think—our homes. Then we move on to the next place where we develop our thinking— preschool and then into elementary and secondary education. And then finally, we consider the dynamics of brain development as we enter into our professional spaces and retirement.

Early Childhood Development

Brain development begins in utero and continues exponentially throughout infancy and early childhood. The brain reaches full maturity around age 25 and continues to engage in neurogenesis (building new brain cells) throughout adulthood and even into late adulthood. According to their review of the literature, Fair and Schlaggar (2010) report that "humans exhibit substantial brain growth between birth and adulthood. Adult brains are approximately four times larger than that of infants. This brain growth is not linear. Maximal growth rates occur at full term birth, and by 6 years of age the brain is approximately 95% of the adult size" (p. 320). By age 10, they provide evidence supporting that the brain's volume (size) is the same as an adult—even though it is far from fully developed or mature by then. There are critical periods of growth for the human brain, and certainly in utero and infant development are crucial, but our development continues through our lifetime. Fair and Schlaggar also report that the number of synapses (connections between brain cells/neurons) of a child is about 140% to 150% of an adult. As learning takes place, and the brain develops, synapses are "pruned" to become more efficient.

There is no question that the period from late gestation (30 weeks) through about age 2 is a period of remarkable growth and development. Research on the brain during this period shows "substantial growth in the number of synaptic contacts throughout the cortex"—in short, babies and toddlers are making neuronal connections and developing patterns of synaptic firing at rapid speed and perhaps more than at any other time in development. But toddlers and babies do not have the same cognitive abilities as older children, adolescents, and adults. In addition, during this period of infancy, we experience "infantile amnesia"—meaning, we don't remember anything prior to about age 2. Experts are still struggling to explain this phenomenon of infantile amnesia. Could the infant brain be trained to remember or is there something fundamentally physiological that prevents this from happening? This is still unknown. We do know much about the capabilities of the infant brain, however. Bringing together cognitive and brain science, in *The Scientist in the Crib*, the authors show that

> babies persistently explore the properties of objects. Six- or seven-month-olds will systematically examine a new object with every sense they have at their command (including taste, of course). By a year or so, they will systematically vary the actions they perform on an object: they might tap a new toy car gently against the floor, listening to the sound it makes, then try banging it loudly, and then try banging it against the soft sofa. By eighteen months, if you show them an object with some unexpected property, like a can that makes a mooing noise, they will systematically test to see if it will do other unexpected things. And, as we saw, children will quite spontaneously sort different kinds of objects into different piles. (pp. 87–88)

Could these young children be taught to develop their thinking more explicitly? Can they sequence? Examine cause and effect? Describe? Compare and contrast? The research literature on infancy suggests yes. Infants do appear to have innate cognitive capabilities in these areas. We would not be able to intervene or "program" thinking at infancy, but infants at birth are thinking. They certainly can discern between their mother's voice and that of a stranger, by comparison and contrast. They can differentiate between sounds of words within their own culture and cease to recognize certain sounds that are not within their native language, if they are not exposed to a live model speaking that language (Kuhl, Tsao, & Liu, 2003). Infants live by cause and effect (e.g., sucking on this nipple will give me milk, if I cry I will get help). Infants mimic the sequential patterns of movement. These cognitive processes and thus patterns identified in the Thinking Maps model appear to have roots that are innate to the brain. Kuhl and her colleagues offer that the comparison between scientists and babies helps us back map our understanding of brain development through cognitive development: "Scientists are such successful learners because they use cognitive abilities that evolution designed for the use of children" (p. 239). "We think that these distinctively human cognitive emotions—the agony of confusion and the ecstasy of explanation—may be the mark of the operation of the natural cognitive system that allows us to learn when we are very young" (p. 251).

During early childhood in most regions of the brain, no new neurons are formed after birth. Instead, brain development consists of an ongoing process of wiring and rewiring the connections among neurons. New synapses between cells are constantly being formed, while others are being pruned away. This "pruning" of the hierarchical networks happens throughout our lifespan as we learn new things—basically the brain has a "use it or lose it" focus to its pruning. Babies as early as 8 months have around 1,000 trillion synapses (connections between neurons), many of which are pruned away as they grow, develop, and become more efficient thinkers. Babies at this age have been shown in research on language learning to lose the ability to hear certain key sounds in languages if they are not exposed to them. The research on Babies conducted by Kuhl and her colleagues has shown, for example, that English-speaking babies at this age, when exposed to sounds unique to the Japanese language, will continue to recognize them, but if they are never exposed to these sounds their brains will not even process them. They have found this repeatedly with various language sounds from a variety of cultures.

Early learning experiences are critical to prevent overpruning—that is, where the brain eliminates areas that are not being used or developed. "Surgeons now remove congenital cataracts as early in infancy as possible because they know that if they wait until the child is older, the neural connections between his eyes and his brain will fail to develop properly and he will never be able to see" (Kuhl, Tsao, & Liu, 2003, para. 6). Neuroscientists are still working to determine exactly the causes of pruning and how this wiring and rewiring happens. This understanding does call for at least investigating early facilitation of thinking in infants and young children.

Emotional development and healthy attachments also influence brain development. Learning is intimately connected to the emotional centers of the brain, so if these fail to develop normally, then learning will be difficult. We do know from longitudinal studies such as the University of North Carolina's

"Abecedarian Project" that those children at risk because of poverty and low maternal interaction and education levels improve their IQ scores from targeted interventions. The impact of these early interventions are long lasting—well into adulthood, where the participants still showed a clear cognitive advantage over the control group (Ramey, Campbell, & Blair, 1998). However, good, targeted educational interventions during this period of early childhood can make a difference in cognitive development. How then, do we intervene?

Young children do unconsciously engage in the cognitive processes grounding Thinking Maps and other visual tools based on cognitive processing, although they may not recognize it explicitly. They sequence, examine causation, make comparisons and analogies, engage in spatial reasoning, description and categorization, and define in context. Can they be taught to recognize when their brains are engaging in these activities? Absolutely. Can young children learn the fundamentals of thinking and recognize and build their skills with help from adults? Yes, they can with a consistent language and scaffolding and support from adults as they learn the language.

And as with learning anything new, it should be fun, as the Habits of Mind model created by Costa and Kallick propose. There should be wonder and awe, and humor, and interdependent engagement in learning environments. As Daniel Pink (2009) argues in his book *Drive,* to motivate learners, activities should have three components: opportunities for autonomy, mastery, and purpose. Of course, the fun or pleasurable feelings the brain gives from pleasure chemicals (neurotransmitters) come from successful mastery and opportunities for mastery and purpose. Look at what children choose to do when left to their own devices. They like to "play." Children like play because it is autonomous, they can master or get better at what they are doing (think monkey bars or video games), and they have a purpose (making friends, maybe the sheer endorphin rush from exercise, etc.). It has been observed that in the absence of adult intervention, children redefine the rules of a game in the moment to keep playing, despite the presence of an obvious "victor." The game's the thing, as a paraphrase of Shakespeare offers. A game, in other words, is "dynamic inquiry" or "problem solving" for self and with others. (This is one reason why video games are so enticing, and sometimes addicting: The opportunity to be challenged and gain mastery is *always* available.) Enhancing thinking through play is a great lesson from childhood that we can take throughout our lifespan. A learning task shouldn't be painful. If it is, learning will be short-circuited by the learner. This is how our brains are wired.

The cognitive work that young brains are being asked to do on a regular basis as "digital natives" is also different from that of the earlier generation (digital immigrants). As Prensky (2005) argues, digital natives use quicker "twitch speed" to go back and forth between ideas and technological gadgetry more rapidly versus the more "conventional speed" of the digital immigrants. In addition, and perhaps even more important for engendering the capacity to "think about our thinking," digital natives tend to engage in more "parallel processing" where they are able to multitask with several electronic devices and interactions at once. Whereas traditional or "digital immigrants" tend to engage in more linear processing and linear thinking that trends toward text-based learning, digital natives tend to look at connections and look for graphics first. That is, rather than "text-first" strategies of digital immigrants, digital natives tend to seek pictures, visual representation, and graphics first (Prensky, 2005) with text embedded. Now more than ever, this generation of digital natives craves visual representations—these are what they are used to; to ignore this cognitive expectation within a formal learning context would be a mistake likely to lead to rapid disengagement. Extensive cognitive science research has shown that the brain is dominantly visual. Of course, the recurring, common, and dynamic visual display of patterns for each *Thinking* (cognitive pattern) *Map* (dynamic visual networks) thus plays to the strength of a visual brain of many young learners, who are now all digital natives.

Are preschoolers already thinking like digital natives? Robyn Zevenbergen (2007) in her literature review concludes that the answer is a resounding yes! In her article "Digital Natives Come to Preschool," she discusses the implications for education. She argues that educators sometimes fail to recognize such differences, but if we pay attention to these differences, there is potential for important gains in learning. She proposes that "early childhood settings need to reconceptualize pedagogy and learning opportunities for the new generation of learners" who have "grown up in very different social conditions from previous generations, mainly through the saturation of digital technologies" (p. 19).

Early Thinking in the Home

What does all this mean for infants and young children in the home and at day care centers and preschool? First, we know that early intervention matters and that the young brain has tremendously adaptive plasticity, and the impact we have on the young brain's development can be long-lasting. We know that the brain is pruning fast and furiously during this time period of early childhood. We know that emotional centers and emotional development is being developed during this time. So what can we do? We need to help even very young children recognize the thinking that their brains are doing and provide them skills to recognize certain types of thinking and when each is needed. In addition, we need to assess young children's cognitive strengths and follow their development in each of the cognitive areas. We can directly introduce them to their own cognitive processes in playful, engaging ways. We need to make learning fun. This can happen using Daniel Pink's advice about motivation—making experiences autonomous with opportunities for mastery and a sense of purpose. Naming forms of cognition (e.g., "this is sequencing and this is describing") for young children can help, so when they go to school they have an awareness of their thinking and are ready to be more purposeful . . . and metacognitive.

To this end, my colleagues and I developed an early childhood and lower elementary series of stories for children for use by parents and adults that we are in the process of piloting in Thinking Schools. Playing off the classic "farm animal" scenario, we empowered each of eight animals, respectively, with eight specific cognitive processes. We have called these animals *Thinking Friends*, who work together on the farm with Farmer Framer to create their own school, think through and solve problems together, and "learn how to learn" new content about thematic topics such as the weather and veterinarians.

In specific terms, Thinking Friends are eight animal characters, living life on a farm, with each animal having the personality, respectively, of a single fundamental thinking/cognitive skill (sequencing, defining, describing, cause and effect, comparing/contrasting, classifying, examining parts of objects/spatial reasoning, and using analogies) and style. As children engage with the Thinking Friends, they learn to identify and think about their own thinking (metacognition). These explicit lessons about their thinking allow them to become more skillful thinkers and successful learners as their young brains mature. At the same time, children are becoming more attuned to the different ways others approach thinking. The education goals are quite clearly stated for parents and teachers:

- Children will become aware of the different thinking processes they and others use in their daily lives—specifically, sequencing, defining, classifying, describing, comparing, and explaining analogies, causes and effects of events, and parts of whole objects
- Parents and teachers can assess children's cognitive strengths and weaknesses
- Children become more purposeful and grounded in cognition/thinking rather than just on content
- Children will build early skills in mathematics and science concepts through the content of the stories
- Children will build early literacy in reading and making sense of stories and nonfiction text
- Children will be able to use their Frame of Reference to explain the source of their knowledge and provide evidence for their ideas

First, young children are introduced to each of the characters and his or her individual cognitive strength. As young children become more familiar with the characters, and more aware of their individual cognitive styles, the stories become more complex. The Thinking Friends begin to think and work together to improve and expand their own thinking, content learning, problem solving, and social-emotional approaches to building relationships. Along with the characters, the children learn to appreciate the complexity of ideas, the different perspectives that can be taken, and the value of working cooperatively.

Here are the eight primary characters and their respective, primary cognitive strength:

Farmer Framer/Framer—His cognitive/thinking contribution to the stories is that he *frames* problems and looks at *perspective taking*—Farmer Framer surveys the perimeter of the barnyard "framing" the topic, issue, or problem under consideration in a story or script. He helps the Thinking Friends identify how they know what they know, surface the factors that influence their ideas, and formulate conclusions and insights from their experiences.

Snakey Sequencer—His cognitive/thinking strength is *sequencing*. Snakey puts things in order and focuses on the sequencing of ideas, things, numbers, alphabet, events, and so on.

Doggie Definer—His cognitive/thinking strength is *defining* or *understanding context*. Doggie focuses on defining or understanding a given situation or context. He brainstorms everything he knows about a concept or the questions about it that he would like to find the answers to.

Chicky Comparer—Her cognitive/thinking strength is *comparing and contrasting* the similarities and differences between different people, animals, places, and things.

Cowsie Cows N Effect—Her cognitive/thinking strength is *examining cause and effect*. She examines the causes and effects of actions and events.

Donkey Describer—His cognitive/thinking strength is *describing*. He uses adjectives and the five senses to describe the attributes and qualities of people, places, and things.

Kitty Categories—Her cognitive/thinking strength is *categorizing*. She categorizes or groups together ideas, things, events, experiences, and animals.

Pony Parter—Her cognitive/thinking strength is examining *parts of whole objects* and considering how objects fit in space.

Rooster Relationships—His cognitive/thinking strength is examining *analogies* or analogous relationships between and among ideas and things— that is, he helps identify the "relating factor" that connects different ideas to each other, thereby expanding the meaning of those ideas.

Because we do not use only one thinking process to solve problems as we go through our day and lives, the final three stories in this guide show the Thinking Friends working together with Farmer Framer. Important to note, over many weeks and months, each of the characters has already been introduced to children through their respective story. For example, in the story introducing Snakey Sequencer, Snakey engages with Farmer Framer in thinking through the best order for the Farmer to plan out all the priorities for the day on the farm. By the time of an advanced story, Thinking Friends are beginning to "think together" about how to define and describe a veterinarian, compare and create an analogy between a veterinarian and a human doctor and the different categories of veterinarians, and the causes and effects of getting shots (which don't hurt so much!). In the end, Snakey Sequencer asks the question about which animal will be first, second, and third in line for a shot!

In these stories, the Thinking Friends think and problem solve interdependently and begin to develop the thinking skills that each of the others represents. The Farmer "frames" the question for the Friends, who work together using their thinking styles to contribute solutions. Ultimately,

Farmer Framer embodies one of Costa and Kallick's Habits of Mind, the disposition of metacognition: He helps all the Thinking Friends think about their thinking and engage with each other through questioning for collaborative inquiry. Beyond solving problems together, they learn to appreciate each other's thinking strength and learn the importance of working together. They also learn that everyone has different things they do well, each can improve their range of thinking processes, and every one of us animals can contribute to the group!

This is just one example of how to explicitly surface cognitive processes that work in parallel to the basic processes the brain is using at much more complex and unconscious levels. Children, through this kind of engagement, are not only learning about words associated with farm animals, or the weather, or veterinarians, but they also are learning the language of thinking that they can begin to transfer to any other story they read, any content they learn, and to their own evolving story of development. They are learning about how to coordinate these processes as they work in groups to solve problems, and ultimately, they are becoming ever more reflective on their own strengths as thinkers and learners, and where they need to improve.

Where We Are: Childhood, Adolescence and Content-Focused Schools

As young children enter school, they are bombarded with cognitive tasks. Suddenly they need to be independent in their thinking too. They need to manage social and academic cognitive demands. The whole field of "cognitive load" is now surfacing as we realize how working memory relates to long-term memory and the influences of multitasking. This can be overwhelming for children. Guiding children in recognizing the thinking they are doing in a given challenging situation can help.

One of the most important and challenging tasks for children's brains to do when they enter school is to learn to read. There has been a great deal of research on how the brain learns to read in childhood and some of the difficulties with this task. The good news is that studies have shown that children who are struggling readers (including those with reading disorders such as dyslexia) can actually rework, and thus rewire, their brains to read more like typically developing readers with proper early intervention (see the work of Sally Shaywitz and Benita Blachman).

The brain in childhood is going through a period of neurogenesis and pruning as well as further myelination of the synapses (which makes the neuronal signals travel faster and more efficiently). Some children's nerve cells myelinate more quickly than others, and thus they may be quicker (earlier) in their cognitive abilities than others. Older children in classrooms typically have the speed advantage and as a result tend to get more opportunities to engage and answer questions than younger, cognitively slower but still maturing students. This cycle tends to advantage those developing at a quicker pace cognitively.

Reading involves so many complex forms of cognition. Regarding the underlying cognitive processes grounding Thinking Maps, students must be able to recognize and identify letters *in context; describe* their sounds; *compare and contrast* different letters and their sounds; *sequence* letters to make words; sentences, paragraphs, and so on; *classify* types of letters, sounds, words, chunks, parts of speech, and so on; and recognize *analogies*/relationships between and among types of letters, words, pieces of writing, and so on. The maps thus provide a range of student-centered visual tools that, like the Thinking Friends discussed above, become the conscious support mechanism for transferring thinking processes into practice.

There can be a breakdown in cognition at any point in these different forms that would affect the way a child learns to read. For example, one child with whom I have worked has very strong spatial reasoning skills. As a result she tries to look at the whole word form and shape and guess based on that rather than defining each letter sound in context and sequencing each sound. Once we identified the problem in the cognition, we were able to help her sound out each letter sequentially to read the words and read the phrases. As she becomes stronger as a reader, she can remember entire word chunks and rely on those to sequence. We can use the same strategies described above in early childhood—that is, using the cognitive portrait to determine cognitive strengths using the Thinking Maps.

The Adolescent Brain in School

The area of adolescent brain development has received a great deal of attention from researchers and policy makers alike. Discussions of the possibility of the juvenile death penalty in the *Roper v. Simmons* case in 2004 sparked a flurry of discussions about the implications of the research on the teen brain and how fully developed/mature the brain really is during this period and whether or not it can be held accountable for its actions. The adolescent brain is far from fully mature. Consistently the research shows that the period of puberty is marked by much brain development:

> During this time, gray matter—areas of the brain responsible for processing information and storing memories—increases in size, particularly in the frontal lobe of the brain, as a result of an increase in the number of synaptic connections between nerve cells. Around puberty, however, a winnowing process begins in which connections that are not used or reinforced begin to wither (hence the "use-it-or-lose-it" hypothesis). This pruning, which begins around age 11 in girls and 12 in boys, continues into the early or mid-20s, particularly in the prefrontal cortex, an area associated with "higher" functions such as planning, reasoning, judgment, and impulse control. As Dr. Jay Giedd of the National Institute of Mental Health has said, the real cognitive advances come with paring down or reducing the number of synaptic connections. During adolescence, the amount of myelin, a fatty, insulating material that coats the axons of nerve cells—similar to the way insulation coats a wire—also increases, improving the nerve cells' ability to conduct electrical signals and to function efficiently; this too continues into adulthood and occurs later in "higher" regions of the brain, such as the prefrontal cortex. (Schaffer, 2004, para. 3)

Pruning and myelination continue throughout adolescence and affect the way the adolescent brain functions. Abigail Baird and colleagues (2005) have shown that the way the adolescent brain processes decision making can be quite different from that of adults. Adults, for example, when asked whether "swimming with sharks" is a "good idea" or a "bad idea" respond with the emotional brain and instantly—far more quickly than the adolescent brain. Adolescents try to think about questions like this with their more rational brains and come up with mixed responses and take longer. In focus groups for example, students would respond with comments such as "well, maybe if you're with a friend it could be a good idea to swim with sharks." Clearly the adolescent brain has a lot of developing to do before it reaches full adult maturity.

While the spike in synaptic connections in early childhood (around age 3) is well-known, less well-known is the spike in the production of synapses (synaptogenesis) that happens just prior to adolescence. In their landmark study "Brain Development during childhood and adolescence: A longitudinal MRI study," Giedd et al. (1999) examined the brains of 145 healthy boys and girls from age 4.2 to 21.6. They postulated that this period of preadolescence through adolescence "may herald a critical stage of development when the environment or activities of the teenager may guide selective synapses elimination during adolescence" (p. 863). Basically, because this is a critical period of brain growth and pruning, experiences of the brain during this time are crucial.

ASSESSMENT OF COGNITION AND ■ COGNITIVE PORTRAITS

Across schools, and especially in the environment such as in Thinking Schools where fluency with processes such as Thinking Maps, Habits of Mind, and questioning techniques used in collaborative inquiry are developed, teachers and students alike can effectively learn to use the tools for formative assessment of student thinking and content learning. We call this *bifocal assessment* (Hyerle & Williams, 2008) because students and teachers can focus simultaneously on content learning and their cognitive strengths, and refine ways to collect and create cognitive profiles to deepen strengths and further develop weaker cognitive areas. Ideally, these cognitive profiles could be used to engage in differentiated instruction to improve thinking and learning for all learners.

As shown throughout this book, with Thinking Maps there is the added benefit of the visual tools being the actual structures for academic language and content concepts, and over time to purposefully assess cognitive strengths and areas that need improvement. To effectively use the maps as a strategy for assessing student strengths, students must be fluent with all eight maps and the frame of reference. Without a high level of fluency it would be difficult to determine if the student performance on certain thinking tasks is a result of limited proficiency with the maps or a cognitive skill, or simply an area that is underdeveloped. Teachers need to offer many opportunities for students to demonstrate all the eight forms of cognition and collect as much evidence as possible in each of these areas. Collaboration across disciplines can be helpful because student thinking can be influenced by the subject matter as well. As teachers collect student maps, they can consider the tree rubric below to determine the degree to which a student chooses a given map, uses it correctly, and represents thinking fully within it (see Figure 3.1).

If a student is scoring "never" or "rarely" in each of these three categories, there may be a problem with that cognitive area. Collect student work samples that demonstrate their best thinking in these areas. Create "thinking portfolios" where students choose their most representative thinking. Once identified and once work begins to rectify the problem, then evidence should be collected to demonstrate improvement. Thinking portfolios and cognitive portraits can also be used to differentiate instruction for all learners, but particularly learners with special cognitive needs. If it turns out that a student has a serious cognitive deficit and, despite interventions, shows minimal improvement, it may be necessary to help tailor instruction to meet those needs. School psychologists and special education teachers are often familiar with whom to scaffold and improve cognitive skills, while many regular classroom teachers, though familiar with this area, normally are so focused on content-specific learning that they may not know how to zero in, assess, and support students in this area. Because of this situation, many students who may not be coded "special education" remain in remedial classrooms because their cognitive strengths and weakness are *never* assessed, thus never directly mediated and improved.

For example, a college student with whom I work intensively has a serious nonverbal learning disability. Despite consistent work to build his understanding of causal reasoning, he still struggles mightily in this area. We still work to build his causal reasoning with the Multi-Flow Map—focusing on either "causes" or "effects" but rarely both in the same map. Sometimes, when mapping challenging reading for his college-level history courses, rather than focus on causes and effects of events, we look at categorizing information into a Tree Map as "good" or "bad" or "potentially problematic" or "potentially positive" and so on. He has become quite good at categorizing using the Tree Map (this is not uncommon, I've found, among social science majors). Then we use the Multi-Flow from

Figure 3.1 Tree Map Rubric for Assessing Cognitive Challenges Using Thinking Maps

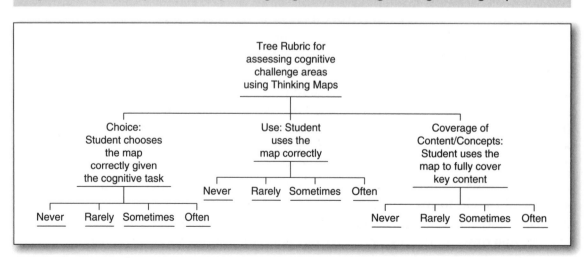

these positive outcomes or problematic outcomes to build the Multi-Flow and look at the "effects."

I have worked with a different college student who has a great social science mind but has repeated a statistics course because he struggles to understand the formulas. We started capitalizing on his strength in sequencing (using the Flow Map) and his strength in classifying (using the Tree Map) to sequence and classify key ideas in statistics using words rather than numbers. As a result, he understood the ideas so well conceptually that he could explain why these different formulae worked and when they were appropriate to use. When he would get stuck in a problem, he would use a Flow Map to sequence it using words and classify where this type of formula fit in the larger theoretical framework of statistics. He developed into one of the best students in the class, and the teacher would call on him to explain difficult concepts to his classmates. These examples show how we can capitalize on students' cognitive strengths to leverage them to build and improve their cognitive weaknesses. The maps help with the diagnosis and the intervention and with the assessment after the intervention.

ADULTHOOD: TEACHERS, LEADERS, AND ■ PARENTS HAVE CHANGING BRAINS, TOO

The brain continues to learn and form new memories throughout adulthood and into old age. A relatively new finding in neuroscience is that adults continue neurogenesis (creation of new brain cells) until death. Fair and Schlaggar (2010) contend from their extensive review of the literature on brain maturation that "brain development is dynamic. Interactions between brain regions are constantly changing over age, leading to an assortment of adjustments with regard to the contribution of a brain region to any particular task" (p. 327). This finding offers promise—we can continue to build on our cognitive strengths and enhance our weaker areas of cognition. Identifying those strengths and weaknesses using the Cognitive Portrait can be useful for adults as well as students. As teachers, administrators, community members, and parents, we are all continuing to learn and grow as we help young people learn and grow. As we interact, understanding our own cognitive strengths can be very useful to our ongoing personal and professional development—basically to improving our thinking. For example, if a teacher or a parent has cognitive strengths in classification and sequencing, he or she may overly rely on cognitive tasks that focus on these two areas at the expense of the other six. Recognizing this cognitive style bias will help teachers and parents develop their own cognitive skills across all areas, and in turn help develop these cognitive skills in their children and/or students. As we discussed above with the Thinking Friends example, we need to focus on the full range of cognitive processes for every child. Looking for learners' cognitive strengths and drawing on them exclusively *or* identifying cognitive weaknesses (often called the *deficit model*) and just trying to improve these few processes leaves learners in both situations without a full array of possible cognitive processes that they will certainly need to draw on over their lifetime.

As adults, we are all cast in the role of leader at one point or another—at work or as parents or caregivers. How can we best function in that leadership role? The Thinking Maps have been shown in the research to enhance the productivity, efficiency, and clarity of groups working with a leader trained in the Thinking Maps model (Alper, Williams, & Hyerle, 2011). The leader, as a skilled thinker, can identify the kind of thinking required in a given task and then choose the correct map(s) to engage in collaborative thinking with a group or person to resolve an issue, plan a project, problem solve, and even make the most difficult of decisions (read Chapter 10 by Larry Alper and David N. Hyerle about this research). The leader can capitalize on his or her cognitive strengths and enlist those with complementary strengths to help facilitate in other areas. For example, let's say a leader is strong in sequencing and classifying but less strong in spatial reasoning. Perhaps there is a plan for a new addition to the school. The leader may want to enlist as members of her team those strong in spatial reasoning to help with the physical design of the space. The use of the Thinking Maps encourages collaborative leadership as people work together using their cognitive strengths to solve problems and engage in planning. Working together on the same canvas of thinking, the brainpower of many can be harnessed by a skilled thinking leader. The results are impressive. Leaders using Thinking Maps say that their work with groups is more effective and efficient and the level of thinking is enhanced.

The vision of Thinking Schools is centered on this idea that all participants in a school are consciously engaged in the improvement of their thinking, and maintaining an awareness of cognitive science and brain research that informs this endeavor, all framed by an understanding that each of us has a range of unique qualities. The interplay of thinking processes, dispositions, and inquiry is the ground on which students, teachers, administrators, board members, and parents can play. If we are to facilitate the rich complexity of the human brain, we will need to turn our focus to these kinds of avenues for growth and shift away from rote learning by students, lower-order questioning and lesson design by teachers, and leadership driven in schools by positional power and not the collaborative empowerment catalyzed by thinking together.

■ LATE ADULTHOOD: KEEPING THE BRAIN ACTIVE AND ENHANCING MEMORY

One of the biggest cognitive challenges in later adulthood is enhancing memory. Sometimes the difficulty may be in memory retrieval (e.g., "I know that, but I can't come up with it") or creating new memories (e.g., "I need to remember to pick up some milk on the way home"). Either way, developing a deeper understanding of the cognition needed and of one's cognitive strengths can help with memory.

First, recognizing what kind of thinking is needed to enhance memory retrieval or creation can be a useful first step. The challenges and preferences depend on one's Cognitive Portrait. Nonetheless, using the Thinking Maps to help create or form new memories can be helpful—whether the cognitive task is relatively simple or complex— in identifying the thinking needed and then creating the maps accordingly to help form the memory. For example, let's take a fairly routine task of going to the grocery store that more than one teacher has told us about: Teachers have reported that they categorize the items needed using a Tree Map (e.g., produce, meat, dairy, etc.) and also create a Flow Map for thinking through the sequence of their day, which includes grocery shopping. Of course, comparison shopping is a common challenge, particularly when buying large items such as a car or a house, or even helping chose between colleges for a daughter or son. Drawing out a Double-Bubble Map has helped many people we know think through decisions. One teacher in Florida actually used all eight maps to fully understand her marriage! The added benefit is that Thinking Maps can help get the ideas into memory as one creates them.

As far as memory retrieval, the Thinking Maps are helpful because the brain remembers patterns, especially when linked to images. As you look around your room, take a mental snapshot and then close your eyes. You can basically recreate the image in your mind, much like a camera. (See Temple Grandin's amazing book, *Thinking in Pictures*, to learn more about the amazing visual memory capacities of the human brain.) The same is true of the Thinking Maps. Once a map is created by hand or on software and learned, most learners of any age can close his or her eyes and recreate the image to enhance memory retrieval. Deborah Burke's research on "tip of the tongue" phenomena (when you can't quite come up with a name or thought or idea that you know you know) suggests that as we age these experiences are a result of a weakening of neural connections responsible for what we process and retrieve. She also offers recommendations about how we can improve memory retrieval in these instances: build associations and connections. Thinking Maps can help with these associations, too, by mapping out what you're trying to remember and kick-starting those weak linkages by looking at the patterns of associations with it. Of course, you can always use Google to find it in a nanosecond. But for things we can't Google and would like to remember—names of acquaintances, important dates, items on a to-do list, and so on, the Thinking Maps can help activate the weakened network of associations.

THINKING SCHOOLS: THINKING BRAINS ■

The fulcrum on which Thinking Schools balances plays out with these questions: What if we were to design schools with a focus on teaching students how to *think*—that is, the focus was on *thinking* rather than on content-specific knowledge? What would that look like? How might it be different? What might the outcomes be for students? For future democratic participants?

Let's imagine that students first learn the basic universals of thinking—that is, the cognitive universals outlined in the Thinking Maps model (as well as Habits of Mind and inquiry strategies). The theory, research, and practice of Thinking Maps over the past 25 years is already well-developed and may be referenced by visiting www.thinkingfoundation.org. These are cognitive strategies that have been described and supported by cognitive psychologists for decades. Thinking Maps have been used from pre–K to college and in the workplace, so there is already a rich history to draw from. Unfortunately, the implementation of Thinking Maps, though based on whole schools, does not always move from school to school with the student. While many school districts have focused on feeder patterns for continuity of a thinking approach, this has not always been the norm. Schools should continue to build on these thinking skills throughout a child's schooling, for what Hyerle has called *continuous cognitive development*. Such is the case with dispositions, questioning for inquiry, philosophical approaches (Philosophy for Children) and other high-quality models for different pathways for facilitating thinking.

■ CONCLUSIONS: THINKING HOMES, THINKING SCHOOLS, THINKING WORLD

Picture a future where purposeful thinking is prioritized in our homes, schools, workplaces, and beyond, one in which our minds learn to identify the different kinds of thinking that are needed in a situation and use that thinking purposefully (either individually or collaboratively) to determine the best possible choices, outcomes, and so on. We would become much more reflective and metacognitive about what our minds are thinking. We could become more efficient, purposeful, and productive. We engage and efficiently use our brains to improve the function of our minds—throughout our lifespan.

We need to first name our thinking, then represent it using a language that is universal, and finally determine and use the best thinking in any given situation. We become a world of intentional, productive, and collaborative thinkers. From there, the possibilities are endless. We could create thinking homes, thinking schools, and a thinking world. As we discussed at the beginning of this chapter, the facilitation of thinking does not wait for preschool or those first days of kindergarten. Thinking comes with each and every birth, with the first breath before the eyes open, and a brain that is already actively wiring and firing. Also, as we project into the near future, thinking has already been richly developed in the mind of the parent holding this newborn, a parent who has learned how to *think for themselves* and with others as part of the journey of a Thinking School.

QUESTIONS FOR ENQUIRY

The walls of schools have literally and figuratively been built on a foundation of content. While not entirely set in stone (Williams points out how content has shifted over time), content has remained the focus or the building block. What might be the implications for "schooling" as content becomes so easily and universally accessible? How can the physical and figurative walls of schools be transformed into opportunities rather than become impediments for learning?

Williams states that a "compliance-driven system" dilutes learning by influencing teaching in a particular way. What are ways that assessing student learning or demonstrating understanding can be used to promote learning rather than retard it?

If, as Williams claims, "the brain learns as the heart beats," what might be the unintended ways the brain is being influenced by experiences in schools as they are generally constituted today? How might the current understanding of how the brain works be used to shift patterns and structures of teaching and learning in schools to better align them with who we are as human beings and the challenges and opportunities in today's world?

REFERENCES AND FURTHER READINGS ■

Alper, L., Williams, K., & Hyerle, D. (2011). *Developing connective leadership using thinking maps.* Bloomington, IA: Solution Tree Press.

Baird, A., Fugelsang, J., & Bennett, C. (2005, April). *"What were you thinking?" An fMRI study of adolescent decision making.* Poster presented at the annual meeting of the Cognitive Neuroscience Society, New York, NY.

Dewey, J. (1933). *How we think: A restatement of the relation of reflective thinking to the educative process.* Boston, MA: D. C. Heath.

Fair, D. A., & Schlaggar, B. L. (2010). Brain development and CNS plasticity. In D. Borsook, L. R. Beccera, E. Bullmore, & R. J. Hargreaves (Eds.), *Imaging in CNS Drug discovery and development: Implications for disease and therapy* (pp. 319–335). New York, NY: Springer.

Giedd, J. N., Blumenthal, J., Jeffries, N. O., Castellanos, F. X., Liu, H., Zijdenbos, A., . . . Rappoport, J. (1999). *Brain development during childhood and adolescence: A longitudinal MRI study.* Retrieved from http://www.math.tau.ac .il/~dms/Longitudinal/brain_MRI.pdf

Gopnik, A., Meltzoff, A. N., Kuhl, P. (2001). *The scientist in the crib: What early learning tells us about the mind.* New York, NY: HarperCollins.

Hawkins, J. (with Blakeslee, S.). (2004). *On intelligence.* New York, NY: Holt Paperbacks.

Hyerle, D., & Williams, K. (2008). Bifocal assessment in the cognitive Age: Thinking maps for assessing content learning and cognitive processes. In D. Hyerle & L. Alper (Eds.), *Student successes with thinking maps: School-based research, results, and models for achievement using visual tools* (pp. 204–216). Thousand Oaks, CA: Corwin.

Kuhl, P. K., Tsao, F. M., & Liu, H. M. (2003). Foreign language experience in infancy: Effects of short-term exposure and social interaction on phonetic learning. *National Academy of Sciences, 100*(15), 9096–9101.

Piaget, J., & Inhelder, B. (1969/2000). *The psychology of the child.* New York, NY: Basic Books.

Pink, D. P. (2009). *Drive: The surprising truth about what motivates us.* New York, NY: Riverhead Books.

Prensky, M. (2005). *Digital natives: How they think differently.* Retrieved from http://coe. sdsu.edu/eet/articles/digitalnatives//start.htm

Ramey, C., Campbell, F., & Blair, C. (1998). Enhancing the life course for high-risk children. In J. Crane (Ed.), *Social programs that work* (pp. 184–199). New York, NY: Russell Sage Foundation. [Note: Additional statistics are cited on the Abecedarian Project's website at http://www.fpg.unc.edu/verity/]

Schaffer, A. (2004, October 15). *Head case:* Roper v. Simmons *asks how adolescent and adult brains differ.* Retrieved from http://www.slate.com/articles/health_and_ science/medical_examiner/2004/10/head_case.html

Williams, K., Alper, L., & Hyerle, D. (in press). *Thinking friends: A teacher's and parent's guide for developing thinking in children.* Lyme, NH: Designs for Thinking.

Zevenbergen, R. (2007). Digital natives come to preschool: Implications for early childhood practice. *Contemporary Issues in Early Childhood, 8*(1), 19–29.

4

Criteria

Editors' Introduction

In the last two chapters, Lisa Dellamora and Kim Williams offered a challenging "ripple effects" view of future schooling if we continue to pursue a vision of learning based primarily on the teaching and testing of knowledge in the isolated silos we call content areas while disregarding what we now know about 21st-century learning needs and neuroscience research. Many of the innovations that surface to shift from this antiquated view seem as isolated: Bring in a "new" program, more supervision and evaluation of teachers, reduced class size and/or school size, promote technology use by student, privatize schools for more competition and innovation, apply isolated "brain-based" research to practice, focus on "best practices" by teachers, develop consistent curriculum and units of study based on new standards or the "common core," and engage teachers as leaders. Schools and systems have attempted to do some or all of these things and often with some success. But these trials, errors, and successes are often measured against the existing paradigm of 20th-century learning rather than projecting forward into the rapidly changing landscape of global education in the cognitive age. If the focus of the whole school still remains fundamentally imbalanced toward "content learning," then we have improved on that which is antiquated rather than transforming schools toward a new paradigm.

What is the alternative? Professor Emeritus Bob Burden of Exeter University in the United Kingdom has been investigating this question for most of his career. As one of the world leaders in the field of dyslexia, he paralleled this primary research area with close attention to the evolving field of cognitive-based teaching, learning, and assessment. Bob's extensive international work has informed his respect for the cultural contexts that frame individual growth, classroom practice, and whole school change. Bob's deep understanding of the practice and theory of a range of dimensions of thinking and practical classroom approaches to thinking give us the grounding for comprehensive definition of and criteria for Thinking Schools. Few have the experience to attempt, to even risk defining that which seems so diffuse. Bob offers an explicit answer to the question What constitutes a Thinking School? The 14 criteria that Bob has developed for use by any school around the world is used as a reflective framework—not a template or checklist—for schools that want to map out their own vision. Schools may also engage in the collaborative process of becoming accredited as a Thinking School. Does this sound odd? Not really, because Bob also conveys that the process of accreditation is a journey that proceeds forward with continuous development, and not an end point.

CRITERIA FOR A THINKING SCHOOLS APPROACH

Bob Burden

INTRODUCTION ■

By far the most rewarding aspect of developing a 'Thinking School Culture' has been the impact on our pupils' attitudes towards learning, on their motivation and their growing sense of themselves as learners. We are constantly amazed by their sharing of their thinking and (teachers) no longer make assumptions about pupils' capacities to learn. Pupils have become increasingly more involved in their learning with teachers becoming more confident in relinquishing their control, giving greater choices to our pupils.

You've got to jump in with two feet, it's got to be a whole school approach, otherwise it won't work . . . (Affley, p. 2).

The first decade of the 21st century has witnessed the beginnings of a mini-revolution in curriculum planning and pedagogy in schools across the globe. Wearied by the constricting demands of overprescriptive national curriculums and the invidious requirements of continuous government-set examinations, many within the teaching profession in the United Kingdom and other countries have become conscious of the transformational nature of cognitive approaches to learning as an alternative to transmission-based teaching. The ideas of such luminaries as Matthew Lipman (Philosophy for Children), Edward de Bono (Lateral Thinking), and Reuven Feuerstein (Instrumental Enrichment), previously considered to be "on the fringe" of educational thinking, have increasingly come to be seen as offering valuable insights into the fundamental connection between thinking and learning.

Similarly, in the United States the revolutionary ideas of the Harvard Project Zero team, stimulated by the leadership of David Perkins and Howard Gardner (Multiple Intelligences), alongside the inspirational writings of Art Costa (Habits of Mind) and Robert Sternberg (Triarchic Mind), and others of a similar mindset, have filtered through to many educational establishments while making a wider global impact on such curriculum innovations as the *International Baccalaureate*. On the whole, however, the global impact of all these luminaries might best be described as somewhat piecemeal and, as yet, rather muted.

Attempts to introduce thinking skills into schools are certainly not new. As far back as the mid-1980s, reports emphasized the need for schools to produce more independent thinkers and problem solvers, a demand repeated in more recent years from around the world.

In the United States, there was a "thinking skills" movement in the late 1970s and into the early 1990s cresting on the wave of Piagetian "constructivism" that was well-documented in the comprehensive book *Developing Minds*

(Costa, 2001). This edited book contained entries by dozens of educational leaders, university professors, and practitioners describing their theories, research, and practice of the explicit development of students' thinking abilities. A U.K. government–sponsored inquiry carried out by Carol McGuiness (1999) toward the end of the century came to very similar conclusions and suggested the integration of thinking skills into the mainstream curriculum as one possible way forward.

Meanwhile, however, research into the effectiveness of such approaches appeared to produce, at best, equivocal results. The "thinking skills" wave crashed. A typical scenario was of initial enthusiasm by "converted" teachers withering on the vine of others' indifference or even downright hostility. This was not helped by lack of "hard" evidence showing formally acceptable learning outcomes or long-term uptake of cognitive approaches other than as supporting high-quality teaching and learning, but not a central driver for transforming schools. Each of these approaches and many others have become to a certain degree embedded in the everyday practices of classroom teachers today. So, in one sense, the impact of the rise in the research and practice of thinking process approaches has been wide, though maybe not so deep. There is now a higher awareness of multiple intelligences, including emotional intelligence and cooperative learning; the need to focus on dispositions for thinking, or habits of mind; and the use of a range of graphic representations that support different learning modalities through visual tools such as Concept Mapping and Thinking Maps. The use of Bloom's Taxonomy of Cognitive Objectives as a framework for designing curriculum and asking students questions that go well beyond simply factual responses has been central to this work, as teachers attempt to engage students in the processes of analysis, synthesis, evaluation, and reflection through a metacognitive perspective.

SO WHAT, THEN, IS A "THINKING" LEARNER?

Given this brief historical background it becomes essential to answer a fundamental question: What is a "Thinking" Learner? First, let us dismiss a possible answer: that a thinking learner is just *any* learner, since, by definition, a learner has to be thinking. Actually, learning and thinking are complex activities, and their definitions are not so clear-cut. Perhaps more learning is done unconsciously than we realize. But this chapter is not the place for a comprehensive, complex analysis. The point is that some learning is clearly more *thoughtful* than other types of learning. Compare, for example, classic "rote" learning of tables, e.g., multiplication or elemental, with scaffolded learning of the principles behind such tables. There may indeed be degrees of "thoughtfulness," but it is an aspiration to operate at the *higher* end of such a continuum that underpins the notions of the Thinking School and the Thinking Learner.

One aspect, then, of the development of the Thinking Learner within a Thinking School could well be a sharing in the wide recognition of differences between lower-order thinking and higher-order thinking. The main categories of Lorin Anderson et al.'s 2001 revision of the Bloom's Taxonomy of Cognitive

Objectives (remembering, understanding, applying, analyzing, evaluating, and creating) might become commonly used, if not displayed, in classrooms. Many approaches to the development of a Thinking Learner often begin with an investigation of Bloom's Taxonomy, though few remember that these are *cognitive* objectives.

But it is important to emphasize that such schemes and terms should be used *meaningfully,* with a view to *learners* becoming more aware of the level of task they are being asked to perform by teachers. Younger children, for example, might be put off by words such as "apply" or "analyze" but could be encouraged deliberately to extend their thinking by questions such as, "Does anything we have learned in this lesson make a *difference* to how we live or think?" or "What were the main things we learned in this lesson, and how do they *connect?*" The goal, ultimately, is not simply for learners to address the individual tasks successfully or even thoughtfully. It is for them develop a cognitive stance when faced with any new learning experience within and beyond the formal structure of school.

One example, the language of Thinking Maps, which has been used extensively with other visual tools by schools focused on student-centered development of thinking, can be particularly helpful in developing such student awareness. As visual representations of eight fundamental cognitive processes activated by graphic patterns that expand on the page as the student develops connected information, each Thinking Map explicitly names and defines fundamental cognitive process and how they are used together for reading, writing, and thinking across all disciplines. For example, seeing analogies (using the Bridge Map) is naturally creative, and particularly seeks the application of an idea in different contexts; relating parts to wholes (the Brace Map) clearly involves analysis; describing specific attributes or qualities of things (the Bubble Map) and comparing and contrasting using these characteristics as a filter or rubric (the Double-Bubble Map) also involves analysis, and, with guidance, leads to evaluation. The addition of the visual "frame of reference" that is used around each map offers students a concrete tool and a visual, metacognitive space for identifying and exploring what is influencing their perceptions and seeking to understand ideas from multiple points of view held by other classmates or by material presented in the texts or on the web.

It might also be noted that Benjamin Bloom was interested in objectives in the affective domain (emotional awareness and development) as well as the cognitive, again listing them from lower order ("receiving" or just attending) through "valuing" (showing interest or appreciation) to "characterizing" (taking on a particular value or belief as part of their character). A Thinking School takes this domain just as seriously, aiming to develop their pupils' *"interest in their work, positive attitudes towards school, enjoyment and confidence in learning"* (11th of 14 criteria described below). One could even say that among the values and beliefs that characterize Thinking Learners would be those that make up what Carol Dweck calls a *growth mindset* (Dweck, 2006). This may be seen as a series of values, stemming from the prime belief that *intelligence can be developed,* much as the brain has a high degree of plasticity. Cognitive challenges, then, are welcomed as means to this end; effort and persistence are valued in meeting such challenges; and mistakes and criticism are viewed positively, as opportunities for learning.

Other ways of developing the affective alongside the cognitive would be to focus on Costa's 16 Habits of Mind (which include adventurousness, persistence, and openness). We have found that Art Costa's Habits of Mind model has been used by many schools focusing on thinking because it engages learners and teachers alike in a new vocabulary for dispositions that directly affect how they approach problems, how they collaborate, and how they respond to new information and problems for which understanding is not immediately apparent. These dispositions are essential for living in a complex, highly networked global communication system, wherein people from different countries, cultures, and languages are working in teams via texting, Facebook, and Skype. A recent book, *The Power of the Social Brain: Teaching, Learning, and Interdependent Thinking* (Costa & O'leary, 2013) on just one of the Habits of Mind, *interdependence,* is a comprehensive investigation of how students can elevate their thinking capacities when explicitly focused on dispositions such as the development of patience, persistence, clarity of communication, and empathy. Guy Claxton's 8 Character Strengths and Virtues for the Learning Age (which include imagination, courage, and experimentation) is another model that gets to this intersection of cognitive processes and affective dispositions uniting to support a Thinking Learner. Another framework is afforded by the P4C model (Philosophy for Children)—Critical and Creative, Caring and Collaborative Thinking—which can be practiced in dedicated "communities of enquiry" and which ripple outward into learning across the curriculum. Such lists of thinking virtues can seem a little daunting but schools that are, or aspire to be, Thinking Schools, will already have signed up to them in principle. They will have begun to *explicitly* discuss these dispositions and consciously use them as reflective signposts for developing high-quality thinking and improving interdependent, collaborative thinking of all students within the community.

The value placed on the ability of learners to demonstrate critical and creative, caring and cooperative (collaborative) thinking is clear. But perhaps a final emphasis should be placed on the practice of *reflective* thinking. This is a vital quality of the Thinking Learner, clearly distinguishing her from the "rote," or the passive, learner. A reflective thinker/learner is one who is independently and actively reflecting on both the process and the content of her learning. This may begin with identification of her preferred learning styles or modalities, but would work toward deepening awareness of self, especially her dispositions, and of her relationships with others in her learning community.

Schools could encourage such deepening in various ways. They might, for example, take it to be an essential component of a good Personal and Social Education/Development program with a spotlight being shone on "self-awareness."

Or some schools might prefer to broach these ideas in even greater depth within a dedicated "thinking" or "study skills" program. The ideal offered here is that reflection (or review, as distinct from revision) would take a more routine place in all lessons, with every teacher using "Wait Time" (or "think, pair, share"), to consolidate the content of learning and occasionally to reflect on the process of learning. By such means learners increasingly see themselves as creative agents in their own learning.

That, in short, is the ideal of the Thinking Learner: one who has realized that "learning" is for herself (not *for* her parents or her teachers—and still less *by* them!); but, moreover, that it is an active process, involving persistent collaboration with her teachers and with others, to construct better understandings; and, finally, that her own understanding will grow precisely in line with the fundamental dispositions to enquire, to share, and to reflect.

THE ROLE OF EXETER'S COGNITIVE ■ EDUCATION CENTRE FOR THINKING SCHOOLS

The Exeter University Cognitive Education Centre was established in 2005 with a number of aims in mind. Its location in one of the most prestigious teacher education departments in the United Kingdom made it ideally placed to introduce thinking skills into the curriculum of prospective teachers. At the same time, there was a desire to make available to schools across the United Kingdom the latest information about cognitive program developments and research findings, and to act as a hub through which interested schools could contact each other and share ideas and experiences. Finally, there was the expressed intention to seek ways of assessing the impact of thinking approaches on a wide range of learning and behavioral outcomes with a view to helping schools maximize their effectiveness. This latter aim led us to begin our search by seeking to identify how and why attempts to introduce thinking skills into the curriculum had so much promise, and only a minimal impact.

Our preliminary analysis of why so many thinking skills initiatives either petered out or simply failed altogether led us to conclude that the problem did not necessarily lie within the program, model, theory, or approach to implementation themselves. Feuerstein's theory of *Structural Cognitive Modifiability* is one of the most impressively constructed theoretical frameworks for cognitive change that has ever been produced with 50 years of remarkable research. The foundations of Lipman's *Philosophy for Children* and Communities of Enquiry stretch back to Dewey and to Socrates. There is plenty of anecdotal evidence that the creative tools and techniques within De Bono's *Lateral Thinking* approach and *Six Hat Thinking* has been shown to bring about remarkable improvements in business organizations and schools worldwide. Art Costa and Guy Claxton have demonstrated the efficacy of focusing on dispositions. The effectiveness of the cognitive process model of Thinking Maps developed by David N. Hyerle has been demonstrated through extensive documentation and research across whole schools. If each of these approaches has been effective, then where did the roots of the problem lie?

The conclusion that we reached was that the obstacles to the successful implementation of any thinking "program" designed to teach children to "learn how to learn" were almost entirely systemic. There was little wrong with many of the approaches themselves, but rather the ways in which they have been introduced into schools. Firstly, there was what Georgiades and Phillimore

(1975) referred to many years ago as "the myth of the hero innovator." In a highly influential article, they pointed out that innovations are often introduced by enthusiastic individuals, possibly teachers returning from a conference or course, who seek to impose their newfound enthusiasm on an unresponsive audience of skeptical colleagues. In a telling phrase, these authors commented that "organizations, like dragons, eat hero-innovators for breakfast" (Georgiades & Phillimore, 1975). Thus, deprived of support or nourishment, and experiencing even downright hostility from other colleagues, the innovation will inevitably fail. This was clearly exemplified in Blagg's (1989) study and a more recent case study evaluation by Burden and Nichols (2000) of one school's attempt to introduce thinking skills into the curriculum. In the latter study, we were able to identify by means of an illuminative evaluation some key factors preventing the successful uptake of the thinking skills approach. Here it became apparent that forceful leadership that had not won over the hearts and minds of the teaching personnel, particularly in a large secondary school, was almost certain to fail. If key stakeholders have a different set of priorities and different views about the nature of the teaching/learning process, then the students are likely to become confused at what they see as mixed messages. Moreover, unless those attempting to teach thinking skills and strategies are themselves completely committed and demonstrating a high level of expertise, the students are unlikely to be convinced.

Secondly, within the United Kingdom and in the United States as well, the ever-increasing demands on teachers to meet various externally imposed targets (the ever-increasing focus on standardized test results) left little time or opportunity for creative curriculum planning, or for further reflection and innovation. It was only when frustrated with a national curriculum that gave the impression, at least, of focusing mainly on the regurgitation of information by means of formalized assessment tasks that teachers began to cast their eyes widely for more process-based approaches to teaching and learning. However, although cognitive (or, as they are more commonly known, *thinking skills*) approaches appeared to many to offer more promising alternatives, advocates of some isolated thinking skills programs often fell into the trap of appearing to claim that they could provide the answer to all traditional schooling's ills. While most approaches, models, and/or fully developed programs offered something special to the cognitive curriculum, what was often not realized was finding ways for them to complement each other rather than being mutually exclusive. This understanding was central to our work of promoting systemic change.

The need, therefore, was to seek ways of combining the benefits of a range of high-quality programs rather than focus on just one. As one head teacher reported in his review of the Thinking Schools approach,

> The key to whole school success is a whole school approach to thinking skills. They need to be taught both discretely and immersed into subject delivery; this can only be achieved by a comprehensive in-service program that includes the sharing of good practice across the school through workshops. (Thinking Schools International, n.d., p. 3)

By taking a piecemeal approach to teaching thinking and "study skills," the danger became one of adding the occasional stimulating lesson devoted to thinking skills as a kind of add-on, bolt-on, "sticking plaster" solution, while at the same time conveying a set of mixed messages to the students. This would be analogous to the long-practiced ritual by teachers of offering "brain teasers" as the end-of-the-day activity rather than explicitly and fundamentally shifting and refining the focus of teaching and learning toward the development of thinking. Before long, those who had begun so enthusiastically trying out new "techniques" or programs were in danger of finding themselves asking, in the words of the immortal Peggy Lee, "Is that all there is?"

The breakthrough came from an unexpected direction. The literature on school effectiveness and school improvement, since the early work of Michael Rutter and Peter Mortimore and his colleagues at the Institute of Education in the United Kingdom, later summarized by Teddlie and Reynolds (2000) and built on by Michael Fullan (1982) and others had more or less come to similar conclusions on how to recognize an effective school and what needed to be done to achieve a school's vision. In their excellent summary of what is known about effective schools, Reid, Hopkins, and Holly (1987) identified a number of key factors. Strong leadership that is curriculum-focused is vital. The school has to be well-organized with a happy, efficient staff, who all should have a common purpose and a guiding value system and ideally be involved in collaborative planning and implementation. Regular in-house professional development training also has an important part to play in ensuring high quality, up-to-date teaching. There should be clear goals and high expectations set for *all* students across the whole ability range. Regular feedback on performance needs to be given to every student by means of a clearly understood system for monitoring performance and achievement. Students should be encouraged to participate in the running and organization of their school as a means of helping them identify with it and the staff, thereby building a sense of mutual respect and more positive learning and behavioral features. Additionally, the quality of the actual learning environment (clean, attractive, well organized, and not overcrowded) warrants serious consideration. Complementary to these findings, a report in 2001 prepared for the International Academy of Education by Stella Vosniadou titled "How Children Learn" identified key factors to be active, constructive involvement of the learners, their social involvement, meaningful activities, the development of learning strategies, engagement in self-regulation, and being reflective.

What was much more open to speculation was how exactly these aims could best be met. Here the literature on school improvement (in contrast to school effectiveness) has provided many helpful ideas about the process of implementing change (Fullan, 1993, 1999), but little on the actual nature of the curriculum itself. It was the recognition of the potential value of combining the lessons from the school effectiveness/improvement literature and cognitive education approaches that gave rise to the concept of the Thinking School. Out of the fusion of these two sets of ideas, we were able to construct our definition of what a Thinking School would look like, sound like, and feel like, and to identify a number of criteria that a school would need to meet to fulfill that definition.

■ A DEFINITION: WHAT IS A THINKING SCHOOL?

The definition of a thinking school that emerged is one of

> . . . an educational community in which all members share a common commitment to giving regular, careful thought to everything that takes place. This will involve learning how to think reflectively, critically and creatively, and to employ these skills and techniques in the coconstruction of a meaningful curriculum and associated activities. Successful outcomes will be reflected in students across a wide range of abilities demonstrating independent and cooperative learning skills, high levels of achievement, and both enjoyment and satisfaction in learning. Benefits will also be shown in the ways in which all members of the community interact with and show consideration for each other and in the positive psychological well-being of both students and staff.
>
> To achieve this goal, a whole school approach will be necessary whereby all stakeholders (including parents and school governors) are fully committed to the school's aims and how they can best be achieved. Staff will need to be specially trained and methods will need to be introduced into the curriculum for teaching the skills of thinking and associated cognitive and metacognitive strategies. The widest possible application of these skills and strategies should underpin all other aspects of the curriculum and should guide behavior policies and expectations about human interactions at every level and care for the environment. (Burden, 2006, pp. 2–3)

It can be seen that such a definition contains a number of necessary elements. First, and perhaps most important, is the notion of a community where everyone shares a common commitment. In this instance, that commitment is for everyone in and associated with the school to learn as much as possible about thinking and its relationship with learning, with the aim of building together what is learned into the curriculum and sharing this knowledge with the students. It assumes that learning and behavior are inextricably linked and that these new cognitive skills and knowledge will pervade all social as well as academic interactions that take place within the school at every level. Thus, worthwhile outcomes can be measured in terms not only of improved academic results, however measured, but also in terms of love of learning for its own sake, confidence in meeting new and unforeseen learning tasks both in and out of school, respect for others and their ideas, and a general sense of positive well-being.

Working with such pioneers as Gill Hubble from St Cuthbert's School in New Zealand (see Chapter 5: Journey Toward Becoming a Thinking School), who had already formulated many of these ideas based on Art Costa's vision of "School as a Home for the Mind," together with a group of thinking skills practitioners and trainers from the Kestrel organization in the United Kingdom, we followed this definition by constructing criteria for identifying and achieving a successful Thinking School. In sharing these criteria with various schools that had already started on the journey, the idea of Thinking School accreditation became the logical next step. Fourteen criteria were established, and schools were offered the opportunity of producing a portfolio of evidence to demonstrate how these had been met. Important to note, each school would create a substantive action plan for their own unique development and outcomes as related to the criteria and share this with our team for feedback and recommendations. These plans were made with benchmarks, projected timelines, and a process for collecting evidence of attaining their own stated goals. When the school, after multiple years, came to a place where they had clear evidence of attaining their goals, they sent their portfolio in for review, feedback, and formal accreditation. A follow-up visit to the school by a member of the Cognitive Education Centre team made it possible for teachers, classroom assistants, school governors, parents, and pupils to be interviewed, lessons to be observed, and pupils' work to be shared. The very production of the portfolio makes it clear whether the set criteria have been met and, if so, the follow-up visit becomes more of a joint celebration and dialogue with "critical friends" rather than an inspection or formalized evaluation. In a sense, it is the whole school's opportunity to share with a knowledgeable and interested outside expert the benefits of their approach to becoming a thinking, learning, caring, sharing community.

At the completion of this process, a report is produced for the school. This is followed by a certificate and trophy, and the right to print the CEC logo on any formal school literature for a period of 3 years, when reaccreditation is required. This process is thus not an endpoint but marks a step along the way in the journey of transformation from a school community focused on learning content toward one that is authentically dedicated to all students, staff, and administrators exploring a lifetime journey, individually and collectively, learning how to learn.

CRITERIA FOR ACCREDITATION ■
AS A THINKING SCHOOL

The identified criteria (See Figure 4.1), their reasons for selection, and the kind of evidence needed to show that they have been met are presented below. These criteria have been used over the past 10 years and offer guideposts but no linear route toward the process of growing a Thinking School. This is not a checklist but an array of actions and descriptors, expressed as commitments that may be redefined and translated across cultures and countries.

1. **Leadership.** There is a need for the principal/head teacher to have made a formal commitment to cognitive education as a means of school improvement as a central aspect of the school's development plans. This is because all the school effectiveness/improvement literature identifies the crucial importance of leadership in the change process. This is most readily shown in the printed documentation that the school makes available to current and prospective parents and to reports to the school board members/governors. It will also become endorsed by an interview with the principal about her or his underlying values and future plans in the follow-up visit to the school.

Figure 4.1 Criteria for a Thinking School

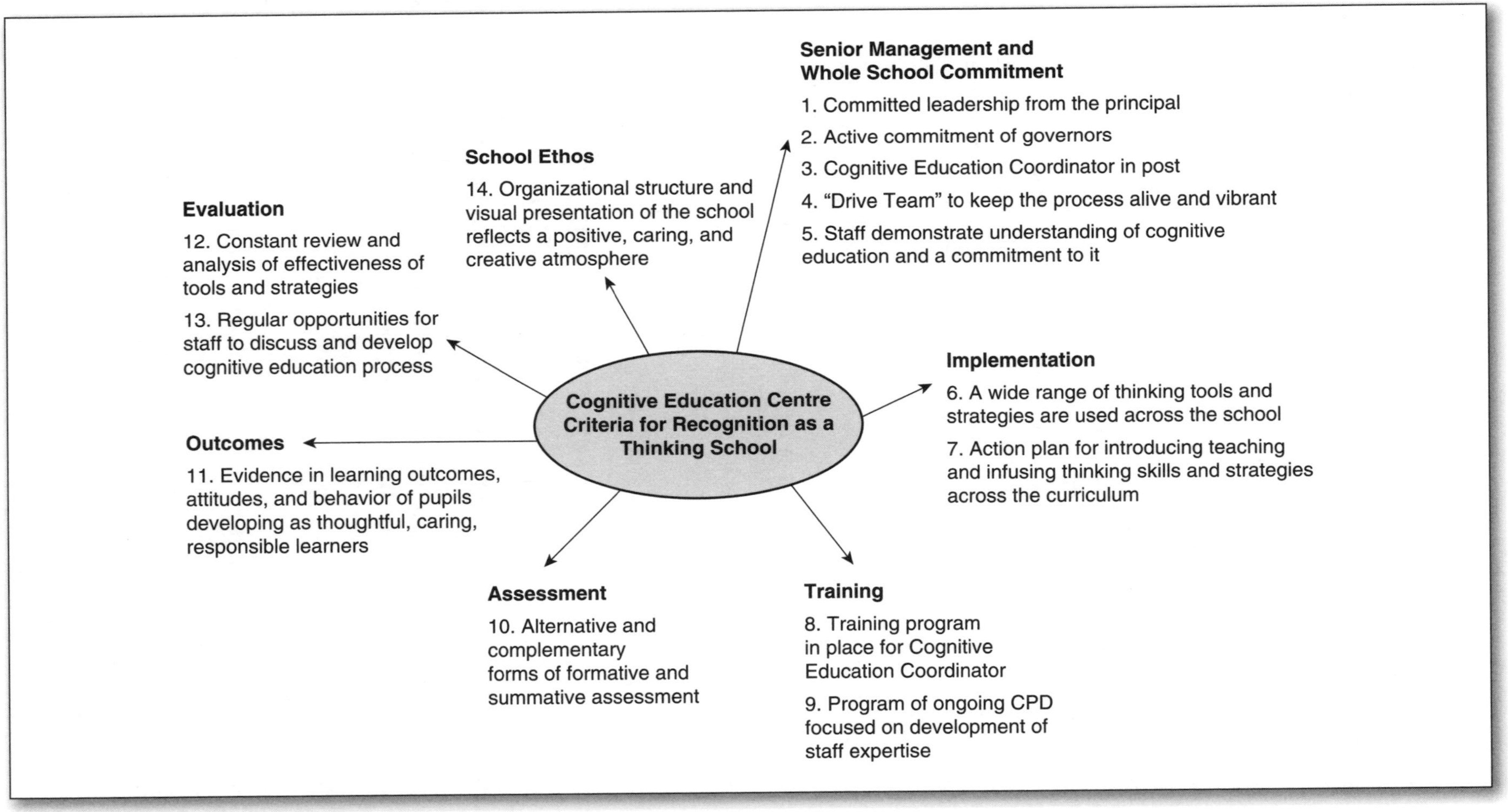

**Senior Management and
Whole School Commitment**

1. Committed leadership from the principal
2. Active commitment of governors
3. Cognitive Education Coordinator in post
4. "Drive Team" to keep the process alive and vibrant
5. Staff demonstrate understanding of cognitive education and a commitment to it

Implementation

6. A wide range of thinking tools and strategies are used across the school
7. Action plan for introducing teaching and infusing thinking skills and strategies across the curriculum

Training

8. Training program in place for Cognitive Education Coordinator
9. Program of ongoing CPD focused on development of staff expertise

School Ethos

14. Organizational structure and visual presentation of the school reflects a positive, caring, and creative atmosphere

**Cognitive Education Centre
Criteria for Recognition as a
Thinking School**

Assessment

10. Alternative and complementary forms of formative and summative assessment

Evaluation

12. Constant review and analysis of effectiveness of tools and strategies
13. Regular opportunities for staff to discuss and develop cognitive education process

Outcomes

11. Evidence in learning outcomes, attitudes, and behavior of pupils developing as thoughtful, caring, responsible learners

2. **School Board.** This commitment to cognitive education must have the explicit support of the community school board members. In the United Kingdom, the school board members together are called the *governors* and are the body most responsible for all aspects of the running of a school. There have unfortunately been occasions when an enthusiastic principal/head teacher has been frustrated by a governing body that has failed to see the full benefit of a cognitive approach but has been more influenced by a drive for examination success at all costs and has seen information transmission and rote learning as the only way to achieve this. For this reason a formal statement of support by the Chair of Governors is necessary, together with evidence of ongoing support from the governors in the minutes of their meetings, which may well include a record of how they themselves have been informed about or even trained in the cognitive approach. Again, at the visiting stage, it will be necessary for the Chair of Governors and, if possible, one or two others to be interviewed.

3. **Coordinator.** It is necessary for each school to have a well-respected leader as the formally appointed member of staff as their Cognitive Education Coordinator to organize and oversee the implementation of the cognitive education development agenda. There are several reasons for this. It is usually impractical for the principal to take on this role, but unless it is seen as a highly prestigious post within the school, particularly in large schools, research has shown that the cognitive agenda can be easily sidelined or undermined by competing demands. Here we are looking for details of the appointed person's background and experience, particularly with regard to their previous and current training in different cognitive approaches. It will be the responsibility of the Cognitive Education Coordinator (titles sometimes vary) to prepare the portfolio of evidence about how the set criteria for recognition as a Thinking School are met.

4. **Task Force.** One of the first tasks of the Cognitive Education Coordinator after their appointment should be to establish a task force or subgroup of colleagues, from across curriculum subjects in large schools, to ensure that communication and cooperation takes place across the school and that discussions amongst staff and the teaching of thinking skills and strategies can occur by means of a cascade model. The requirement in the United Kingdom for all schools to devote a specific number of hours each term to the in-service training of staff means that cognitive education can readily become a regular aspect of professional development sessions. This will help overcome the dangers of the hero-innovator tendency and will prove vital in leading to a committed "critical mass" of cognitively oriented staff. Evidence here should take the form of listed names and roles, together with recorded details of inset sessions, discussions and planning meetings.

5. **School-Wide Design.** This should in time lead to the vast majority of the school staff, including learning support assistants, demonstrating a clear understanding of what is meant by a Thinking School, why it has been undertaken, and how they can best contribute to it. This should be demonstrated in their pedagogy and in the nature of the tasks they set and the quality of the work produced by their students. The evidence portfolio should demonstrate

the work of students across a range of subject areas and/or topics, as well as examples of work across the ability range.

6. **Implementation of Models/Programs.** Implementation of a cognitive curriculum is most likely in the first instance to be by means of an examination of the major cognitive programs. This should lead to the adoption of a least two approaches, models, or programs over a 3-year period. This may involve some degree of trial-and-error learning, that is, by deciding to reject one or another of the programs and favoring others that seem to fit more readily with the school's vision and action plan. (Clarification: *Program* in this case means that schools identify a model, an approach, and/or a guiding theoretical framework that is research-based and practical and it is implemented across the school in a systematic way and integrated with the daily life of the school. It is not simply an "add-on" set of activities or "best practices," or a rigid and isolated curriculum separate and apart from the flow of classroom and school-wide activities. The approach must also not exist to simply improve teaching, but a coherent design that is student-centered so that students become fluent in the approach.) At the time of writing, the most popular and well-founded programs in the United Kingdom appear to be David N. Hyerle's Thinking Maps, Edward de Bono's Six Hat Thinking, variations of Matthew Lipman's Philosophy for Children, Art Costa's Habits of Mind, and Guy Claxton's Building Learning Power. However, none of these programs is considered to be either necessary or, by themselves, sufficient; each school will develop its own unique approach to the curriculum, which will inevitably include some "homegrown" activities.

i. Schools tend to vary in the order in which they begin, but no school achieving accreditation has yet indicated that any one program fulfils all the requirements of a cognitively oriented curriculum. Two is an absolute minimum to start with, but gradually schools find that they can build on their growing confidence and expertise by taking on complementary programs like Adey and Shayer's Cognitive Acceleration through Science Education (CASE), Cognitive Acceleration through Mathematics Education (CAME), and Let's Think programs—Thinking Through History, Geography, and so on, constructed mainly at Newcastle University—or by developing their own homegrown approaches. The evidence of this process and the reasoning behind the adoption and/or rejection of different approaches should be clearly documented.

7. **Action Plan.** All this should be part of an Action Plan that has been drawn up by the Cognitive Education Team, endorsed by the principal and governors, and shared with every member of staff, including support staff, playground helpers, and building supervisors. A drive team that consists of a leadership team including teachers representing various dimensions of the school is essential for developing this plan and assessing the integration of the approach over time.

8. **Developing Expertise.** It is obviously important that a Cognitive Education Coordinator needs himself or herself to be highly trained and confident in a range of potentially useful programs and detailed techniques and

should see this as an essential ongoing aspect of his or her role. It is not enough for someone in this position to have attended a preliminary training course in a particular technique and expect to remain ahead of the game. Details of this person's ongoing Continuing Professional Development program must therefore be made available, including details of how they are keeping abreast of current thinking and pedagogy.

9. **Continuous Professional Development.** All staff should be encouraged to attend external courses or should receive constant in-house training by the home team and/or highly rated external consultants. Documented reports of such training and its outcomes should also be available for public scrutiny.

10. **Alternative Assessment Approaches.** Taking a cognitive approach to the curriculum carries with it assumptions about alternative forms and outcomes of assessment; formative assessment for learning should be the norm running alongside more conventional assessment of learning outcomes. We would also expect to see an emphasis on pupil self-assessment and peer assessment as part of the regular assessment process. Most schools have found that Anderson's revision of Bloom's Taxonomy provides an excellent framework for this form of assessment. A Thinking School will also have considered possible alternative and complementary ways of assessing learning outcomes such as enhanced pupil self-esteem and increasing enjoyment in learning and increased staff satisfaction in teaching.

11. **Evidence.** At the end of the day, there is a requirement for evidence of positive learning outcomes, attitudes, and behaviors of the pupils to indicate that they are operating as thoughtful responsible learners who are able to articulate how and why thinking skills and strategies are a vitally important aspect of all that occurs in their schools. This can be seen in the nature and quality of the pupils' work (including homework), interest they show in their work, positive attitudes toward school, enjoyment and confidence in learning, good attendance and behavior records, a significant decrease in bullying, and improved attainment and exam results, where this is clearly necessary. Much of this can be revealed during the evaluation visit to the school, when interviews with individual and groups of students plays a significant role, but will also require careful record keeping of critical incidents and other indications of change.

12. **Continuous Growth.** Few innovations ever work completely smoothly from start to finish. In fact, becoming a recognized Thinking School does not signify the end of the journey, merely a significant moment along the way. This implies that there will be a need to constantly review the effectiveness of the thinking programs and tools employed in developing pupils' metacognition and wider thinking strategies. A Thinking School will constantly be on the lookout for additional or useful approaches to enhance their children's learning, and for ways of evaluating these.

13. **Participation.** The whole school approach means exactly that. Here we are looking for evidence that all members of staff are being encouraged to discuss on a regular basis the processes of thinking and how it can be maintained and improved. During the accreditation visit, the evident enthusiasm of all staff

members (as well as that of the students) for the cognitive approach and their ability to identify its benefits will be a significant feature in illustrating how well this is working. This will apply also to the way in which new staff are recruited and inducted into this way of working.

14. **School Ethos.** All the above should be manifest in the whole ethos of the school, in the way it conveys a positive, caring, and creative atmosphere to all stakeholders and visitors, while at the same time demonstrating that careful thought has been put into its organizational structure and visual presentations. This is likely to be shown in examples of the pupils' work and displays that adorn the school, the way that visitors are received and treated, and the general "feel" of the way in which everyone goes about their business.

■ EVALUATING OUTCOMES: SURVEY RESULTS

By the end of July 2013, more than 90 schools across England, Wales, Northern Ireland, Australia, Thailand, and New Zealand had successfully navigated the accreditation process. The ratio of primary to secondary school stands at about 5:1, but every level of socioeconomic and cultural background has been represented. Some are small, three-teacher schools, others cater for more than a thousand students with over one hundred staff. Of the secondary schools, four are single-sex schools, while three are comprehensives. Almost all are within the public school sector and about a quarter are faith-based.

In 2013, the CEC at Exeter University issued findings drawn from surveys of 55 accredited Thinking Schools that responded to our request for feedback (see Appendix). In summary, the preliminary results are encouraging because there is an overwhelmingly positive reporting by schools of the influence on their schools, academically in the area of increased attainment and in quality of instruction (lessons by teachers), and there is notable feedback from schools about the importance of the whole school approach.

The survey focused on five key areas, as follows:

1. Satisfaction with the Thinking School approach by accredited schools

2. Attainment

3. Thinking Schools International approaches adopted by Thinking Schools (i.e., Thinking Maps, Habits of Mind, Philosophy for Children)

4. Evaluation Methods of the Thinking School approach

5. Major benefit and issues of the Thinking School approach

Summary of Key Findings

- 100% of primary and 87.5% of secondary accredited schools are satisfied with the Thinking School approach; none are dissatisfied.
- 90% of all accredited schools reported an improvement in the quality of lessons; none have seen lesson quality adversely affected.

- 89% state that the Thinking School approach raises attainment; 3.5% state that it does not raise attainment.
- All five major Thinking School International programs are reported to be highly effective.
- 82% of accredited schools would welcome more support with their evaluation methods.
- Benefits greatly outweigh issues.

When we look more closely at the survey results, we see some of the highest marks in the areas of student self-confidence, involvement, collaborative learning, and, significantly, "reflection on learning." A very high percentage of schools also reported that both teacher-questioning and student-questioning skill rose across their classrooms. Of course, often these powerful indicators of outcomes in a school get overshadowed by the quantitative reporting of test results. That 89% of the surveyed schools stated that they say a direct link to improved attainment is thus important to note. As one head teacher stated:

In our last inspection report, the school (Cardiff High School) was awarded 7 grade 1's, the highest number possible. In the year we were inspected, the school achieved the highest percentage of grade 1 lessons for any secondary school in Wales, and this was attributed largely to our thinking skills approaches . . . Despite our pupils becoming far more diverse, ability wise, over the last ten years, our exam results have gone up year on year. (Thinking Schools International, n.d., pp. 2–3)

In addition to our survey, there is also detailed reporting from Thinking Schools that have been evaluated by Ofsted, the government's education evaluation unit. In the United Kingdom, all schools are required to make themselves available at short notice for full-scale inspection by a team from Ofsted, Her Majesty's Inspectors of Schools. These inspections are intensive and focus on a number of aspects of a school's organization, which are subsequently judged to be outstanding, good, adequate, or inadequate. Schools are rated on their overall effectiveness, on their capacity for sustained improvement, on pupil outcomes regarding their attainments and the quality of their learning and progress, and whether the pupils enjoy learning, feel safe, demonstrate positive behavior, contribute to the school and community, and are developing workplace skills for their future economic security, as well as the extent of their moral, social, and cultural development. The quality of teaching is also assessed, involving the use of assessment practices to support learning and the effectiveness of care, guidance, and support. Finally, a judgment is made of the effectiveness of leadership and management, engagement with parents, and the effectiveness of the governing body in encouraging equality of opportunity and fostering community cohesion. Statistics show that 9% of primary schools and 13% of secondary schools inspected will receive a rating of good or outstanding. The vast majority of the 15 schools inspected soon after achieving Thinking School status were rated by inspectors as outstanding (60%) or good with outstanding features (27%), with many receiving specific mention for the unique contribution of the cognitive approach to the pupils' learning, as is illustrated in the following quotes from publicly released Ofsted reports (see http://www .ofsted.gov.uk/schools), each submitted by different evaluation teams.

> Beechwood Primary School provides an outstanding quality of education. Its identity as a Thinking School is at the heart of its work, whether it is in encouraging children to think about others or to think things out for themselves.
>
> This outstandingly successful school (St Michael's RC Primary) fully meets the aims of its challenging mission statement by being a "creative and thinking school" and giving each pupil a unique educational experience.
>
> Across the school (Monnow Primary) pupils' problem-solving skills, creative skills, their willingness to work with others, and their awareness of how to improve their own learning and performance all have many outstanding features.
>
> An outstanding feature is the focus on "thinking skills" across the school (St Mary's Primary). This plays a significant role in teaching pupils how to learn effectively. It is an important factor in the good progress they make and in their preparation for secondary school and later life.

■ FURTHER DEVELOPMENTS

One of the findings from our survey was the interest shown in gaining more support for new evaluation methods for moving their vision of a Thinking School forward. The search now is for ways of monitoring and recording a range of possible outcomes and of demonstrating the benefits that cognitive education can bring. A number of questionnaires have been developed at the Cognitive Education Centre (CEC) for approaching this task, including the Myself-As-a-Learner Scale (MALS) and Myself-As-a-Thinker Scale (MATS), a scale to measure student reflections on the quality of mediation received and a scale to measure teachers' reflections on the impact of introducing Thinking Maps and other approaches into their classrooms, respectively. At the time of this writing, a considerable amount of data has been gathered from several schools employing these scales without this being fully analyzed, but the following informal outcomes have been very apparent: (1) Where there has been obvious room for improvement, attainments have risen, (2) attitudes toward school and learning have been shown to be positive across the board, and (3) bullying and negative behavior is virtually nonexistent.

The expressed attitudes of more than 90% of the teaching and support staff in every accredited school reflect high personal satisfaction and enjoyment in their chosen profession.

While these outcomes are inspiring, we know that the journey toward becoming a Thinking School has no endpoint. Initial accreditation is provided for a 3-year period, after which the school needs to provide evidence that it has continued to move forward in its quest to demonstrate that an emphasis on the transformational process of teaching and learning offers far more than one in which information transmission rules the day. Several schools have already sought and obtained reaccreditation after reaching the end of this initial qualification period with only three falling by the wayside. The notion of an Advanced Thinking School has subsequently been raised by many of these schools, providing the CEC with the task of finding ways of identifying whether and how well they have moved forward in that time (see Richard Coe's Chapter 6 describing a school that has received Advanced Thinking School accreditation). As well as improved academic standards across the board, high attendance rates and expressed high levels of satisfaction on the part of students, parents, and teachers, one important criterion currently being considered is the production of evidence of student, staff, and/or parental responses by means of questionnaire surveys or homegrown research projects.

Another criterion already taking shape is how well the school has been able to "spread the word" and influence the take-up of these ideas in other schools within their country and around the world. Another may be the way in which the school has been able to apply the Thinking Schools approach to considering "big questions" relating to more global issues of a practical and philosophical nature. More recently, an International Thinking Schools Association is being established whereby worldwide networking between schools taking a similar journey will begin to use modern digital technology to share ideas and experiences. Schools' use of modern technology thus becomes a further area for exploration and development as part of their thinking journey.

It would be unwise to claim too much for what as yet is an exciting and evolving educational movement that is a synthesis of new ideas with past practices and approaches. There have been plenty of so-called educational revolutions that have withered on the vine and are now barely remembered, if at all. The whole school approach to cognitive education, at least in this phase, is still young. The production of "hard" evidence of a range of positive outcomes will undoubtedly help stave off the critics and advocates of the *anciene régime*, but in the meantime, the following quote from the head teacher of Rhydypenau school, reflecting on the having taken this path, leaves little doubt about the school's conviction of its effectiveness:

> Our school has embarked upon a series of exciting initiatives, all under the umbrella of a "Thinking School." This work has involved all children and parents, governors and staff at school, demonstrating the value of all working together to create within our school an ecology of reflection, growth and refinement of practice. It has assisted us in promoting Rhydypenau as a community of confident, enthusiastic learners. . . . our accreditation as a "Thinking School" has been an exciting journey, a journey of challenge and a journey of change: change because teachers have been asked to adopt new teaching tools, develop their own knowledge and skills; challenge because it has involved some changes to the teachers' role from transmitters of information to facilitators of opportunities for children to understand. They have moved from being predominantly "the sage on the stage to a guide on the side." (Thinking Schools International, n.d.,pp. 1–2)

QUESTIONS FOR ENQUIRY

Bob Burden articulated 14 criteria for schools to use as benchmarks for determining the extent to which they have developed as a Thinking School. What other criteria might you use for this purpose?

What critical shifts in how we conceptualize education, locally and globally, need to occur if becoming a Thinking School is not seen as such a radical departure from the prevailing models that exist today?

What are the major trends we see in the world today, and how might Burden's vision for Thinking Schools address or even anticipate these emerging forces?

It's easy to say that a "whole school" approach will lead to transformational change. Beyond specific programmatic decisions, what approaches should a "whole school" engage in that will truly transform it into a Thinking School rather than one that simply strengthens existing paradigms?

■ REFERENCES AND FURTHER READINGS

Affley, P. (n.d.). *Christ the King Catholic primary school: Our thinking journey.* Retrieved from http://www.thinkingschoolsinternational.com/site/wp-content/uploads/2011/12/Christ-the-King-Catholic-Primary-Sch0011.pdf

Anderson, L. W., Krathwohl, D. R., Airasian, P. W., Cruikshank, K. A., Mayer, R. E., Pintrich, P. R., . . . Wittrock, M. C. (2001). *A taxonomy for learning, teaching, and assessing: A revision of Bloom's taxonomy of educational objectives.* New York, NY: Addison Wesley Longman.

Blagg, N. (1989). *Can we teach intelligence?* Hillsdale, NJ: Lawrence Erlbaum.

Burden, R. L. (2006). *Is there any such thing as a 'Thinking School'?* Retrieved from http://www.thinkingschoolsinternational.com/site/wp-content/uploads/2011/12/Bob-Burden-article-Is-there-any-such-thing-as-a-Thinking-School.pdf

Burden, R. L., & Nichols, S. L. (2000). Evaluating the process of introducing a thinking skills programme into the secondary school curriculum. *Research Papers in Education 15*(3), 293–306.

Costa, A. L. (2001). *Developing minds: A Resource book for teaching thinking* (3rd ed.). Alexandria, VA: Association for Supervision and Curriculum Development (ASCD).

Costa, A. L., O'leary, P. W. (2013). *The power of the social brain: Teaching, learning, and interdependent thinking.* New York, NY: Teachers College Press.

Dweck, C. (2006). *Mindset: The new psychology of success.* New York, NY: Ballantine Books.

Fullan, M. (1982). *The meaning of educational change.* New York, NY: Teachers College Press.

Fullan, M. (1993). *Change forces: Probing the depths of educational reform.* London, UK: Falmer Press.

Fullan, M. (1999). *Change forces: The sequel.* London, UK: Falmer Press.

Georgiades, N., & Phillimore, L. (1975), The myth of the hero-innovator and alternative strategies for organisational change. In C. Kiernan & E. P. Woodford (Eds.), *Behaviour modification with the severely retarded.* Amsterdam, the Netherlands: Associate Scientific Publishers.

McGuiness, C. (1999). *From thinking skills to thinking classrooms: A review and evaluation of approaches for development pupils' thinking.* Norwich, UK: Department for Education and Employment.

Reid, K., Hopkins, D., & Holly, P. (1987). *Towards the effective school.* Oxford, UK: Blackwell.

Teddlie, C., & Reynolds, D. (2000). *The international handbook of school effectiveness research.* London, UK: Falmer.

Thinking Schools International. (n.d.). *Observations from senior leaders of Thinking Schools in the UK.* Retrieved from http://www.thinkingschoolsinternational.com/site/ wp-content/uploads/2011/12/observations-from-senior-leaders-of-thinking-schools-in-the-uk.pdf

Vosniadou, Stella. (2001). How children learn. *Educational Practices Series 7.* Brussels, Belgium: Royal Academy of Science, Literature and Arts International Academy of Education. Retrieved from http://unesdoc.unesco.org/images/0012/001254/ 125456e.pdf

5

Journey

Editors' Introduction

In his chapter above, which focused on the background, evolution, definition, and criteria of Thinking Schools, Bob Burden noted that there was one school that was an early exemplar for him for what is possible when educators come together over time to focus on thinking as central to the value system of their learning community. Here is the story of that school, detailing the long journey toward becoming a Thinking School.

The story told by Gill Hubble, one of the key leaders of St Cuthbert's College in New Zealand, begins all the way back in 1992 and takes us through to early 2003. What may be surprising about this decade-long transformational process that continues to this day is that this single-gender girls' secondary school was doing quite well in the national rankings in New Zealand. Yet, after survey and interviewing their "high scoring" post graduates, most of who were in college, they found that many of their students while once testing near the top were not at the top in college performance. Many students also reported that they felt in some areas unprepared for the independent thinking and rigorous challenges of courses. They scored in the 75% to 85% level in their courses, but relatively few could break into the top 10%. Why this discrepancy? The leadership and later the faculty slowly and surely moved forward as a whole to explore new ways of directly supporting their students to think more deeply and independently, autonomously.

As you will see, explore they did! Yet the outcomes of the first few years offer all who want to reframe their schools around thinking a few essential lessons learned about the process. While individual teachers experimented with new approaches and there were many professional development opportunities focused on teaching techniques—and teaching and learning improved—there was little evidence of a coherent, school-wide impact on students, or on their performance. Teachers were more aware of approaches, but students were not learning sets of strategies, or models, that they could transfer, autonomously, into their daily work.

The outcome? By the late 1990s, as the story is told below, St Cuthbert's came to focus on a few good models that they had tested in their classrooms: Thinking Maps and Habits of Mind. More in-depth professional development was conducted for all staff with a commitment that the focus would be on students' fluency with both models working together in an integrated way. Most important, the schools did not depend on merely implementing these models. They developed their own design for bringing the idea of thinking becoming central to the definition of the school, reflected in their understanding that this process was about having a transformation in the environment, the character, the ethos of the school. You will read about their "double-processing" technique, metacognitive lesson planning, multiple intelligences/differentiated learning activities available to students through their intranet, and school-wide focus on inquiry techniques drawn from the Philosophy for Children approach. This demonstrates that it is not only about implementing effective models, or approaches, but rather the process of consciously creating a comprehensive weave of systematic, whole school practices over time.

You should also know that for all this hard work and long processes of change, St Cuthbert's School's ranking went to the top in the nation over time, thus demonstrating that a focus on thinking improves students' thinking abilities as described below, while also positively impacting outcomes on measures of achievement within the traditional evaluation criteria.

This chapter stands as a testament for schools that first look inside themselves for questions and their own answers, while simultaneously reaching out for support and networking with other schools and experts in the field to evolve a design for creating their own Thinking School with rigorous attention to student needs. The teaching, leading, and learning practices have significantly changed. There is good reason why Bob Burden references the experiences described in detail below as key to his thinking about the process of taking this path. This school certainly has also been an inspiration for educators around the world wanting to engage in growing a Thinking School from the inside out.

JOURNEY TOWARD BECOMING A THINKING SCHOOL

Gill Hubble

I have always thought that all schools could become "thinking schools"—schools that consciously and systematically focus on the development of cognitive and critical thinking for all students—via various pathways. St Cuthbert's College in Auckland, New Zealand, the girls' school described in this chapter, piloted and evaluated a range of thinking strategies and approaches as a first stage, before finally realizing that doing a thorough job of introducing, training, and implementing Thinking Maps would actually provide a basis of understandings about cognitive strategies in general. When I was the associate principal and later researcher and consultant for the school, I became aware that this foundation allowed other strategies to be used and in fact strengthened various combined approaches. Over time, this allowed for autonomy for both teachers and students as they selected the best strategies to fit particular purposes. Students using Thinking Maps on their own is a start but is not the end point or long-term goal of becoming a Thinking School. This has been witnessed over the past 3 years as Thinking Maps have been integrated into dozens of schools in England (in coordination with the Cognitive Education Centre at the University of Exeter) that are refining their own evolving definitions toward schools in the 21st century focused on the wide-ranging processes of thinking.

St Cuthbert's has developed many learning approaches, but a solid understanding of the basic thought processes gained through Thinking Maps has been crucial. The other approaches that have been complementary are Costa and Kallick's (2000) Habits of Mind in the behavioral domain and a focus on Bloom's (1956) taxonomy of cognitive objectives to explain to students the steps that can be taken to think in more complex ways. In addition, this school has a focus on philosophy. Originally this was developed through the Philosophy for Children program developed by Dr. Mathew Lipman, but now questioning, building arguments, logical and lateral thinking, making assumptions, generating concepts, and ethical thinking are all given significant curriculum time. Time is also deliberately given to the teaching of various skills using mobile phones and Internet blogs, which allows students to use Thinking Maps and other strategies outside the classroom. This has resulted in a huge expansion of the information-technology department, which services student responses and links both teachers and students together in a sophisticated, flexible thinking community, responsive to and respectful of others' ideas.

The pathway this school has taken has resulted in learning and *thinking* being central to the way everything is done. The school community sees itself as a Thinking School because all the opportunities provided by the school are in some way designed to extend students' thinking outcomes.

■ BEGINNING THE LONG PROCESS

In the later part of the 20th century, our school began an evolutionary process that finally envisioned a community of learners who could move beyond "tacit use" of thinking skills. Through research, practice, personal discoveries, and many rich conversations, we made a multiyear commitment to integrating the Thinking Maps language into our community. Over the recent years, we believe that our school has achieved "reflective use" of these tools—a sophisticated metacognitive use involving reflection and evaluation (Swartz & Perkins, 1989). We have come to believe that if our students functioned as reflective users of Thinking Maps, this would increase their thinking-skills repertoire and encourage autonomy of thinking and collaboration, certainly important if not essential outcomes for every school in a democratic society.

An assumption underlying the explicit teaching of thinking is that instruction in thinking skills can enhance the development of a student's thinking-skills repertoire (e.g., you can identify and teach the skills required for conscious decision making). In a narrow sense, it is always possible to teach thinking-skill strategies and tools and to test a student's cognitive comprehension of these skills or even his or her ability to apply these skills to a given problem. In a broader sense, the vision of many educators and researchers of the thinking-skills movement of the past few decades has been that the direct teaching of thinking is possible and is a necessary next step in the evolution of teaching and learning toward transfer of thinking skills across—and deeply into—content areas, for interdisciplinary problem solving and lifelong learning. Our story is of a school wanting it both ways: direct, formal teaching of thinking skills and explicit transfer into content areas.

St Cuthbert's College is a unique, single-sex, independent school spanning the K–12 grade levels, with a student population of 1,500 girls aged 5 to 18. The college is expected to provide an outstanding education that not only encompasses academic, sporting, and cultural excellence, but also adds the dimensions of character and values education. Thus, the long-term development of a systematic, fully integrated use of thinking skills, ultimately leading to our use of Thinking Maps, took continuous focus and persistent attention to the goal.

There is a high expectation of all involved that we must provide for individual needs and produce graduates who can gain entry to the universities and courses of their choice and approach tertiary studies, and life, with the attitudes and skills that encourage success and personal fulfillment. Parents expect of the school that it retain its traditions and at the same time be innovative. Through the process of our evolution, we have moved from being a high-quality school with strong academic outcomes to being a true learning organization unified by a focus on developing high-quality thinking. Along the way, our academic results have moved us to the top rungs of the educational ladder in New Zealand, but this seems a sidebar to our evolving capacities to seek deeper understandings of how our minds work and to treasure the intrinsic rewards gained from becoming a school as a home for the mind.

Phase I: Discovering Too Many Possibilities

In 1992, staff and management began this process by reviewing the school philosophy guided by the following questions: What kind of learners do we want to produce in this college? What behaviors, attitudes, skills, and knowledge would they have? We agreed that we wanted our students to become adults who were lifelong, independent learners, who approached life's situations and problems positively and persevered to find resolutions and answers. It had been the norm in schools such as ours for teachers to be responsible for writing superb lessons. They were expected to supply students with books of resource notes and to test, train, and, in general, provide opportunities for students to learn. The focus was on disseminating information and expecting students to study and memorize all this valuable knowledge so they could have success in national examinations.

While our school did well in the national rankings of senior secondary examination results, there was a nagging feeling among some staff that our teaching methods were producing graduates who were dependent learners: students who had excellent recall skills, who were prepared to read and study hard, but whose work was careful, methodical, and pedestrian rather than original, inventive, and risk-taking. This idea was supported by the fact that many good students gained fine marks of around 75% to 85%, but relatively few broke into the 90th percentile at the university scholarship level. We decided that we had a responsibility to make a change for our students. We embarked on a project in 1992, which we hoped would lead our students toward being autonomous learners.

First, we made a list of all the qualities such a learner would have. What developed from this was the conviction that effective learners are good thinkers who have a range of internalized strategies they can use to do their work. Then we debated these questions, to achieve the changes required to create the learning community we had described:

- How would this change our teaching practice?
- How would this change how students apply themselves to education?
- What skills or strategies would they need, if "better thinking" were our goal?
- From the range of theorists and practitioners who wrote on thinking, learning, and best educational practice, which should we use as our models, and which of the many strategies should we choose?

By 1992, a range of exciting strategies, methodologies, frameworks, and programs was becoming available for teachers who were interested in encouraging their students to think deeply and independently. A group of our staff read through the available literature and attended courses on best practices. The problem soon emerged: too many possibilities. Everyone who went to a course or read one of these books came to school converted and full of enthusiasm to try out the new ideas. We were all over the place. Across our K–12 school could be found pockets of teachers "doing" such processes as Edward de Bono's CORT program, Mind Mapping, multiple intelligences, and learning styles.

This was all terribly exciting to those of us involved. We held many personal development–training sessions for the whole staff between 1993 and 1994, and some of us became specialists in one process or another. However, by 1994, it became obvious that we had made a great change to individual teaching practice, but had done nothing that made a school-wide impact for students. An individual student could have had some very good lessons from innovative teachers but not have recognized the strategies used or their application elsewhere. In addition, students' thinking patterns or habits would have remained unchanged, and students would not have developed a set of strategies they could regularly use to do their work more meaningfully. We were also quite aware that there was very little conceptual transfer or internalization of the strategies.

Phase 2: Focus on Transfer and "Double Processing"

As a staff, we decided to focus on transfer: We would all focus on a selection of strategies, teach them across all disciplines at the same time, practice them, and explicitly identify them, so students could see the transfer links and how useful they could be in different situations. We selected some of the lessons from several programs and had developed the firm belief that students who processed work in a number of different ways gained a deeper understanding of the content. We called this "double processing": If a lesson involved written notes in linear form, then homework could be to talk to parents about it. If a graphic organizer was used in class, then linear notes could be used for follow-up. At this stage, the graphic organizers we used were such things as the fishbone, the Venn diagram, sequence boxes, and Mind Mapping (or concept mapping). None of us had really associated these wide-ranging, disconnected graphics with a cognitive function because they were used by staff to sort content information given in class or for homework. They were prescriptive: Students were told to fill them in.

In 1998, we again reviewed our thinking program. So much had been done, but somehow it still seemed more like a personal development program for staff to improve teaching strategies than for the explicit development of autonomous learning for students. Had we gone wrong? Better teaching had led to better marks for all, but it seemed to us that we were not making enough of a difference for *all* students. We referred again to Costa's (1991) vision of a school as a home for the mind as a reference point. Here was a vision of everybody in a school community working together to make thinking central to the way everything was done. What we needed was a common, school-wide language that we could all use, which could be built on from age 5 to age 18 in greater depth. We had a unique opportunity to introduce good thinking skills early and develop them over the years so they really made a difference, but which approaches were out there that could do this?

Phase 3: Uniting the School With a Common Language

In 1999, we decided to have a research year where interested staff would examine the various approaches, programs, and strategies that could form the basis of an effective thinking program. We focused on the primary elements of thinking from the critical, creative, and caring/affective domains. Thinking Maps appeared to be an excellent way to focus on eight basic cognitive processes and the use of the Frame of Reference for metacognitive development. The challenge for us was to get both staff and students to see these as effective thinking processes, united together as a language rather than as isolated graphic organizers. Our goal was to gradually teach and implement these over 3 to 5 years so students would have a range of strategies to employ.

Year 1: Introducing Thinking Maps in 1999

To introduce a common visual thinking language to the whole K–12 continuum of St Cuthbert's teaching and learning needs was an ambitious undertaking. We chose to introduce Thinking Maps through a three-year implementation cycle, by first teaching the use of Thinking Maps explicitly within noncurricular contexts. We chose this method of introduction since research (Perkins & Salomon, 1989) revealed that cognitive skills are not automatically acquired unless they are taught explicitly. This was a formal approach carried out by everybody—expected, planned, and agreed on by staff. Following the initial training, teachers were grouped into departments to find applications within subjects and units and were supported by follow-up sessions as they gained confidence. They began with a narrow view of what an isolated map could do—and what the maps could do together—and we encouraged them to focus on students gaining confidence and experience in use across the curriculum.

We also established a Department of Thinking and employed a thinking coordinator to manage the program and write the lessons using a six-step methodology: (1) label the strategy (the cognitive skills and map), (2) explain the purpose, (3) practice (provide practice experience and feedback), (4) transfer (put into different content contexts), (5) evaluate, and (6) reflect. Teacher attitude was crucial, and where the teacher was confident and prepared, the lessons proved very successful in teaching the strategy.

While the primary school staff and students had a positive attitude toward the Thinking Maps approach, some secondary staff expressed reservations. Secondary staff had concerns about teaching skills in noncurricular contexts; they disliked the imposition of creating "artificial or forced" opportunities for conceptual transfer. In turn, some secondary students questioned the need to learn about the maps separately because "the teacher shows us how to do them in class anyway." These older students said, "We already know how to think, and we don't need you to tell us." Generally, this is a situation easily overcome by confident, persuasive teachers who believe that the processes they are teaching can make a difference, but it is very difficult when the teachers themselves are unsure as they integrate the tools into their repertoire.

Despite these difficulties, we achieved our goal of having every child in the school introduced to the maps in an explicit way. Students are able to use all the maps as required in a range of situations and when use of the maps is genuinely integrated and flexible. Most staff members model metacognitive processes by saying, "I need to analyze this information—which maps do you think would be useful here?" Consequently, we see much greater choice and flexibility of use, including the use of a range of maps to reach a decision or to extend an idea.

We believe that our earlier work of encouraging teachers to get students to doubly process notes also paid off: During some lessons, students were to take notes only in map form and then for homework write up the information in linear form, and vice versa. We saw excellent collaborative work develop, as some groups elected to take class notes in map form and work as teams to develop the ideas as fully as possible. It is much easier to see ideas being extended when they can be presented visually, and students enjoy adding to a collaborative map.

We also had considerable success in working meaningfully with departments to help them create units and lessons that used the maps in subjects. These "transfer" lessons were almost always valued highly by staff and students. The goal was to demonstrate how a thinking tool could be used right across the curriculum—how it could be used for homework and study, in assessments, and to help make real-life evaluations of problems in context and make decisions.

Teachers began to see how useful a map was in eliciting prior knowledge. Students are now often asked to draw a map early in a lesson and then at the end of the lesson. By comparing the maps, students see and evaluate their own progress, thereby developing a sense of personal efficacy of themselves as learners. Metacognition and evaluation! Students also feel positive as they choose which maps to use when given a task. Secondary school staff members who initially were not enthusiastic about the maps because they said they had their own subject-specific processes became more positive when they saw that the maps could clearly reveal where thinking had gone wrong. All students benefited from this opportunity to analyze the merits of each other's thinking processes.

Year 2: Evidence of Independent Use in 2000

In the second year, we were confident that students knew what a Thinking Map was (tacit use), but we were uncertain of the degree to which students used the Thinking Maps independently. We wanted to know the extent to which students had moved from tacit use of Thinking Maps, to aware use or even strategic use. Students could use the maps when asked, but we suspected that they did it without clear intent. The challenge for the year 2000 was to gather evidence of the existing students' independent use of the Thinking Maps.

To determine the extent to which a fluent and "reflective" student's use of maps occurred in problem-solving situations, we had students use their 20-minute thinking-skills time to collaboratively solve a long-term problem using Thinking Maps. For example, one teacher created a challenging activity on endangered animals playfully presented through a Gary Larson cartoon:

> Imagine you are a member of a team of researchers charged with reversing the population decline of the endangered "balloon" animals that have a hard time surviving in a harsh landscape. Use Thinking Maps as tools for generating, organizing, and assessing factors that might affect the population size of the balloon animals (e.g., physical factors, catastrophic events, food supply, disease, competition, ecotourism). Develop an action plan, based around your Thinking Maps, to help reverse the population decline.

The students' efforts were assessed, and prizes for fluent and flexible use of Thinking Maps were awarded. One group of four students created the example, shown in Figures 5.1 through 5.5, of using multiple maps to analyze this problem.

The purpose of the activity was to evaluate how students, working in cooperative groups, could apply multiple thinking processes via Thinking Maps to gain a solution to the scientific problem found in cartoons and nature. This sample of student work is representative of the quality of work received and reveals how these students could employ the tools for multistep problem solving and decision making. Although some students showed strategic and even reflective use of maps, the majority still struggled to show the fluency we expected in their map use.

Year 3: Reviewing and Moving Forward in 2001

Our review of student applications revealed that there was still a need for more explicit teaching of these tools. The development of autonomous transfer of thinking skills does not happen over just a year or two. It happens during the evolution of a student's educational career and lifetime. Our evaluation of

Figure 5.1 Factors Affecting Size of Population of Balloon Animals

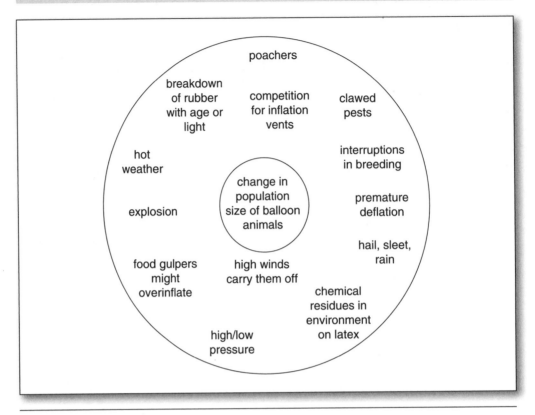

Source: Hyerle and Alper (2011).

Figure 5.2 Categorizing Factors Affecting Size of Population of Balloon Animals

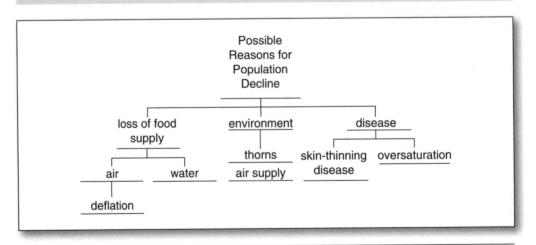

Source: Hyerle and Alper (2011).

student map use in the year 2000 indicated that many students and some staff were not as confident or competent in the use of Thinking Maps as we believed possible and necessary to reach the goal of being authentic, independent thinkers. We needed to revisit individual maps for fluency.

Figure 5.3 Causes and Effects of Population Decline of Balloon Animals

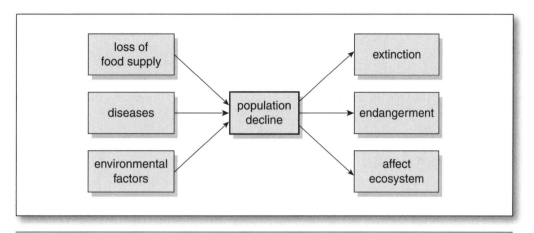

Source: Hyerle and Alper (2011).

Figure 5.4 Comparing Possible Solutions to Population Decline

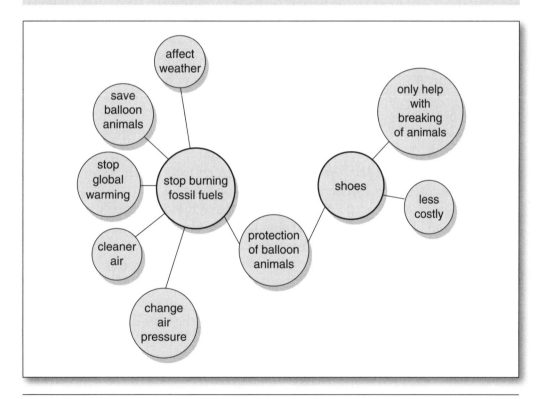

Source: Hyerle and Alper (2011).

Though there was a risk of repetition for both teachers and students—the risk that many schools do not take for long-term change—we created a more authentic, thematic learning experience for senior students based on their reflections on the "Big Day Out," a 12-hour music festival that many students and their friends had attended. We also carried out in-school research during

Figure 5.5 Making an Analogous Relationship With a Possible Solution

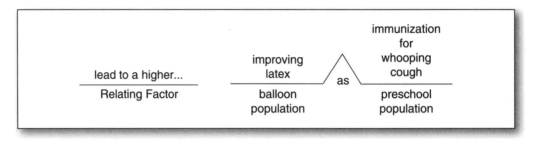

Source: Hyerle and Alper (2011).

the year using a questionnaire to ask students about the maps they had used, about the subject areas in which they used different maps, if they had used maps to organize their thoughts in situations outside school, and whether they believed their thinking had been developed through learning about Thinking Maps.

In the junior school, students were positive about Thinking Maps, had experienced their use in many different settings, and almost uniformly enjoyed using them to enhance their thinking both at school and at home. In the senior school, the results were predictable: Students who had experienced staff who valued the maps and provided opportunities for transfer into several different curriculum areas were positive about the usefulness of the maps and optimistic about map-related improvements in the way they solved problems or sorted issues. In contrast, students who had been provided with few opportunities to use the maps in curriculum areas or who had had teachers who avowed "grudging compliance" saw the maps, and the thinking-skills lessons, as "boring and a waste of my time." Without opportunities for transfer, senior students marginalized the maps and considered them pointless.

Once again, it was evident that teachers make the difference to the implementation and effective use of a learning strategy. In 2001, in the senior school, we also moved toward more departmental autonomy. Secondary departments were asked questions such as the following: What kinds of thinking do you most value in your department? What are the most powerful experiences to encourage this thinking for students? What Thinking Map activities will you use to develop these skills? How might you show the effectiveness and value of your thinking-skills focus for students' learning?

Departments were required to add their "thinking focus" to their departmental plan, and staff could choose to be apprised of this thinking focus. Individual departmental choice was interesting. The technology department chose to improve its students' metacognitive thinking through developing links between sequencing (Flow Maps) and the design process. The art department wanted to use maps to strengthen problem finding and metaperception. In social sciences, pattern finding was valued, with a focus on Flow Maps for sequencing and Double-Bubble Maps for comparing and contrasting, and in the music department, there was exploration of the use of Brace Maps to better teach musical notation and intervals.

Years 4–5: A Common Language in 2003

Through our continued focus and retraining, by 2003 we had achieved a common visual-thinking language across the school, with staff and student competence with the maps much increased. The Department of Thinking expanded to two full-time teachers supported by a team of staff. Examples of student use of Thinking Maps continued to be displayed in every teaching space. They were regularly used in assessments and curriculum lessons. In the secondary school, we saw more experimentation in flexible map use than in the early years, with several maps being linked and used to process a task. In the junior school, the majority of students showed fluent map use by Year 6, and students were adept users of the Thinking Map software (Thinking Maps, Inc. 2006).

Thinking Maps continued to be explicitly introduced in the junior school. However, after three years' implementation, the map knowledge base in the senior school was considered to be such that teaching of individual maps was only required for new students. Flexible catch-up training for new students and new staff was provided each year, and ongoing support from the thinking coordinators was provided on an individual and departmental basis.

By 2003, we were able to recognize some significant advances in the way the maps were being used, especially since St Cuthbert's College had expanded its professional development time to 1.5 hours a week. There was planned training for teachers in how to link the maps to other thinking or learning strategies. This encouraged students to use a wider range of strategies together to engage with the content knowledge. When several approaches are used together—such as linking Costa's (1991) 16 Habits of Mind with Thinking Maps—the emphasis on isolated tools lessens and changes to an emphasis on whole thinking and learning processes. It also extends the quality of the thinking involved. Here is a sampling of some of the spin-off benefits of our evolution. Teachers have been experimenting with the following:

- Developing a metacognitive lesson plan, where teachers identify a specific learning goal and the questions they can ask students that will allow them to identify for themselves appropriate Thinking Maps to use.
- Encouraging greater infusion by creating intranet-based learning activities. Students can call up a page of lesson activities available for a task, click on a hyperlink, and be presented with a range of links to higher-order thinking, Thinking Maps, and multiple intelligence-differentiation activities. They can then download these directly into their responses.
- Encouraging flexible use by having a school-wide focus on "applied thinking," where a philosophical real-life problem is analyzed using the maps and inquiry techniques.

These examples reflect the inherent rigor and flexibility of Thinking Maps and the empowering nature of the change process that was allowed to mature naturally over time. The learning outcomes for our students based on fundamental thinking processes and learning approaches have been remarkable. Academic results in New Zealand's national league tables have risen consistently, with the college a national academic leader, placing 1st or 2nd in

New Zealand in every senior external examination category for the past 5 years, up from 12th at the start of our evolutionary process. We have also seen improved results on international tests and PATs (reading, listening, and comprehension tests), the high level of acceptance and approval from students and parents, and the continued use of double processing using the maps and linear writing from our students who now attend universities.

Yet the most powerful outcome has been the move to collaborative and interactive classrooms where students—and teachers—are confident to discuss their learning and to learn from each other. We now know that students are much more willing to share their work with the class when it is developed visually, collaboratively, and through a flexible, common language for thinking that is the foundation for the evolution of our community. And, as teachers and school leaders, we are able to work deeply in our own content areas, with focused collaboration in teams. After 10 years, we are still living the never-ending ebb and flow of change and thriving as an evolving school as a home for the mind.

QUESTIONS FOR ENQUIRY

Art Costa urges schools to become a "home for the mind for all who dwell there." In what ways did St Cuthbert's School respond to this urgent call and engage the minds of all members of the school community? How did their approach into becoming a Thinking School establish the foundation for how their instructional practices would be transformed?

Interestingly, the students in St Cuthbert's College were already performing at a high level before the school embarked on its journey of becoming a Thinking School. What, then, were the sources of their motivation to do so and what were the barriers they needed to remove or look beyond to genuinely embrace this process and its potential?

If St Cuthbert's stands as a model for what a Thinking School can be, how might you describe its distinguishing attributes and qualities? What evidence was presented in this chapter that would support your descriptors? If you were to compare your own school with St Cuthbert's, what might be the most significant similarities and differences? What conclusions can be drawn from this about your own school and the opportunities/areas for future growth and development?

■ REFERENCES AND FURTHER READINGS

Bloom, B. S. (Ed.). (1956). *Taxonomy of educational objectives: Handbook: Cognitive domain.* New York, NY: Longman.

Costa, A. L. (1991). *The school as a home for the mind.* Palatine, IL: IRI/Skylight.

Costa, A., & Kallick, B. (2000). *Activating and engaging the habits of mind.* Alexandria, VA: Association for Supervision and Curriculum Development.

Hyerle, D., & Alper, L. (Eds.). (2011). *Student successes with thinking maps* (2nd ed.). Thousand Oaks, CA: Corwin.

Perkins, D. N., & Salomon, G. (1989). Teaching for transfer. *Educational Leadership, 46*(1), 22–32.

Swartz, R. J., & Perkins, D. N. (1989). *Teaching thinking: Issues and approaches.* Pacific Grove, CA: Midwest.

Thinking Maps, Inc. (2006). Thinking Maps: Technology for Learning. *Thinking maps software version 2.0 user's guide.* Cary, NC: Author.

6

School

Editors' Introduction

The engaging, challenging, exploratory journey described by Gill in the previous chapter of her school evolving slowly over more than 10 years' time and still going toward balancing content learning and thinking processes approaches is a powerful example of a shift to a new paradigm for education. Yet a question you may be asking yourself is this: Is this long process of discovery what every school needs to do to make this kind of significant change? We find a full array of answers in this chapter about the conscious efforts of Rochester Grammar School faculty to make "the shift." As described by Bob Burden and more fully in Chapter 4, Thinking Schools International drew from the work of Gill Hubble and many others to synthesise a dynamic approach to clarifying, accelerating, and systematically sustaining the transition of any school wanting to make the shift. Richard Coe, then a drama teacher at Rochester, describes how his school went through much of the same hard questioning, reflective change processes that had occurred over a 10-year span, as documented by the pioneering work at St Cuthbert's that left key trail markers as guideposts. Thus, they were able to avoid some missteps and could focus energies on creating a more efficient and equally effective path toward a common goal.

As you will see below, Rochester School was able to draw on many new resources and lessons learned not available to Gill's school and thus was able to move much more quickly toward their own established goals. Bob Burden, through Exeter's Cognitive Centre, offered support and feedback on the 14 criteria for Thinking Schools as they developed a plan for accreditation. Thinking Schools International (then known as Kestrel Consulting) offered an introductory workshop (now called Growing Thinking Schools from the Inside Out*) and planning documents for staff. When requested, and as one dimension of the process, specific training in research-based approaches such as Thinking Maps, higher-order questioning, Habits of Mind, Six Hats Thinking, and Philosophy for Children were readily available through certified trainers, many of who could work with Rochester staff to help blend these approaches together in the practice of classroom teaching. What is also not to be underestimated is that Rochester was not alone. They were able to join a dynamic network of schools working off a common vision, but each taking their own route to get there. These schools have been unified in their belief that "the shift" toward balancing deep content and conceptual learning and a student-centred thinking process was absolutely essential for students of the 21st century. While the school had the natural growing pains and some early struggles as they shifted, Richard ends this chapter with an insight: that for Rochester to continue to grow over time and evolve as a Thinking School they needed to engage students as teachers of thinking for each other and the faculty needed to move beyond their own hallways to reach out to give back around the world through the Thinking Schools global network across the United Kingdom and on to Malaysia.*

Note: This chapter is by a British author. The text is in British English.

THE TREE OF LEARNING

Richard Coe

■ THE STARTING POINT

Despite working in a school where students have achieved high-quality results, over the years many of our staff came to feel frustrated by our students' inability to think critically or creatively without significant scaffolding. Yes, the students were great at remembering lots of information, taking tests, and writing essays, but if you talked to them, many did not actually have a way of expressing their thoughts clearly in unfamiliar situations or nonexamination contexts. They didn't have a language for discussing how they were thinking. In retrospect, clearly students had not developed a *metacognitive* stance toward their own thinking. This is because *we* had not done so purposefully. We therefore made the decision to embark on a journey of thinking for our students and for ourselves: developing, discovering, and transforming our school for the long run, not the short-term gain.

We researched a number of projects and approaches and discovered the Cognitive Education Centre at Exeter University, in the United Kingdom. Further exploration uncovered a unified approach for schools that was led by Thinking Schools International (TSI), in association with the university. This approach was not presented as simply a course, or programmatic. Our school could work in collaboration with TSI and develop a long-term plan that reflected our needs, yet also offered structures that we adapted as we moved forward over the years. This ultimately resulted in accreditation as a Thinking School through Exeter University. Though this accreditation recognised the evidence we gathered showing where we had come on our journey over the previous 3 or 4 years, it was not intended to mark our arrival at a permanent resting place. The longer-term project toward becoming a Thinking School is thus not about implementing a program or about a formalised "designation," or for that matter, reaching a final destination. It is an ongoing, focused process of growth, reflection, and further development.

The Rochester Grammar School (RGS) is a school in Medway, England. Medway came into existence as a unitary authority in 1988, located on the southern bank of the River Thames, bordered by Kent and with its own river, the Medway, flowing through it. It forms one of the largest regeneration projects in Western Europe, the Thames gateway. It has higher levels of deprivation than neighbouring Kent partly due to the closure of its dockyard in the 1970s, causing high levels of unemployment and depression—an area with its fair share of socioeconomic issues.

We started our transformation toward a Thinking School in 2006. Of course, we are proud that our school has received positive recognition from outside evaluators as we have changed our focus. In 2008, Rochester was judged to be outstanding in all areas by Ofsted. (As discussed in Chapter 4 by Bob Burden, Ofsted is the U.K. government's independent body that inspects schools for standards in teaching, learning, progress, health and safety, and personal well-being.) Inspections are run by lead inspectors who view ALL public schools against four ratings; Outstanding, Good, Satisfactory, or Unsatisfactory. Then we were accredited as a Thinking School by Exeter University in December 2009 and later became the first English secondary school to gain advanced Thinking School status in October 2011. These "outside" points of evaluation only point to the "inside" changes we have made that are strong and enduring. On reflection of our process over the years, we have come to see that our vision to begin the journey to develop thinking as a central animating principle of our school was drawn from several causes and intended effects as shown using the Multi-Flow Map.

We used the following broad definition of a Thinking School, as offered by Bob Burden and the Cognitive Centre 2 as a starting point:

> A thinking school is a learning community in which all members share a common language; where thinking strategies and tools are used across the curriculum . . . where all students are developing and demonstrating independent and cooperative learning skills; where the school generates high levels of achievement and an excitement and enthusiasm for learning.

Figure 6.1 Multi-Flow Map of Causes and Effects of Rochester Grammar School's Decision to Undertake the Journey of Becoming a Thinking School

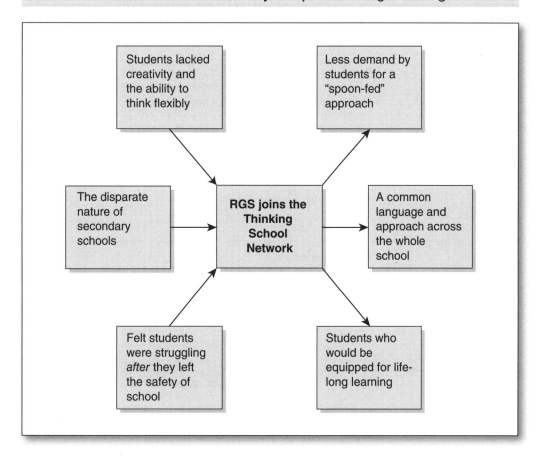

Using this definition, our drive team started by creating a comparative table as we first embarked on this process. The descriptors in italics are taken from Arthur Costa and Bena Kallick's Habits of Mind model, which has been highly influential in shaping our approach from when we started our journey until this very day. This is because, as with the other models and processes we develop, the language and tools we have used have become internalised within the culture or ethos of our school, shaping the core of our identity.

How Did We Begin the Journey?

The decision to put "thinking" at the heart of our school was taken in the academic year 2005–2006. Although at this time the school had just achieved some of its best results ever at A (Advanced) level (Senior years 12 and 13)

Figure 6.2 Comparative Table Showing Before and After Introduction of Thinking Schools in RGS

Before Thinking Skills program	Impact of Thinking Skills program
Teacher led lessons	A clear student voice Student presentations Student taking lessons Students *questioning and posing problems* Students *gathering data through all the senses*
Lack of variety in students work	A range of visual tools, creative and challenging stimuli, tasks on all levels of taxonomy scale
Work in isolation	*Thinking interdependently* *Applying past knowledge to new situations* Thinking Time for reflection
Lack of engagement and enthusiasm by students	Passionate response, debate, confidence, respect for learning *Responding with wonderment and awe* *Taking responsible risks* *Acting with persistence* *Finding humour*
Lessons dominated by content	Lessons dominated by learning through thinking activities *Thinking flexibly* *Thinking about thinking (metacognition)*
One paced lessons	Starters, plenary and task that shift and develop
One task fits all	Extension tasks for the most able—using Bloom's Taxonomy
Subjects in isolation	Transferable skills and languages Joint homework tasks Project-based learning

and GCSE (General Certificate of Education 14–16, years 10–11), it was felt by the leaders of the school that somehow we were still not challenging the minds and creativity of the students. Ges Hartley, the Deputy Head Teacher, began by planning and implementing a number of cross-curricular projects, or *rich tasks* as they have now become known as. The first task was based on the Fibonacci Sequence. Students were instructed in the theory of the sequence and then created posters to try to bring this theory to life in a visual way. Students were encouraged to make connections between the sequence and everyday life: Where would they see the sequence "in action"? Drama, music, and media were then all used to bring these posters to life and also brought together mathematics and ICT with drama and media in a new and innovative way. The project was called the *Phi factor*. Our students were finally transferring skills and abstract concepts from different disciplines and applying past knowledge (one of the 16 Habits of Mind) to move forward with their creative projects. A focus was placed on group work and skills of collaboration (*interdependence,* as this would later be known, using the Habits of Mind model). Students were assessed on the quality of their work represented through posters, compositions, film sequences, and presentations, but were also asked to identify and describe degrees of creativity and personal growth.

The success of the *Phi factor* project was revealed as students worked collaboratively in groups on very open-ended tasks that required both analytical and creative thought. It was also one of the first times where students were making in-depth, thoughtful connections between their learning in one subject with another curriculum area. This experience led to further projects using rich tasks such as one on migration, titled *Crossing Borders,* which combined history, geography, music, and art. It also included an independent project for Year 7 students (age 11–12) based on the buildings of the Thames south bank, titled *Perspectives of London.* It was clear that the school was beginning to look at learning in a new light and that students were being asked to reflect and hold value with intelligent dispositions and thoughtful strategies, not just for the formative outcomes and assessments. However, at this point we were not using any specific thinking tools or models for approaching thinking explicitly across our school—just generally fostering independent research, curiosity, and creativity. This is a key dimension that makes us now a Thinking School as distinct from where we were in the past, challenging our students to think deeply every day, every year using specific models of thinking: Simply challenging student thinking through rich curricular tasks and/or high-quality teaching techniques does not mean that students—as independent and interdependent learners—are *consciously* internalising their capacities to identify, apply in context, transfer, and reflect on the full range of their own fundamental thinking processes. This was the shift we determined we needed to make.

As a teacher, I became interested and, to a certain degree, successful as a lead practitioner in presentation skills and creative thinking. This "success" was determined by faculty input whereby a whole-school approach to presentation skills was developed including criteria that were created by a range of teachers and students. There was clear evidence of students and teachers using PowerPoint software in a more creative and less intrusive way; students were no longer reading prepared speeches but using notes or even no notes in order to engage with the audience more through eye contact and open body language. This work across the whole faculty and student body was instrumental in the school deciding that we needed to take this experience to a new level. I was soon appointed as the Director of Independent Learning and given the charge of researching other possible approaches and programs for the school to take school-wide. As a first step in the process in March 2007, a lead consultant from TSI was invited to work with our school and introduce the key ideas about becoming a Thinking School. This was met with much enthusiasm. As a lead teacher, I attended follow-up sessions with educators from other schools that were engaged in the process and with Exeter University's Cognitive Education Centre and began to see the wider sphere or range of differentiated approaches that were possible as a school began to weave together its own unique design, from planning to school-wide implementation. The "tool-based" approach was something that inspired the RGS faculty to follow a whole-school, embedded approach to thinking rather than simply an "additive" approach or the implementation of a single, isolated "thinking skills" program. Our intentional use of the term *tools* meant to us that there was no additional curriculum for us to teach or programmatic workbooks and additional assignments that students had to use. Because of the whole-school approach, we could immediately and over time teach the tools to students and they could immediately apply and transfer these tools in ever more sophisticated ways as they became fluent as tool users.

We were beginning to discover that which we didn't know we were looking for: not simply a catchall collection of tools as you might see scattered around on a floor, but a variety of connected tools that are well defined and organised by research-based models, much as you would see a doctor, carpenter, chef, or mechanic with a professional bag or box of tools for use. We began to see that we, as teachers working in a coordinated manner, could integrate these tools together over time and fit the needs of our students as 21st-century learners. It also meant that we had to build our own internal expertise if we were truly going to transform our school over time so that students could also become expert.

Our drive team and faculty members identified Thinking Maps as a key starting point, because the language of cognition seemed very much focused on a whole-school approach. In the past, many of us had dabbled with Tony Buzan's brainstorming Mind-Mapping techniques, and this had been a good starting point but did not offer an array of patterning tools nor was it based on fundamental thinking processes. We were also interested because there was a systematic approach set up for teaching students the tools without "add-on" activities and worksheet assignments. In fact, the whole process is one of directly training students to apply each map to immediate work at hand. Also, Thinking Maps had been well received by other schools in our network, and faculty members from those schools talked passionately about their impact in their own schools. There was a ready support network in the area, which seemed important for our first exploration into thinking tools for developing Thinking Schools. We began to build an implementation model that started with developing "in-house" expertise. By the summer of 2007, six teachers were trained so they could then trial the approach and be able to train their colleagues in how to integrate Thinking Maps into the day-to-day life of classrooms.

The following year, Thinking Maps were introduced across the whole curriculum at all stages by all teachers. This was reinforced through performance management targets, individual professional development portfolios (CPUs), and a change to the environment: Thinking Maps posters were put up in each classroom by teachers along with the initial training to support student fluency with the tools, but important so that all could *see* that this was a school-wide priority. Despite some initial reluctance on behalf of some staff and students (who likes significant change in their lives?) the maps started to have a visible impact on the processing of content knowledge *and* thinking by students and staff. Below are some of our first attempts with maps by Year 7 in the subsequent Perspectives of London project. The implied thinking processes that had been embedded almost out of sight in the original project had now become visually explicit with students having to represent their ideas, plans, and processes in Thinking Maps.

As the maps became more commonly used in the school, they started to "pop up" in other places: hallway displays, public presentations by senior staff, and professional development presentations. It was then that we started to feel that both staff and students were becoming more fluent with the maps. We were taking our first steps in shifting from a traditional, teacher-centred,

Figure 6.3 Student Flow Map From Study of London

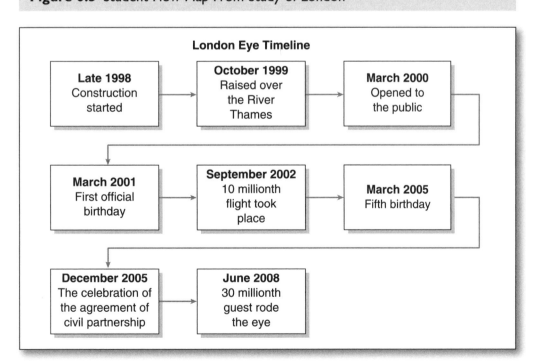

Figure 6.4 Student Tree Map From Study of London

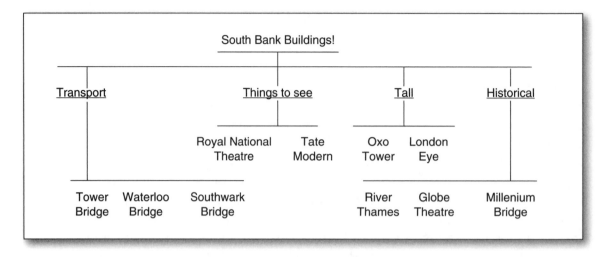

Figure 6.5 Student Double-Bubble Map From Study of London

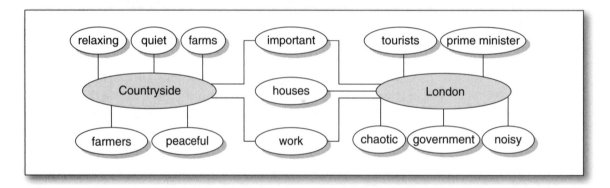

Figure 6.6 Personalized Learning and Thinking Skills Tree Map

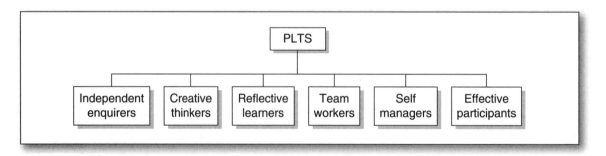

"strategies" view for improving learning and for incremental change to a more student-centred, "thinking-tool" approach. This happened within the context of a larger, school-wide commitment: developing our own unique vision of a thinking school.

This school-wide commitment surfaced in this PowerPoint slide that shows a tree map. What is significant here is that this was the first Thinking

Map used in a presentation to the School Board (called *Governors* in the United Kingdom) about why we were interested in becoming a Thinking School. Personalised Learning and Thinking Skills (PLTS) was an overarching goal for school change and was all the rage across the United Kingdom in 2008, so combining the two ideas was a powerful strategy for us to use. This was the first time that we were publicly practicing what we were preaching to those responsible for the long-term, overall well-being of the school. It was also evident from the exemplar material and observations that we collected and presented that the students were beginning to understand the link between visual tools and the actual thinking process and the effects in classroom performance. For example, the seemingly simple bubble map focusing on adjectives really led to improving the descriptive quality of students' written work. Previously, students had always taken the thinking skill of "description" for granted and as a vague, broad term with little rigor, and therefore had not given it any thought. By focusing and generating their thoughts on description via the bubble map, their vocabulary became richer and more considered. Their ideas (as well as ours to the Board of Governors!) became *public* because each student had dynamic tools through which they could visually map out their descriptors, reflect on the array of adjectives and adjective phrases, and actively share their unique patterns of thinking with other students. Of course, the maps also enabled teachers to directly facilitate, mediate, and assess both the content of the map as well as the process of thinking. As a result, the Maps are now seen as a language of vital tools—not isolated content area strategies—held in high regard by both staff and students.

A closer look at Thinking Maps and the implications for RGS over the past 7 years is key to understanding the depth to which we integrate a range of approaches in the core of our school. The practice of thinking in depth described here is essential to the larger vision of a Thinking School: There needs to be congruence between research from the cognitive-neurosciences, the big picture of a Thinking School, and the refined, everyday implementation of models and specific tools. Research tells us that humans are intrinsically visual beings—the eyes contain almost 70% of the body's sensory receptors and send millions of signals every second along optic nerves to the visual processing centre of the brain. Therefore, it makes sense that students remember, understand and apply concepts for longer if they have some visual way of exploring them. Thinking Maps have helped our students capture processes and thoughts in a clear and highly flexible way. The key to their usefulness and inherent value is that they are transferable across all curriculum areas. The students (as well as teachers and administrators) therefore share in what at first seemed an odd thought: Thinking Maps is a "common visual language."

For example, Thinking Maps have been particularly useful for "Edexcel" examination board drama portfolios I have assigned to my students. The Circle Map is used for seeking context. This tool enables students to generate relevant information about a topic represented in the centre of the circle and is often used for diagnosing knowledge, or literally *drawing* from prior knowledge (one of the 16 Habits of Mind). For example, at the very start of a topic such as when students learn about pantomime, physical theatre, monologue, or mime, each student and/or groups of students create circle maps reflecting what they already know (or think they know) about the topic. All the information is recorded and displayed, the students' responses nested within the concentric circles. Many teachers may say, "We brainstorm all the time," which is a fair point, but there are several elements that separate this tool from standard brainstorming. First, students have already learned the map as the "go-to tool" for generating ideas. Second, the visual circles carefully avoid linear listing, which can lead to hierarchical ordering or simply the shouting out of ideas. Third, the use of the "frame" of reference drawn around the Circle Map immediately moves students to a metacognitive stance not only about "what" they know, but also "how" they know it.

The *frame* is a metacognitive tool that allows students to reflect and evaluate *how* they know something rather than just what they know. When students draw a frame around any map they are then engaged to consider and explicitly state why they said what they did: Where are they coming from? Where did they receive this information? Is it reliable? Are the answers dependent on other factors, such as personal histories, culture, belief systems, and influences including peer groups, the media, or parents? This metacognitive process can then lead to thoughtful, critical reflection, questioning, discussion, and further exploration. This is just one example of how a number of thinking tools and strategies can work in combination. The Thinking Map provides a cognitive process and a way of working visually—in this case a circle map without hierarchy. A focus on questioning though is vital here for taking a potentially arbitrary piece of work and making it a critical and evaluative tool allowing both staff and students to climb the taxonomy ladder. What is really at play here is the notion of students "thinking about their thinking," yet another example of Costa and Kallick's Habits of Mind. Teachers often come back to the circle map midway or at the end of lessons as a grounding in the content being learned by adding to it or eliminating other ideas dependent on what has happened during the lesson.

The Circle Map with the frame is reminiscent of "role-on-the-wall." This is a technique established by Jonathan Neelands used in experiential drama. The outline of a person is drawn on the wall, and over the course of the drama the outline is "filled" with what students discover—age, name, background, and so on—essentially defining this role. Around the outside of the figure, students can pose questions that they would like to find out about this role, but it can be used for all those ideas that are not about individual characters, such as themes or genre.

Frames of reference can also be easily linked to another model of thinking we use at Rochester Schools, de Bono's Thinking Hats model and certainly the Habits of Mind of *metacognition* or thinking about your thinking. By asking which hat to "put on," it engages students in approaching a task from six possible points of view, from analytic to creative to critical "hats" or ways of seeing—or framing—a problem. The hats become part of the reflective frame of reference for the students' thinking. This also helps students (and us as teachers) to continually journey toward the integration of different yet overlapping approaches to facilitating thinking. This integration is just one isolated example of the focus on integration of models.

FROM THINKING MAPS TO HABITS ■ OF MIND... AND BEYOND

After we as a school became fluent with Thinking Maps, we continued our journey by investigating our next steps as a Thinking School. Several of the faculty attended a Thinking Schools Network Conference on Creativity that was held at Exeter University, and another conference was held on Habits of Mind in Birmingham. Through his keynote address and follow-up workshop, Dr Art Costa, developer of the Habits of Mind model, inspired further reading and research in how we would implement Habits of Mind. Staff were surveyed and introduced to the concept, and six of the 16 Habits were chosen as "termly themes" for the 2008–2009 school year. The Habits—acting with persistence, listening with empathy and understanding, questioning and posing problems, thinking and communicating with clarity and precision, skills of interdependence and creating, imagining and innovating, in that order as well—were introduced formally to students from Year 7 to Year 11 through our vertically integrated house system. By then we had developed an implementation initiative of integration to promote thinking and creativity across the school and renamed the Habits of Mind as "Habits of Excellence" to link explicitly with our mission statement and thus further our efforts at aligning our unique school environment and, thus, terminology.

Weekly sessions introduced different ideas on the "habit" for that term and asked students to reflect on their own behaviours, make links with their own experiences and wider world, and partake in a wide range of activities such as role play, creating songs and dances, poster competitions, group discussion, or analysing film clips. We also ensured that students reflected on the Habits of Mind as they were using Thinking Maps to promote the integration and not separation of thinking processes and approaches. Students were invited to plan sessions alongside the Director of Learning, and an online forum was introduced so students could comment on the sessions and how they might be improved or adapted. The head teacher, Heads of Key stage, and Heads of House also supported the "termly habits" through assemblies, notice boards, and commendations so that these tools and Habits of Mind were not simply modeled but actually used in significant and visible ways around the whole school. The distinction between "modelling" new tools rather than meaningfully integrating the tools into the everyday life in the tapestry of the school is instructive for those wanting to make sustainable change in schools.

The Habits of Mind, at first, were harder to embed into the school than other approaches, and it would be true to say that many students were very reticent and a few students were vehemently opposed to this new way of looking at thinking. While we often think about the difficulty of making changes in how we teach, it is also challenging at times to engage students in changing "how they have done school" for 10 years on end. But the drive team perceived students voicing their views as quite a healthy response, because it was at least provoking passionate responses from the normally passive profile of students at our school. Given our interest in keeping an open-minded, critical stance across the school, a forum was set up during the 2008–2009 school year to allow this debate to continue further, which we believe brought the discussion of how we teach and learn to a metacognitive level of engagement.

Students responded quite positively to this opportunity to voice their opinions. Their comments were thoughtful, reflective, and respectful. Not only did students provide critical feedback, they also took time to offer suggestions for improving the implementation of the work with Habits of Mind. One student recommended a more subtle approach, offering advice on how to introduce the Habits of Mind in a less "in-your-face" manner in order to achieve greater receptivity. This was followed by a comment from the same student who was careful to say that she was not trying to offend anyone but simply offering constructive feedback. Another student suggested that teachers not belabor the introduction of the Habits of Mind. She welcomed the explanation of the Habit of Mind from the teacher, she explained, but then wanted the broader lesson to continue without constant reference to it.

Other students provided insight into how they personally connected with the Habits of Mind and linked them to other aspects of the school's program as well as to everyday life. Some of the students' comments specifically referenced the metacognitive impact of the work. They acknowledged how the Habits of Mind enhanced their ability to be aware of their thoughts and actions during a lesson so they could monitor their learning. They recognized, too, how the work with Habits of Mind, while not embraced with enthusiasm by all their peers, was useful to them. They could identify specific instances where the focus on the Habits of Mind contributed to quality of interactions in the classroom.

Gwynn Bassan, the Director of I Learning and the new Assistant Head Teacher of Teaching and Learning, monitored the quality of these feedback sessions through learning walks, number-crunching evaluations, and review of the forums. I also held open sessions for the most cynical students to come and openly express their views. These students were used to a process of proof reading the next term's lessons and giving suggestions on how these might be improved or amended so a good feedback process was in place. Gradually, students began to see the Habits of Mind as meaningful ways to consciously think and reflect on how to behave intelligently. Important to note, this kind of engaging and forthright discourse on new approaches to teaching and learning with students became an essential dimension of our journey as a Thinking School. Students must become advocates for themselves, for how they learn best, and for those strategies that work for them as well as taking guidance from teachers.

After becoming familiar with Thinking Maps and Habits of Mind across our school, we began to understand how we could also begin to bring in other approaches, and students began to be more open to learning new approaches.

A new stage in our development came with the introduction of another set of tools: "Thinking Keys" to a Thinking Club for Teachers. Thinking Club is a voluntary group of like-minded teachers who enjoy discussing teaching and learning ideas and strategies. It is an informal sharing of ideas where teachers from a range of disciplines can help or ask for help from their peers. Developed by Tony Ryan, the Keys are 20 ways, all titled and having a specific function, to unlock creative and critical thinking across the curriculum. Thinking Keys, unlike more developed models, are simple, require minimal planning or resources, and really help unlock students' critical and creative thinking. They can be adapted for all curriculum areas. Again, using the area of drama, here are three examples:

1. *The reverse.* This key asks students to consider what *would not* be seen or included in specific contexts. For example, what would you not see in a production directed by Stanislavski or what do you not want to see in your own devised performance? By using a different approach, students are made to step away from the usual checklist approach—you are assessing knowledge through the back door.

2. *The alphabet.* Students create an A–Z for a given topic; this sounds simple, but it is a great starter or revision activity. Students create an alphabet on key words in our exploration of *AS texts* (AS stands for Advanced Subsidiary—the first year of senior school—year 12—and in this context texts are plays), key words for analysing performance, attributes of a good drama student, and so on. Sections of the alphabet may be used selectively over a term as a quick starter or use the work as a display, which can be referred to throughout an exploration or year.

3. *The picture.* Take a picture at random and show it to students. Then ask them to try to make connections between the picture and whatever you might be studying at the time. For example, project a picture of jelly and ice cream and ask students how to link this with rehearsal process. It is amazing how creative and analytical students can be when challenged with such an abstract idea. It is a great way of introducing complex concepts like symbolism or Brecht's theory of montage while getting students' brain pathways working. It is particularly useful to explore character emotions for texts at the Advanced-Senior Level. Once practiced, teachers can then set this as a homework task by asking students to bring in seemingly unrelated pictures that they think can show how a character feels at a certain point in a play.

All along the way of introducing and implementing these different approaches, one by one (and not all at once!) the Rochester drive team made sure to support the journey with ongoing professional development opportunities for teachers. This is essential, because these approaches are not simply isolated activities, but processes, tools, and techniques that are being taught explicitly to students. Continuing Professional Development (CPD) sessions were run on the Thinking Keys, which was seen as a valuable and creative way to incorporate simple but effective thinking tasks into all lessons. A further CPD session focused on the Habits of Mind where successful strategies were shared as part of a Thinking Carousel as teachers from a range of curriculum areas took one idea and systematically shared it around as in a carousel within small groups. These included incorporating Habits of Mind into learning objectives, assessing the Habits, and using Habits to evaluate trips or workshops. Developing Thinking Maps and supporting the work of Habits of Mind was again an integral part of all staff performance management targets, giving the approach some real gravitas and leading to rigorous monitoring by the Director of I Learning, all administrators, and curriculum leaders.

■ THE NEXT STEP: SELF-ASSESSMENT, DEEPER INTEGRATION, AND REACHING OUT

During 2009–2010, I transitioned to Associate Assistant Head Teacher and initiated with a supportive faculty the next step on the journey towards Advanced Thinking School Status. I had become a trained trainer, so I was able to lead two workshops for staff on Thinking Maps. During the summer of 2008, all Curriculum areas had been asked to choose from the 16 Habits of Mind those that were most relevant or prerequisites for their specialisation. This was followed by further professional development and our own presentations at regional conferences on the development of Thinking Schools. The focus for these days was on how to promote and then assess the key Habits for each curriculum area, finished by presentations from all teachers on how they were going to tackle this. Assessing key Habits became a focus for 2009–2010 and again was an integral part of all teachers' performance management.

We then began by researching Community of Enquiry (adapted from the foundations of the *Philosophy for Children* program) and other approaches and models. This was in direct response to Professor Bob Burden's report in 2009, when we were accredited as a Thinking School. The University of Exeter's Cognitive Centre (as described in Chapter 4 of this book) engages as "critical friends" in supporting schools in planning and assessing their own journey as a Thinking School. As a school, we thus become researchers, with university support, in the professional development of becoming self-assessing using these kinds of questions:

1. To what extent have we met our milestones and goals for becoming a Thinking School?

2. What evidence is there of this growth across the whole school and not just with a few teachers?

3. What have we learned, and how does this inform our next steps?

Teachers volunteered to take part in the research group focused on our development, which was the most popular choice for CPD during that year. The teachers were from across the curriculum including business studies, psychology, French, and technology. Strategies were piloted and evaluated by these teachers throughout this academic year. During the 2010–2011 school year, more extensive focus on de Bono's thinking tools such as "Cort 1" were introduced. We are already seeing that these new tools are having a significant impact on the teaching, learning, and leadership of the school.

A major development at this time was devised by Gwynn Bassan, which linked Habits of Excellence to what we call the Rochester Learner Profile for each student. The learner profile parallels the Aims of the International Baccalaureate Diploma with goals for students to leave our school as well-rounded human beings (communicators, knowledgeable, risk takers, caring, principled, etc.). There are 10 aims in total that can be seen as the final outcomes, or the branches of the tree. The Habits of Excellence are seen as the roots—those behaviours that need to be practised so that the outcomes are achieved. This development led by Gwynn has made all our initiatives come together under one core purpose and has given the school a clear vision for the future. This learning tree is in all classrooms and staff offices as a constant reminder of our vision and represented in the RGS Tree of Learning.

In addition, in 2010, Denise Shepherd, the head teacher for all these years, became the Executive Principal of RGS, which has allowed her to stay engaged with leadership at Rochester and to work with primary and secondary schools in the area in raising standards and attainment. Denise is also able to work more now on national and international projects while maintaining overall strategic control of RGS. This past year, Denise and I were part of a team from TSI to go to Malaysia and systematically train teachers in three pilot schools using the whole-school approach. We were able to work with each school faculty for a whole week, introducing Thinking Maps, questioning for enquiry approaches and collaborative strategies, as well as engaging them explicitly in how to begin the journey toward whole-school transformation. Denise also just finished a 2-year consultancy at a local underperforming secondary school. With colleague Gwynn Bassan, they helped move the school from failing to the level of "satisfactory with good elements" using some of the very same processes we have learned over the many years.

This means that the last during 2 years we have begun to spread the Thinking School message far and wide. We have come to see and believe that our mission is not simply to help improve our own school but to reach out and to work interdependently with schools in the region, nationally, and internationally. Below you can see a Tree Map classifying the institutions where we have worked and some details on the focus of our work there. The internal CPD that we have here at RGS is one of our greatest strengths, and since the rise of Thinking Schools, the opportunity to share good practise has become a vital aspect of our work and development. At the same time, we feel honoured to have recently been awarded the CPD excellence Kite Mark by Kent University, and we are currently creating a Masters in Arts in professional practice in collaboration with the university.

Schools are always changing, so of course, all new members of staff have a full-day introduction to the range of thinking tools used at Rochester. This is followed up by a session as part of our new teacher induction, and they are constantly learning from colleagues across the school and from students themselves as they have internalised these processes and tools into their own lexicon of learning. This year, I am running a five-session course for all new staff on

Figure 6.7 Tree Map of RGS Dissemination of Practice and Outreach

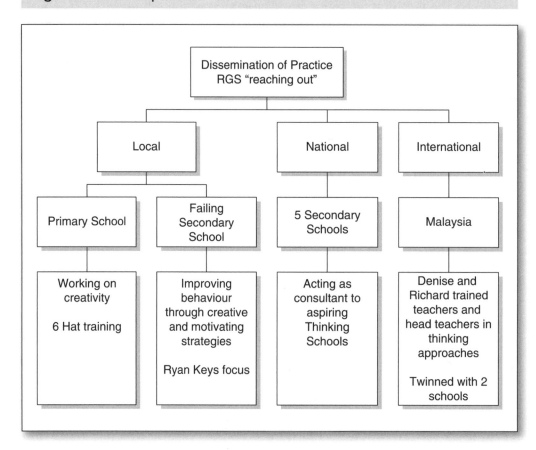

Thinking Maps and Thinking Hats. It is essential that the sustainability of our approach as a Thinking School is part of our plans and thoughts.

While this shift in teachers and teacher leaders had been key, our team also began to think about the *students* as change makers. Every year a team of staff travels to the national conference—to present, to attend workshops, to cogitate, and to plan. Every year the group arrives back at school with a new-found muster, armed with great ideas and new strategies to play with. It always seems a pity that the end beneficiaries do not get the same opportunities, which is why the idea of a student conference was muted in the first place. We wanted this conference to replicate the energy and sense of collegiality present at educators' conferences and try to "bottle" this for students. So our final showcase last year focused on bringing our best thinking forward for others while engaging youth leadership by hosting a "thinking conference" for students—led by students!

Eighty students from four different secondary schools all came together for a wonderful day of thinking, exploring, debating, and networking. The schools that were invited were local and had begun their journey toward becoming Thinking Schools. We tried to make the conference as corporate as possible so that students were treated as "delegates"—there were built-in opportunities to network and plan ideas moving forward. Each student was given a delegate pack on arrival with a plan for the day, corporate pen, corporate notepad with the Thinking School watermark, and a "brain bag" lunchbox, which included foods and liquids associated with high levels of performance. A postcard explaining the choices of each item in the brain bag was also included.

To take the idea of replicating a professional atmosphere further, the two principle leaders from TSI volunteered their services as keynote speakers. Richard Cummins opened the conference by setting the local, national, and global scene, really allowing the student delegates to appreciate that they were part of something much, much larger than the conference. David N. Hyerle led a reflective session at the end of the day, sharing his observations and reflections and, more important, allowing students to create these for themselves through mapping, discussion, and collegiate discussion about the day. It was clear that students felt privileged and empowered by this session, and it highlighted just how important it is for our students to hear from, talk with, and learn from key practitioners in the field of cognitive education rather than teachers always assuming that we are best placed for this type of activity.

Workshops were devised and led by the students themselves, and we had a wide range of ideas being explored—from how Thinking Maps can be used metacognitively, to using Philosophy for Children techniques to explore decision making, through exploring Bloom's Taxonomy, to Habits of Mind, to activities highlighting brain research and how the brain works. In teams of three or four, our students from Rochester conducted workshops throughout the day for groups of 20 students. These visiting students rotated through sessions so that by the end of the day they had been exposed to four different approaches to the direct development of thinking. While there was some support by faculty members, our students became teachers in highly dynamic and engaging ways by offering interactive workshops integrated with video clips, hands-on activities, discussion, and much humour. This conference was a key landmark in our journey as a Thinking School and perhaps was the fundamental shift we were striving for from the outset: students becoming their own teachers in a way that draws on student leadership, student passion, wonderment and awe, collaborative networking, and, above all, a deep-seated willingness and desire to learn and be inspired.

END NOTE: FINDING HUMOUR ■
IN METACOGNITION!

As we are writing this chapter, today is the last day of the autumn term and we are about to break for Christmas holidays. Every year our most senior students devise an end-of-term performance satirising the staff and initiatives of the school. Imagine if you will, two students lost in the Rochester Grammar parallel universe (think Dorothy and the Wizard of Oz) and are on a quest to get home. Along their journey what should they come across? Well, for starters there was the Thinking Maps *Bridge Map to Enlightenment* followed by a trip to the *Tree of Knowledge* just by the *Multi-Flow River Map of Rochester!* But that was not all: our intrepid explorers were helped along their journey by the *7 Hobbits of Excellence.* In support, one of our teachers, Mr Divall, gave clues by putting on his *Thinking Hat*—which could change colour, of course! This was topped off by students playing on the Habit of Mind, metacognition, offering the question, *"Meta-what's it called?"* about their experiences.

We returned happily to our office to write the conclusion to this chapter, safe in the knowledge that thinking is so embedded in the school it actually has become a central comical character in the most important performance of the year.

QUESTIONS FOR ENQUIRY

What were some of the "lessons" Richard Coe and his colleagues learned from St Cuthbert's experience, and how did they use them to inform their decisions on the path to developing as a Thinking School?

How might networks such as the one that Thinking Schools International provides for its member school be used most effectively to promote ongoing growth and development?

A unique aspect of Rochester's approach to developing as a Thinking School was its focus on student empowerment. What implications does this major shift have for decisions regarding all other aspects of a school's approach to developing as a Thinking School? What other ideas might you recommend for schools that want to focus on this particular shift?

7

Systems

Editors' Introduction

It is extremely difficult to make significant changes in a school—to take that fork in the road away from generational norms in an educational paradigm—based on project trends for the needs of future generations. It seems especially difficult when we realize that with information technology, dynamic social media, and global travel, as Neil Postman pointed out decades ago, "change has changed" and that a child born today may well live into the 22nd century. It is even more difficult for a whole school system to make significant shifts in direction when representing a larger community and thus multiple schools. The superintendent's leadership team of East Minoa Syracuse School District in upstate New York, including the authors of this chapter, garnered the support from their schools over time and made changes that improved learning and teaching in their system. They began by implementing Thinking Maps as a new set of tools over 3 years from pre-K to graduation. They could have been satisfied with the growth at this first order of change. But after seeing that wider field of education was calling for a dramatic shift toward "21st-century learning," they realized that the change they really needed was at a completely different level.

So they began investigating "thinking" as a foundational pillar for "learning" in their classrooms. If 21st-century learning is about the 4 Cs of Critical thinking, Communication, Collaboration, and Creativity, had they implemented Thinking Maps for these purposes or merely for improving outcomes based on those established by a 20th-century paradigm for learning? Thus the animating question of their experience and of this chapter is an ongoing enquiry and a question for us: What is the relationship between learning and thinking?

Donna J. DeSiato and Judy Morgan engage us in their "school system" story that reflects what Richard Coe surfaced for us in the previous chapter in how his individual school shifted over time. While this story of transformation offers an avenue for understanding the ideal of Thinking Schools, the authors also take us outside the classrooms of their schools and into the courtroom. This chapter ends with an engaging story of the practical transfer of thinking processes and complementary tools from the school system into the judicial system. The question of the difference between "learning" and "thinking" is answered by a real-life parable. The capacity to develop thinking carries into our adult lives, and how we think drives the way we solve problems and make life-changing decisions.

A SYSTEM-WIDE VISION FOR THINKING

Donna J. DeSiato and Judy Morgan

As educators, we often say that we believe all children can learn and improve their abilities to learn. Do we believe all children can think and improve their abilities to think? What is the relationship between thinking and learning? What do thinking and learning look like in our classrooms?

In summer 2005, as we grappled with these questions, we convened building and district level leaders to analyze our student achievement data. The analysis of the data revealed a 6-year trend of mid-range scores in English Language Arts (ELA) and math. Despite the hardworking efforts of many, a significant gap existed between the abilities of our students and their performance. Dissatisfied with these results and determined to change this bleak pattern, we asked ourselves: What action needs to be taken to change the results of student learning in a positive direction? Searching for solutions and seeking to better understand the world we are preparing our students for, as a leadership team, we read *Good to Great* by Jim Collins and Thomas Friedman's *The World is Flat*. Inspired by these writers, we reflected on how to best prepare our youth for a complex, interconnected, changing world, which led us to explore the impact of explicitly focusing on thinking toward the improvement of student learning. We reasoned that our students are facing an ever-increasing content knowledge base through a range of technologies and a future that envisions the need for people in college and the workforce to be highly adaptive, collaborative, self-reflective, creative, and analytic.

As we confronted the brutal facts of student achievement, we recognized the need to clarify our goals, identify research-based effective practices to address the learning needs of our students—for the present and future—and to engage our stakeholders in the process. We also realized that we needed to implement these practices systemically. We began with three district goals to focus our work on student learning and achievement, as well as to measure our results:

Goal 1: Increase student achievement through high expectations supported by consistent, comprehensive focus on teaching and learning.

Goal 2: Increase student achievement by building capacity within the system to support and nurture a continuum of learning through the implementation of research-based practices.

Goal 3: Increase student achievement by strengthening parent engagement and community partnerships to support learning.

As we embarked on a journey of continuous improvement in student learning, we introduced a District-wide School Improvement Planning

Model. School Improvement Teams were formed in each school comprising teachers, instructional support staff, parents, and administrators. Our School Improvement Team leaders studied and integrated the research of Marzano, Pickering, & Pollack (2004) into plans designed to systemically implement strategies for improving student learning. The research affirmed that "effective teaching is a complex endeavor with many components" (Marzano, 2009), and the School Improvement Team members recognized that the selection and systemic implementation of research-based effective instructional strategies and tools were keys to improving student learning. As each School Improvement Team read and reviewed the research, considered the evidence and reflected on the needs of our students, Robert Marzano's meta-analysis show conclusively that a key area for improving student learning is the focus on thinking processes such as identifying similarities and differences, the use of nonlinguistic representations, summarizing and generating hypotheses, and the capacity of students to work cooperatively. The research also reflects what we knew about "great teaching": the capacity within and across classrooms for teachers to provide high-quality feedback, use higher-order questioning, and use cues and advanced organizers to meaningfully engage the students in learning.

While most any single teacher may point to their isolated use of these key findings from Marzano's meta-analysis, we were increasingly aware that students needed a consistent, year-to-year approach to improve their own learning and thinking. Through our search for proven approaches that integrated these key findings, we discovered that Thinking Maps was a model of visual tools for improving student learning in our classrooms while explicitly focusing on the student-centered development of thinking. As a leadership team, we recognized that Thinking Maps provided our teachers and our students with a common language, a set of tools and visual patterns for organizing information and thinking meaningfully about their learning, while also focusing on questioning based in cognitive processes and collaborative work. This, we believed, could lead us to improved student achievement.

We observed positive outcomes across the district as the maps were thoroughly introduced to all teachers at all grade levels within the first 3 years of implementation.

The implementation design consisted of systematic follow-up, sharing of student and teacher work, training of experts in each school, and an immediate focus on using Thinking Maps for content learning and lesson planning. The initial results in student achievement were impressive, and our elementary schools and our middle school were recognized for significant growth. In a letter written to the principal of each of our schools, then New York State Commissioner of Education, Richard Mills stated, "You and your entire school community are to be commended for leading New York forward to accomplish our dual goals of increasing student achievement while closing the gap in student performance."

Figure 7.1 English Language Arts State Standards Comparative Data

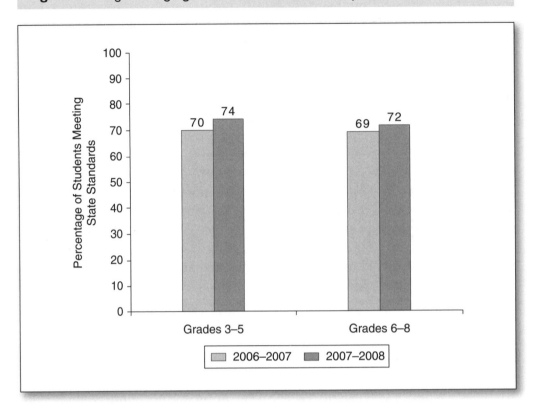

Figure 7.2 Math State Standards Comparative Data

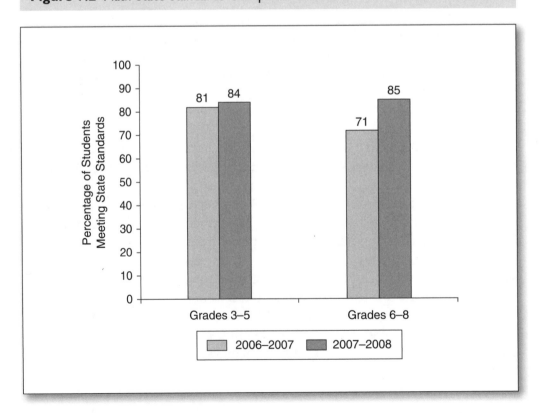

THINKING IN THE 21ST CENTURY ■

While the positive gains in student achievement were notable after these years of implementing Thinking Maps, we recognized the need for improvement and plans were developed for continued growth. As our district embarked on the development of a 5-year strategic plan, we departed from the traditional paradigm of improving the current system. Most often the focus of strategic planning is to strengthen or modify what currently exists. This is first-order change: improvement within the existing paradigm. Certainly, we believe in continuous improvement; however, to embrace the challenges, changes, and opportunities of the 21st century, we discovered that we needed to go to a second order of change: We needed to go beyond our existing system and our current paradigms, which led us to the exploration of what many in the field are now calling *21st-century skills*. This is when we truly shifted from a focus on "improving learning" in a traditional sense, to enabling our teachers to teach for "improving thinking" as well.

Thinking is at the center of 21st-century learning in the shift from mastery of content through memorization and recitation toward internalization of content through application involving problem solving; critical, creative and innovative thinking; communication; and collaboration. Frank Kelly, Ted McCain, and Ian Jukes (2009), in their book *Teaching the Digital Generation*, state that "learning must focus on 21st-century thinking skills" (p. 38). These authors point out that "assessment must encompass both knowledge skills and higher order thinking skills," and they underscore that "assessment of higher order thinking skills must be an integral part of the teaching and learning process" (p. 41).

As we integrated Thinking Maps into classrooms pre-K through Grade 12, our initial intent was to strengthen student learning in the content areas, which happened and reassuringly reflected Marzano's findings about the effects of focusing on key variables as noted above. It was only after the introduction of the idea of 21st-century skills that it became evident that we had not fully used the maps for thinking but primarily for the organization of content knowledge and academic vocabulary toward the goal of improved learning.

But is "learning" within the existing paradigm of teaching, learning, and assessment the same as the development of "thinking"? We questioned: What is the relationship between thinking and learning? What does thinking look like in our classrooms? It became obvious to us as we viewed the use of Thinking Maps in classrooms by students that, by and large, the maps had been integrated across our schools as simply the next generation of "graphic organizers" for organizing and displaying information and had not also risen to the level of application for which they were intended: promoting higher-order thinking. We were still at the first order of change—improving the existing structure within a 20th-century paradigm—and we knew our students of the 21st century needed to go dramatically deeper.

This discovery opened up a multitude of opportunities for exploring and expanding our efforts of improving student learning and student thinking simultaneously using the same tools. In the years that followed the systemic implementation of Thinking Maps as students' progress from one grade to the next and from one area of content to another, the students now consistently apply the eight Thinking Maps as an integrated set of tools for thinking, not just for learning in the traditional sense. Teachers began abandoning a variety of static, disconnected graphic organizers. They slowly let go of these isolated graphics as simply useful for isolated tasks to empower students with "thinking process" tools that concretely transfer across disciplines and through to the eight to 10 different complex jobs they will have over their lifetime. The focus widened to engage students to be active participants in their own learning by explicitly promoting their thinking.

As we developed our next Strategic Plan, we asked the question: What does East Syracuse Minoa (ESM) need to do to shift our educational system to align with the skills needed for success in the 21st century? As we collaboratively examined and reflected on our current practices of teaching and learning, supervision of instruction, and assessment of and for learning, we realized we needed to plan for changes in our system that would integrate 21st-century thinking skills development with the evolution of high-quality teaching and high levels of learning. As we refocused on realigning and strengthening our learning organization, we discovered that we already had the tools needed to enhance, facilitate, and assess critical thinking, problem solving, collaborating, and communicating in Thinking Maps. Along with a strong foundation based in cognitive processes, we also needed to develop dispositions for thinking, high-quality questioning, collaboration, and inquiry. But we were not yet fully implementing the maps to achieve these outcomes. Why not? We realized that to accomplish this, all our leaders would need a deeper understanding of Thinking Maps, their use and application across the curricula, as well as for modeling and applying in their leadership practices and providing meaningful coaching and feedback to teachers in their use of the maps. (Editors' note: See Chapters 9 and 10 for coaching and leadership using Thinking Maps.)

As we planned for our annual leadership institute, we integrated 2 days of professional development grounded in the training guide, *Thinking Maps: A Language for Leadership* (Alper & Hyerle, 2006). *All* our administrators and supervisors at the building and district level were fully engaged and actively participated in this learning for leadership development facilitated by the same consultant who had trained our district-level professional developers for preparing our teachers to use the maps with students. The feedback during the 2 days and follow-up support affirmed that these new visual tools for promoting and organizing thinking were relevant, meaningful, and applicable to all areas of leadership within our district.

Launching the next school year, Thinking Maps became not just our "tools" of choice. Now, students, teachers, principals, and central office leaders were all using a *common language* for thinking and improving our thinking from pre-K children to the superintendent, school board, and community members. The use of the maps to promote thinking and visually communicate began to more deeply permeate our learning environments, exemplified in variety of meaningful ways such as a Tree Map to classify areas needing improvement in a teacher evaluation and a Circle Map to define enhancing staff development in the area of wellness for students, staff, and parents. Our Deputy Superintendent Dr. Thomas B. Neveldine summarized the systemic training in and use of visual language across our learning organization:

> ESM made a commitment to implement thinking maps through extensive professional development and support for practice at all levels of the system. The uses of Thinking Maps are invaluable in working with a variety of school personnel and community groups to produce meaningful outcomes. The process has an understandable logic and provides a roadmap for engaging participants in dialogue around critical issues, providing a visual representation of their thinking. Using the Multi-Flow Map for cause and effect was especially helpful in working with a Citizen's Advisory Committee (CAC) as we analyzed the structure of the school day. This particular Thinking Map was invaluable in analyzing the benefits of 21 distinct transportation and bell schedule options.
>
> Throughout the district, the use of Thinking Maps shifted from
>
> *What map do we need to use?*
>
> to
>
> *What thinking do we need to solve this problem, deepen our collective understanding, or to develop shared understanding and create new knowledge?*

Kathy Southwell, ESM's Director of Teaching and Learning, shared her experience using the maps for the implementation of our Strategic Plan. Her comments directly reflect the shift from using an isolated map in an episodic way toward investigating and focusing on the thinking that surfaces in the high-quality, day-to-day decision making that is required in any school system by different stakeholders to address our complex needs:

> In order to meet our district's vision, we are striving to effectively plan and implement significant educational change. As the facilitator of the Academic Excellence and Rigor Action Team and Subcommittees, I truly believe that the use of Thinking Maps has helped the synergy of ideas, created highly developed recommendations for change, and organized effective implementation plans.

The Tree Map is the work of the Academic Excellence and Rigor Action Team in the 2nd year of implementation of our strategic plan. Teachers, parents, and administrators were starting to feel overwhelmed by the magnitude of the different action items for this group, with questions being raised regarding the connection of some of this work with other ongoing initiatives in our district. This map was created to organize our thinking under the district's vision, show the connection with the five district strategic planning action teams, and make a connection with the DuFour & Dufour (2008) essential questions that have been widely used in our district to shape the work of our professional learning

Figure 7.3 Teacher Improvement Plan Tree Map

Teacher Improvement Plan

Content Knowledge	Preparation	Instructional Delivery	Classroom Management	Student Development	Student Assessment	Collaboration	Reflective and Responsive Practice
-Need to understand the sequence of instruction for teaching difficult children to read -Need to strengthen student understanding of narrative writing -Improve foundational understanding in math	-Need to demonstrate planning for teaching skills to build on prior knowledge -Need to identify learning goals -Need to provide documentation for meetings on student placement	-Need to integrate activities and demonstrate their connection to student learning based on curricula -Need to provide evidence of support for learning over time -Need to demonstrate research-based practices -Need to implement developmentally appropriate practices	-Use effective practices for engagement of all students in learning	-Demonstrate a clear understanding of what students know and differentiate for ability levels	-Use formative assessment -Modify instruction based on what students are learning or not learning	-Collaborate with support staff	-Need to demonstrate evidence of reflecting on instructional practices -Implement supervisory suggestions for improvement based on post observations

Figure 7.4 Circle Map for Wellness Staff Development

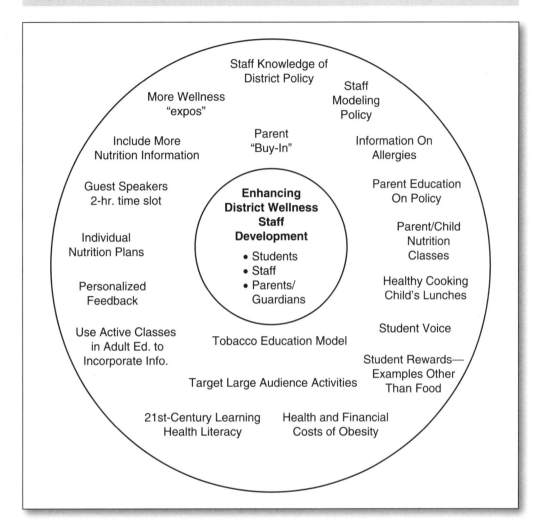

community. Once we established the structure at the top of the Tree Map, our discussion was rapidly focused and organized.

Ken Kay (2010), president of the Partnership for 21st Century Skills, stresses the importance of focusing on the 4 Cs: Critical thinking and problem solving, Communication, Collaboration, and Creativity and innovation. According to Kay, "fusing the three Rs with the four Cs is a national imperative." No longer can we focus solely on the recall and memorization of content. Our students need to know how to access information, ask questions, and apply their knowledge across content areas to make meaning, achieve deeper understanding, and create new ideas or knowledge. Thinking Maps become an essential tool for all 21st-century learners and citizens. Real-life experiences, with the integration skills of critical thinking, communication, collaboration, problem solving, and innovation, are essential for success in our global society. Ultimately, it is not the new technology, a new curriculum, or a reconfiguration of classroom walls that will make the difference. The outcome will be determined by whether or not students can independently and fluently applying thinking processes to

Figure 7.5 Citizen's Advisory Committee's Multi-Flow Map for Cause-Effect Relationships Regarding Structure of the School Day

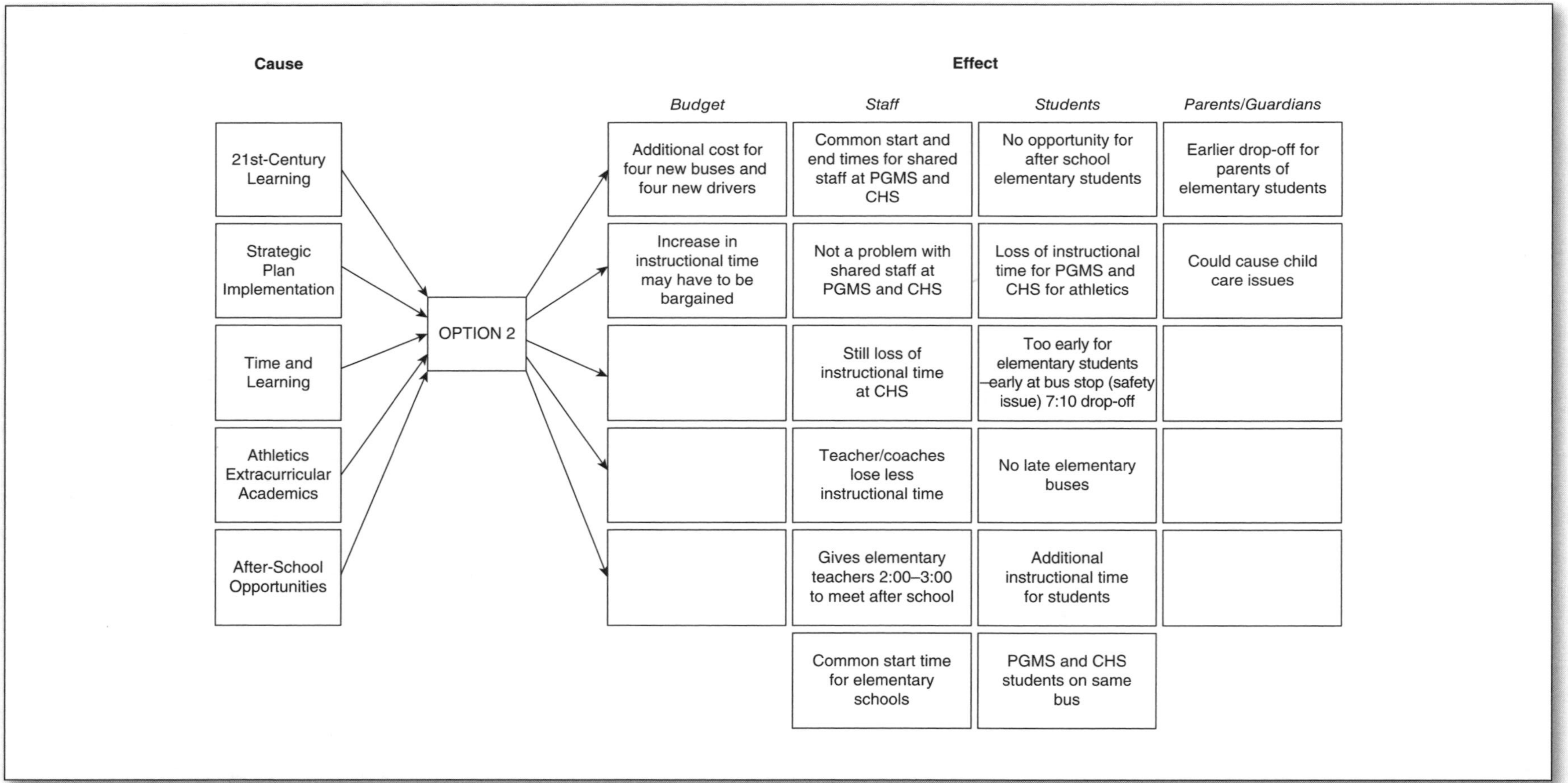

Cause

- 21st-Century Learning
- Strategic Plan Implementation
- Time and Learning
- Athletics Extracurricular Academics
- After-School Opportunities

OPTION 2

Effect

Budget
- Additional cost for four new buses and four new drivers
- Increase in instructional time may have to be bargained

Staff
- Common start and end times for shared staff at PGMS and CHS
- Not a problem with shared staff at PGMS and CHS
- Still loss of instructional time at CHS
- Teacher/coaches lose less instructional time
- Gives elementary teachers 2:00–3:00 to meet after school
- Common start time for elementary schools

Students
- No opportunity for after school elementary students
- Loss of instructional time for PGMS and CHS for athletics
- Too early for elementary students —early at bus stop (safety issue) 7:10 drop-off
- No late elementary buses
- Additional instructional time for students
- PGMS and CHS students on same bus

Parents/Guardians
- Earlier drop-off for parents of elementary students
- Could cause child care issues

Figure 7.6 Academic Excellence and Rigor Action Team Strategic Plan Tree Map

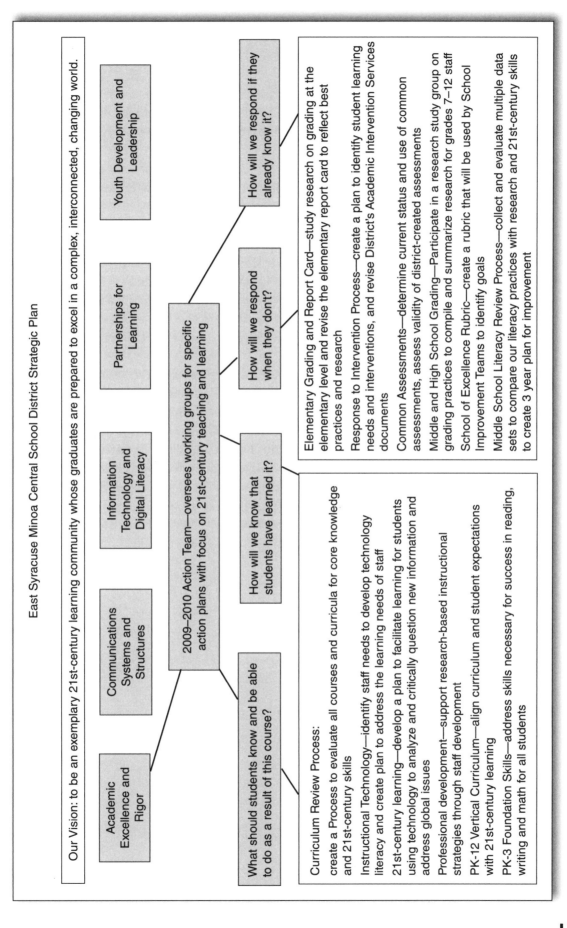

East Syracuse Minoa Central School District Strategic Plan

Our Vision: to be an exemplary 21st-century learning community whose graduates are prepared to excel in a complex, interconnected, changing world.

| Academic Excellence and Rigor | Communications Systems and Structures | Information Technology and Digital Literacy | Partnerships for Learning | Youth Development and Leadership |

2009–2010 Action Team—oversees working groups for specific action plans with focus on 21st-century teaching and learning

What should students know and be able to do as a result of this course?

Curriculum Review Process:

create a Process to evaluate all courses and curricula for core knowledge and 21st-century skills

Instructional Technology—identify staff needs to develop technology literacy and create plan to address the learning needs of staff

21st-century learning—develop a plan to facilitate learning for students using technology to analyze and critically question new information and address global issues

Professional development—support research-based instructional strategies through staff development

PK-12 Vertical Curriculum—align curriculum and student expectations with 21st-century learning

PK-3 Foundation Skills—address skills necessary for success in reading, writing and math for all students

How will we know that students have learned it?

How will we respond when they don't?

How will we respond if they already know it?

Elementary Grading and Report Card—study research on grading at the elementary level and revise the elementary report card to reflect best practices and research

Response to Intervention Process—create a plan to identify student learning needs and interventions, and revise District's Academic Intervention Services documents

Common Assessments—determine current status and use of common assessments, assess validity of district-created assessments

Middle and High School Grading—Participate in a research study group on grading practices to compile and summarize research for grades 7–12 staff

School of Excellence Rubric—create a rubric that will be used by School Improvement Teams to identify goals

Middle School Literacy Review Process—collect and evaluate multiple data sets to compare our literacy practices with research and 21st-century skills to create 3 year plan for improvement problems, engage in sustained inquiry with others by creating their own challenging questions, and draw from a rich array of dispositions, or Habits of Mind (Costa & Kallick, 2000) that will bring about insights and discoveries we will need to solve 21st-century problems.

■ THINKING FOR DEMOCRATIC PARTICIPATION

Important to note, for the adult learners in our school system and wider learning community, the processes and approaches we use must carry some degree of transferability into our daily lives. If not, then how can we say in authentic terms that we are giving students tools that can be used outside the classroom? We have found that Thinking Maps are useful tools, not just in schools, but also in our daily lives. We, as citizens of our world, have a responsibility to make decisions that are mindful, reflective, and demonstrate responsibility for ourselves and others. This transferability is no better illustrated than in the story told in the real-life experience of Judy Morgan, then our Executive Director of Curriculum, Instruction, and Accountability, when she was serving as a juror in a court trial.

A fundamental dimension of democracy is that the representative form of government is an anchor in both political and judicial spheres. The decisions our students as future citizens make in the ballot box may only by rivaled by those they will make as jurors standing as peers in judgment of a fellow citizen. Judy was a district leader who had become fluent with Thinking Maps as tools of collaborative deliberation during important decision-making meetings about the future of our students. Then, as she conveys below, Judy stepped out of that role into a different setting with a similar dilemma: There are often no clear answers to complex questions that we must face throughout our lives as citizens.

As the judge told the 12-member jury that the decision was now in their hands, a sense of fear raced through one of the jurors. The reality began to set in. She was now in a position to determine the future for the plaintiff. Did she have enough information to make the decisions that needed to be made? After listening to testimony for 5 days, what did she really know about this case? There was just so much that had been said, so much that needed to be stricken from the record. What did she really know?

The jurors were escorted to a small room that was just large enough for everyone to sit around a table. This was the first moment that the jurors were allowed to talk about the case. No discussion had occurred prior to this time. The jurors represented the diversity of the community, young and old, inexperienced and very mature, male and female. The room began to buzz with random thoughts, several choosing to speak at the same time. As the one juror listened, trying to take in the essence of each person's interpretation of the sequence of events that had taken place over the past week, she began to ask herself, "What do I really know? How do I sort out fact from opinion? What was the real charge that we were given? How do I make a decision that will affect this person for the rest of her life in a way that is fair and based on fact?" Overwhelmed and confused, her mind was racing. Emotions were high. She knew that she needed to be able to make a decision that she could live with. At a time like this, most of us allow emotions to cloud the issues. She had an overwhelming sense of needing clarity, but how could that happen?

The one thing that the jurors had in common was their desire to "do the right thing." They realized that they held the key to the future for the woman on trial. What would prevail . . . emotions or the facts? How can a decision like this be made? Each of the jurors contributed thoughts about what made the person guilty or not. The one juror, not the foreman, tried to make sense of all the information and thoughts that were being shared.

Her mind was whirling, trying to connect thoughts and facts. It just wasn't coming together for her. She began to make connections as she began to organize information in her mind. She was trying to group and sort information. She needed to be able to organize what she really knew to be fact. She began to use a visual tool that she had learned as a school-district-level administrator. She thought, "Can I use the 'school tool' in this situation?" The jurors needed to regroup and work collaboratively. She decided that it was her turn to offer a strategy for them to think together. She asked the question, "What were we asked to do?" The group agreed that there were 5 charges that had to be taken into consideration. To her it immediately became obvious that she could assist the group by creating a Tree Map. Each of the 5 charges became the category headers. In an orderly manner, the group began to sort out the facts that supported each of the charges. It was amazing how this organizational structure changed the tenor of the group. Each person in a very thoughtful way contributed facts that could be easily sorted into the specific categories. Conversations among the jurors were thoughtful as they questioned a statement or asked questions that helped each member sort out fact from opinion. After about an hour of this organized fact gathering, the foreman asked for the data that was collected to be shared. As the facts were shared, it became very clear what the group knew. The foreman asked for a roll call vote. It was absolutely amazing that as each name was called, the response was GUILTY.

She was in awe of what had just happened. Chaos had been replaced with disciplined thought. Facts had been sorted out from opinions. Clarity had been accomplished through well-defined thinking processes using visual tools.

THINKING AND LEARNING ■

Let's return to our original question, focusing not just on schooling, but the complex and multifaceted dynamics of our daily lives: What is the relationship between thinking and learning? We still are not completely clear about the relationship between the development of students' thinking and what teaching and learning looks like. We are sure that we are on a path of discovering the interdependencies between the two. What is clear is that schools in this country and around the world may continue to teach for the mastery of information and low-level process learning, but this will not transform process thinking for our students of the 21st century. Given the circumstances of a highly competitive global economy and the dynamism of global interdependencies, we must challenge ourselves and students in a new way. We know that this century has placed new demands on how we teach and how students learn. Thinking Maps have provided us with the cognitive and metacognitive tools needed for the successful integration of 21st-century skills into high-quality teaching or what we in the field call *best practices*. Over the years, our students continue to demonstrate growth in student learning as evidenced by their performance on the New York State assessments in ELA and math, in addition to incremental increases in the graduation rate.

Figure 7.7 Student Performance: English Language Arts

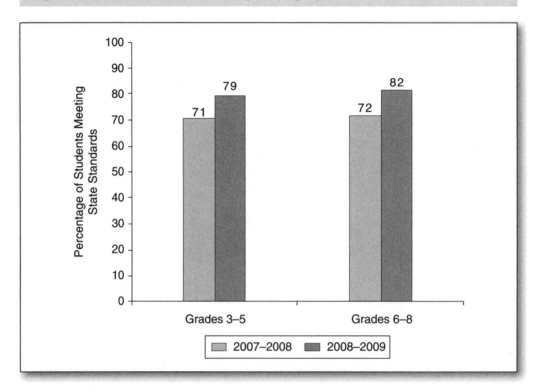

Figure 7.8 Student Performance: Math

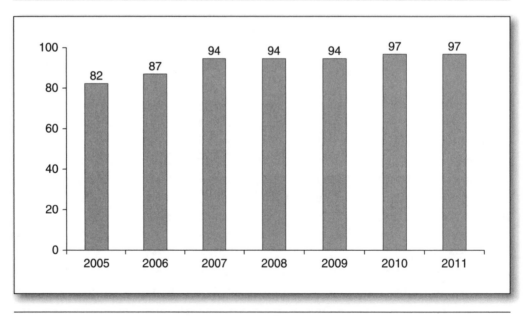

Class of 2005, 2006, 2007, 2008, 2009, 2010 (2002, 2003, 2004, 2005, 2006, 2007 Cohorts) Including Regents, Local, & IEP Diplomas

If we want students to be self-directed learners, to work collaboratively, to explore areas through a creative lens, to explore innovative possibilities, then our schools and whole systems must be focused on the development of

Figure 7.9 ESM Student Graduation Rates

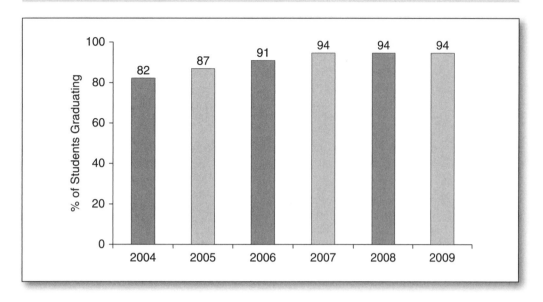

thinking. We must systematically and continuously give them dynamic, organizational, networking thinking tools that go beyond pure analytic reasoning and test-based, closed-answer assessments that focus on content and content-specific skills. Cultivating thinking is the focus of our work for learners at all levels, from consciously developing the dispositions for thinking and the quality of the inquiry in which we situate learning.

The East Syracuse Minoa Strategic Plan guides our decisions and actions toward our vision of becoming an exemplary learning community by preparing students for success in the 21st century. Now, more than ever before, the need to rethink how we are preparing our youth for the challenges and opportunities that lie ahead is critical. Facilitating meaningful, relevant experiences for our students is a powerful model for learning. All children in America—and around the world—need 21st-century knowledge and skills to become effective citizens, workers, and leaders in the 21st century. There is a profound gap between the knowledge and skills most students learn in school and the knowledge and skills they need in typical 21st-century communities and workplaces. To successfully face rigorous higher education coursework, career challenges, and a globally competitive workforce, U.S. schools must align classroom environments with real-world environments by integrating 21st-century thinking skills. Through our strategic plan, ESM is positioning itself to meet this challenge and answer the question: What does thinking and learning look like in our classrooms?

As Judy Morgan revealed in her collaborative decision making with fellow jurors, most problems in life are interdisciplinary, complex, and require clarity of thought and the dispositions of persistence, patience, and above all the capacity for thinking independently and reflectively as one thinks *interdependently* with others. The disposition and growing capacity for reflection, or metacognition—to think about your thinking—is essential to *how* we are as human beings. Judy was using the very same cognitive tools that we now see across our system, used by young children and graduating adults as citizens of the world.

QUESTIONS FOR ENQUIRY

Donna J. DeSiato and her colleagues committed to building a system for learning on the foundation of thinking. The authors identify their shift from first-order change to second-order change as a shift in focus to improving thinking rather than simply on improving learning. Clearly, they had their sights set beyond the classroom. What is the relationship between learning and thinking, and what are the ripples that such a shift in focus creates in our educational structures when a school or system commits to this pathway?

The authors assert that "the disposition and growing capacity for reflection, or metacognition—to think about your thinking—is essential to *how* we are as human beings." The authors purposely chose the word "how," even highlighting it for emphasis. The use of this word suggests that reflection is a dynamic state of being, although in our experience it is not always engaged in consciously. How can this disposition and capacity for reflection be supported in schools in a way that students become truly metacognitive, or reflective in action?

The idea of "interdependencies" is a recurring theme in this chapter as it relates to the new realities of the 21st century and the richly interconnected world in which we live. If, indeed, "change has changed" as Postman asserted, why is it imperative that interdependency—as it relates to content, ideas, and human interactions—be such a central idea to focus on as we think about re-forming the educational experiences for our students?

■ REFERENCES AND FURTHER READINGS

Alper, L., & Hyerle, D. (2006). *Thinking Maps: A language for leadership.* Cary, NC: Thinking Maps, Inc.

Costa, Arthur L., & Kallick, Bena. (2000). *Discovering & exploring habits of mind.* Alexandria, VA: ASCD.

Dufour, R., & Dufour, R. (2008). *Revisiting professional learning communities at work: New insights for improving schools.* Bloomington, IN: Solution Tree Press.

Kay, K. (2010, April 10). *Got 21st Century Skills?* PowerPoint slides presented at conference. Chicago, IL: National School Boards Association (NSBA).

Kelly, F. S., McCain, T., & Jukes, I. (2009). *Teaching the digital generation.* Thousand Oaks, CA: Corwin.

Marzano, R. J. (2009). Setting the record STRAIGHT on "High Yield" strategies. *Kappan, 91,* 30–37. Retrieved from http://www.sde.ct.gov/sde/lib/sde/pdf/curriculum/cali/setting_the_record_straight_on_hield_yield_strategies.pdf

Marzano, R. J., Pickering, D. J., & Pollock, J. E. (2004). *Classroom instruction that works: Research-based strategies for increasing student achievement.* Alexandria, VA: Association for Supervision and Curriculum Development

Postman, N., & Weingartner, C. (1971). *Teaching as a subversive activity.* New York, NY: Dell.

8

Language

Editors' Introduction

It is intriguing to note that in the last chapter the animating questions that Donna J. DeSiato and Judy Morgan offered us drove to the center of classroom practice in the 21st century: What is learning? What is thinking? Are these two dimensions of education the same? In this chapter, Estee Lopez and Larry Alper engage us in a spirited exploration of two equally important questions: What is language? What is thinking? This leads the authors to look closely at the rich interface of these two foundations for learning. These may be more philosophical questions for some, but the reality on the ground is charged in every classroom. It is clear that most of our energies over the past century have been directed toward language, or more specifically, literacy development: reading, writing, speaking. Literacy rates, especially reading scores, are what nations focus on around the world and have become the gold standard for measuring educational changes.

But what about cognitive development? If the importance of the development of thinking abilities, dispositions, and high-quality enquiry and problem solving is key to 21st-century learning, global commerce, and innovation, then why aren't we focusing systematically on these processes? There is urgency in finding answers to these questions in the United States with the growing population of English Language Learners, primary Hispanic children, who come into classrooms with another language in mind. The approaches used by teachers across schools and the performance of these students have now become one of just a few of the central concerns of educators, from rural to suburban to urban school districts. It is also a hot button issue: There is continuing educational and political conflict between those who want teachers to focus on "English only" teaching versus "Bilingual" models that draw from the language of the native speaker to learn English as their second or "new" language. This is a false dichotomy hiding away a third path: the focus on cognitive tools that directly facilitate language acquisition, academic language in the content areas, and higher-order thinking. The authors take us along this third path, an exploration that offers a vision for schools around the world as they shift from a focus on the rote acquisition of content knowledge on the longer journey toward systematically engaging students' thinking.

THINKING LANGUAGE LEARNERS

Estee Lopez and Larry Alper

■ THE CHALLENGE

In today's world of information overload and the need to connect and network ideas across languages and cultures, it is not enough for students as global citizens to know how to simply access and take in information and respond to test items. This is of particular importance for those students around the world who begin school using their native language in a learning community with an unfamiliar, "foreign" language. These students are working *much* harder to perform at grade level or above while being given the lowest level of instruction and coaching, because of limited "language" proficiency. Unfortunately, because their verbal and written communication skills are not yet up to grade level, often, these students are also perceived by educators as also having "intellectual" limited ability. Although they develop simultaneously, literacy development is confused with cognitive development. These students, possibly after many years of gaining basic fluency in the mainstream language of the classroom, have lost years during which their thinking abilities and cognitive development have not been facilitated. The outcome? These students are often left behind in classrooms with curriculums designed to remediate until graduation, if they make it that far.

As the late Paulo Freire warned in a lifetime of work including his influential text *Pedagogy of the Oppressed*, education cannot simply be an act of transmission but must be an act of *cognition* for every person, no matter their background. Freire is not talking about the isolated "skills" of thinking (though these are important), but about surfacing and engaging the deep connections between thought, language, and culture. The learning process Freire named as "conscientization" is elemental to his work: Learners of any age in collaboration with peers and with their teachers must engage through reflective thinking, questioning, and enquiry, through a deepening of critical literacy, framed by the awareness of and respective for diverse cultures and languages. Freire knew this well through his work in adult literacy in northern Brazil with manual laborers. Workers first spoke of themselves as "beasts of burden," but this shifted as literacy rates rose dramatically across the region. But they were also empowered by way of gaining their own voice. Freire's efforts, focused on a high degree of respect and on cognitive processes, linked critical thinking to literacy development. The transformational success of his work, a testament to what is possible, ultimately led to his deportation from Brazil.

Sadly, in the United States at this time, a similar dramatic challenge is not being met in the area of literacy development with students across the age levels, leading to higher levels of dropouts and ultimately, adult illiteracy. English language learners make up an ever-growing proportion of the American school-age population, and with every year a larger part of the labor force and voting public. Most of these students are born in the United States and have attended American schools for their entire lives (Capps et al., 2005). Since the introduction of the federally mandated *No Child Left Behind* (No Child Left Behind, 2001) laws, the changing demographics and the inclusion of English Language Learners (ELLs) participating in assessments has surfaced the need to ensure successful language acquisition. What continues to prove challenging is the well-developed academic language and skills needed for them to master content required for college and career readiness. Over the past 30 years, researchers (Cummins, 1994; Goldenberg, 2008) have demonstrated that ELLs, primarily Hispanics, are the largest minority school-age population in America, yet they are at very high risk of not attaining high levels of academic achievement and progress in their achievement remains restrained.

The challenge of literacy and language development is occurring worldwide as the demands of globalization spread. Educators are finding a common bond in a focus on thinking as a foundation for learning—and language—within their own diverse cultural contexts. So how do we understand and strengthen this powerful intertwining of thought processes and language usage? What are the implications for language acquisition, and more specific, second language acquisition within and across cultures around the world? As we will explore below from evidence from a doctoral research case study (López, 2011), Thinking Maps, as a common visual-verbal model based on cognitive processes, is shown to offer a pathway to success for those students who are simultaneously grappling with learning the conceptual, rigorous, academic language within each content area while learning the new code of a second language. This is key to second language learners. In his work on *Willingness to Communicate,* MacIntyre (2007) points to opportunities for communication in a second language (L2) based on specific moments in time when an individual has the choice to speak in the new language. He states:

> A *willingness to speak* in the L2 at such moments conditions the social interactions among persons from differing language groups and in some respects reflects the success of the interlocutors' language learning efforts. (p. 4)

Thinking Maps have proven to serve as an essential stimulus whereby second language learners on using these visual tools are "willing" to explain and reveal their thinking. The result is a degree of willingness to communicate (WTC) with the potential to demonstrate complexity as the situation changes.

The explicit visual choreography provided by Thinking Maps and guided by the teacher through deliberate instructional actions, including questioning for inquiry and supported by the skillful use of these cognitive tools, evokes purposeful language for meaningful learning by their students, and a higher order of thinking. The outcomes are reflected in the comments of teacher Jeanne Canon (personal interview, February 12, 2013) from the Eastchester Public Schools in New York State:

> Thinking Maps have changed the way I ask questions to my ELL students. The maps helped my students organize their thought processes. I promote higher learning by focusing on the critical thinking skills and

academic vocabulary associated with these eight maps. My students have begun using these maps with my guidance and the work being produced speaks for itself. I have come to realize that I must raise my expectations because my ELL students are capable of so much more, thanks to these wonderful visual tools!

Thinking Maps, introduced in Chapter 1 as one possible pathway in the Thinking Schools process, explicitly supports teachers in seeing the cognitive patterns in academic language and concepts they teach. In many cases, they transcend their own mindsets and perceptions of the thinking capacities of their students. The reframing of education around the vision and practice of Thinking Schools around the world, from the United Kingdom to Ethiopia, South Africa, Malaysia, Lithuania, Northern Ireland, and Norway, is central to facing this challenge: minimal, functional literacy is just not good enough for students of today in an age of high-tech jobs requiring the capacity to think through information, communicate with clarity and precision in collaborative groups, generate solutions to problems, and innovate as entrepreneurs.

Daily, hourly, and in the moment-to-moment interactions in classrooms in the United States, ELL Hispanic students are being underserved by the focus on teaching for basic language learning and literacy while their thoughts, words, and concepts are grounded in their first language, Spanish. This occurs under the long shadow of high-stakes tests based in English, with some accommodations set for ELLs in the testing regimen. The expectations for success may be low in many of these classrooms, partially due to the complex challenge, but also because teachers have difficulty accessing the rich thinking of their students that is hidden behind the silent veil of an unspoken "foreign" language.

In the case study excerpts below, we see how teacher and administrative leaders in the City of New Rochelle public school system (near New York City) focused on the *simultaneous* development of literacy, language, and thinking abilities. Through this shift, we will hear and see how they also transcended some rigid "systemic" restraints, tearing down assumed barriers that interfere with intellectual development and expression among ELLs.

The transformed environment in many classrooms in New Rochelle was toward independent and interdependent learning, supported by a cognitive, visual language, generating rich, academic discourse. Validated as *thinkers,* the English language learners no longer had a fear that their teachers would equate their level of language acquisition to their intelligence and capabilities. Important to note, students did not have to wait for their own levels of English language usage to reach a specific threshold to gain entry into the dynamic realm of knowledge construction with their peers. The universality of language development *and* the universality of the thinking processes associated with it resulted in knowledge and language development, academic achievement, and the facilitation of the intellectual dispositions (Habits of Mind) of learners.

In a very real sense, though not named as such, the New Rochelle schools across the system expanded their focus on language and learning toward becoming Thinking Schools. The foundation of thinking for learning and language growth, the changing mindsets in teachers and dispositions within students, and the evolution toward higher-order questioning and rigorous academic discourse united to bring about significant change.

Reframing Language Acquisition With a Focus on Cognition

The complex situation in the United States is one window into what is happening in other countries around the world with large populations of second language learners. The implications of our investigation into the link between cognition and academic vocabulary development through the use of Thinking Maps and the transformation toward schools focused on thinking development may be linked and applied to the global dilemma of a range of different underachieving populations. And, as people around the world are more mobile and virtual via Skype and other communication portals, the need for highly effective second language instruction is paramount.

In the United States, ELLs face huge challenges when it comes to competing effectively in schools and thus in later life, in college, and in the world of work. We must remember, attempts to raise reading comprehension and writing scores with "mainstream" students has been a challenge, but the gap is huge and is widening for ELLs. In a comprehensive review of the literature in this field, Goldenberg (2008) warns:

> Whatever the explanation for these achievement gaps, they bode ill for English learners' future educational and vocational options. They also bode ill for society as a whole, since the costs of large-scale underachievement are very high. (p. 11)

Every child in the United States is mandated an education regardless of race, creed, economic status, or English language proficiency. The new Common Core Standards are guiding what teachers teach and children must learn, *regardless* of students' language capacity. An essential dimension of these standards is the rigorous demand on students to demonstrate higher levels of thinking and more richly developed expressions of their thoughts in writing. Students must examine texts and extract evidence from the information, not regurgitate a knowledge base. The Common Core Standards recognize that challenging, higher-order questions and inquiry-based classrooms (foundations for the Thinking Schools approach) play an essential role in assisting students in mastering what they are reading through verbal communication. For students to meet these rising expectations, teachers need to provide support and scaffolds that encourage students to take risks, share ideas, and construct meaning. In other words, there is a need to help ELLs not only learn the spoken and written language of the classroom but also to learn a cognitive language for transforming information into knowledge and the maturation of dispositions under what Yvette Jackson (2011) has called a "pedagogy of confidence."

Given the personal, cultural, and societal challenges of educating every child at the highest levels, (including those with severe learning differences) some background research drawn from the New Rochelle case study presented below is essential. This is not a simple problem with a single answer. Understanding the dynamic relationship between thought and language at this time in educational history is key to seeing the urgency of the issue. It is now commonly understood that the skills required of all learners in today's information-technology-cognitive age are those that enable *all* learners to think independently, and with dispositions that nurture collaborative, inter-dependent thinking.

In her book, *The Flat World and Education: How America's Commitment to Equality Will Determine Our Future*, Linda Darling-Hammond (2010) points to the importance of the capacity of people to frame, investigate, and solve problems using a wide range of tools and resources as critical factors in their ability to meet the demands of life, work, and citizenship in the 21st century. She further asserts that people's ability to find, analyze, and use information for many purposes is equally essential to their success. The labor market shows an ever widening gulf between those who have gained a high degree of fluency in language, thinking abilities, and technologies with those who cannot gain the high-skilled jobs.

Within the context of education reform in America, especially with the new demands of the Common Core Standards, ELLs are thus *the most challenged and pressured to perform by educators*. While national standards and assessments will influence the methods and purpose of teaching in the years to come, the search for a clear pathway to effectively meet the academic needs of these young students is paramount. However, school districts are often left with more questions than answers. This challenge is global; many Ministries of Education around the world are also seeing that English has become the universal language of commerce and a primary common language for communication, so approaches to improve academic performance and second language acquisition are required.

The learning strategies that are most needed are not those "micro skills" in each content area that focus only on discrete test items that will raise gate-keeping scores or on rote, repetition learning techniques that have been used for the whole history of public school education. A leader in the field of education for ELLs, Anna U. Chamot (2004) has stated,

> Strategic learners have metacognitive knowledge about their own think-ing and learning approaches, a good understanding of what the task entails, and the ability to orchestrate the strategies that best meet both the task demands and their own strengths. (p.14)

We thus need to *reframe* our approach and develop students' cognitive and metacognitive (executive functioning) abilities, as well as intellectual dispositions such as confidence, perseverance, and reflectiveness directly linked to academic achievement.

If we step back into the past, we find insights informing the dilemma we now face. The American linguist Benjamin Lee Whorf (1897–1941) proposed that there is a profound interconnection between language and thinking. His (1956) hypothesis (the Sapir-Whorf hypothesis) highlights that one's native language determines one's conceptual *categorization* of how the individual experiences the world. It is this intimate language-cognition interface that is the most important dimension evoked when teachers and students, particularly as ELLs, use Thinking Maps that each are based on fundamental thinking processes.

What is this interface? A commonly held assumption is that language shapes thinking. This surface level understanding makes sense, because it is too easy to hear the "foreignness" of another language and all the differences to one's native tongue. Yet underlying every human being and every language are fundamental cognitive processes at work that bridge these languages and cultures together. Within every language community these fundamental cognitive processes are being used moment to moment, often unconsciously: defining in context, describing, comparing, categorizing, seeing spatial part-whole relationships, sequencing, cause-effect reasoning, and analogies and metaphor. Every person around this world thinks through these processes. Languages are in large part structured by these cognitive processes and patterns. The obvious *difference* is that the specific language and cultural context determines how "things" are categorized by use of words, how causes and effects work, how metaphors are being used, and ultimately, how a language community defines "things" *in context,* by way of words.

Few would argue that the very structure and act of language itself could exist without word *groups* (categorization), *comparatives, descriptors, sequences* of words, and *metaphor.* The work of prominent psychologist Lev Vygotsky (1978) reminds us of the psychosocial-cultural aspect of language and cognitive development. The development of thought and language evolves in context and through social interactions. If culture influences the structure and functions of a group's language, the social interaction supports making meaning and clarifies interpretations of what is being learned. This dynamic intersection between cognitive development, literacy, and cultural context is the wellspring of learning.

In the following case study, we explain and analyze the efforts of an urban suburban school district, the City School District of New Rochelle, New York, to enable for all learners, most especially ELLs, to become proficient in academic language and content-specific concepts, and gain access to this wellspring of learning. By developing their students' understanding of fundamental cognitive skills and teaching them how to skillfully apply them through the use of a common, visual language for thinking—Thinking Maps—the district elevated the academic achievement of all its students, including their English language learners. The schools in New Rochelle that are using the Thinking Maps systemically understand the great potential of having a shared, common cognitive language of visual tools with content and language expression.

Research and Practice

The use of Thinking Maps in a whole-school approach creates a language that supports a cognitive-cultural pattern through questioning, clarifying, semantics, syntax, and naming. Cognitive-cultural patterns are cultivated within a learning environment that is engaging. The neuroscience research, at the most basic level, establishes that the brain is a *pattern* detector. To remember, the mind (brain) must sort through information, make and prune connections, and store what is important and discard what is not.

To remember the important parts of text, for example, the English language learner needs to be able to consciously use his or her mind to actively sort the information presented against the cognitive *pattern* in which it is presented.

The failure to do so confronts the student with a wall of text, an undifferentiated mass of information difficult to understand and frustrating, if not overwhelming, to encounter. Extensive research in the area of specific types of text structures (e.g., comparative, categorical, sequential, causal, etc.) gives us the understanding that the structure of text, or thinking *patterns* of the text, offers the reader rich conceptual nets for keeping information in mind. The inability to recognize these cognitive text patterns and the lack of associated tools to mine them for meaning can severely handicap the learner. Understanding and recognizing the highest-level functions and forms of language are necessary to attain the highest levels of learning.

The goal in introducing Thinking Maps in New Rochelle schools was to ensure that ELLs become proficient readers and writers of English. Proficient readers are described as active and purposeful, self-monitoring and metacognitive (Armbruster, 2002). These skills and dispositions, then, need to be explicitly supported by specific, highly developed strategies and tools.

Researchers, educators, and administrators agree that high-quality instruction needed for ELLs to develop language skills and to achieve academic excellence is crucial in order to sustain a productive society (Jamilah, 2000). Yet experts have differing views on the best instructional strategy to teach this population (Norton & Toohey, 2001). The field of second language acquisition has been thoroughly studied by researchers, yet experts remain concerned that deliberate attention has not been paid to cognitive development to improve academic achievement. In their seminal work, *School Effectiveness for Language Minority Students*, Thomas and Collier (1997) point out that while language development is beneficial, to *get the full power* of the content material, students need to be challenged academically across the curriculum. The dilemma is this: How do we challenge students intellectually as they are learning a new language?

Researchers maintain that ELLs need to do cognitively complex, school-related tasks appropriate for their age, while materials must be meaningful for students at their proficiency level in the second language. In other words, *language acquisition and academic learning must be developed simultaneously*. The current failure of our schools to speak the language of the intellect of our ELLs, however, will continue to deny them access to the full range of educational experiences and opportunities. A gap exists between what the research indicates is needed instructionally and the current state of our practices in schools for ELLs in the area of cognitive development and academic language learning. It is imperative that the gap be filled. To meet this challenge, ELLs need explicit instruction in the use of cognitive tools to fully understand and construct meaning from their learning experiences, and to allow teachers to differentiate the application of thinking processes so academic language becomes purposeful, and without which their ability to move beyond the plateau that only suggests proficiency will be severely and, perhaps, irreparably compromised.

Chamot and O'Malley (1987) developed the Cognitive Academic Language Learning Approach (CALLA) as a model to support ELLs. Chamot and O'Malley indicate that the use of learning strategies resulting from a cognitive model of learning assists students' comprehension and retention of both language and content. Consequently, over the past decade, to meet the new standards of No Child Left Behind and now Common Core State Standard, educators across the country have incorporated an efficient model for teaching ELLs: The Sheltered Instruction Observation Protocol (SIOP) (Echevarria & Short, 1999). SIOP is an instructional framework that focuses on both language and content objectives with a structured approach that engages in cognitive academic language learning. The SIOP method, though widely used in the New Rochelle School district, harnessed SIOP's potential by adding a cohesive and consistent tool that focused on cognition *and* academic language development: Thinking Maps.

The City School District of New Rochelle was determined to fulfill the responsibility it had to all the students to enable them to succeed at the highest levels and experience satisfaction as learners. The administrators focused on raising the achievement levels of ELLs, specifically promoting and strategically implementing Thinking Maps as the visual tools to be used in the SIOP model. The agreement between teachers and administrators rested on the concept of utilizing common tools by all teachers for use throughout the students' experience in a school. The intention for utilizing this method to complement instruction systemically was based on fundamental theories of cognitive science and semantics, the foundations upon which Thinking Maps was developed. This cognitive model, along with explicit focus on content and language objectives, created a significant shift in teaching ELLs. Teachers focused on academic language, using tools that inherently differentiated students' thinking and engagement.

The City School District of New Rochelle has various schools with high percentages of ELLs, primarily students of Hispanic background. It is an urban/suburban school district that is representative of the kind of economic, social, ethnic, language, and cultural diversity found in many small city school districts. The commitment to ensure that all students succeed was critical, especially English language learners. Of deeper interest was not only meeting proficiency levels on the New York State English as a Second Language Achievement Test (NYSESLAT) exam, but also helping those students who met proficiency levels yet demonstrated difficulty with academic language in reading and writing. To address this need, the principals with the highest number of ELLs were informed of the value of Thinking Maps. As the Director of ELLs at that time, Estee Lopez, along with principals and other colleagues, began reframing the discussion about teaching and learning, centering it on cognition with a focus on the academic language of ELLs. Effecting change in the schools was like being a "constant gardener," as Estee would explain it, probing, sharing ideas, and slowly bringing people along as the idea to look at another way to support ELLs began to bloom. Moreover, the principals also surmised that the maps would have a positive impact on all the students in the school. In this way, though not explicitly stated, each school was taking on the development of cognitive development and "thinking processes" as a central dimension of their school culture. This led to the strategy of planning for whole-school training.

The cognitive vocabulary inherent in defining and applying Thinking Maps propels students to use academic language meaningfully. The Maps were taught in the children's native language and in the second language. Of particular importance was that the conceptual transferability of cognitive meaning enhanced accessibility and was not bound to language. The student's native language was the asset for thinking.

The effect on transfer regarding the names and purposes of Thinking Maps from the Spanish language into English (López, 2011) through the use of cognates when implementing Thinking Maps was significant. Each map is associated with a specific cognitive term and function; for example, the Thinking Map used to "describe" is called *describer* in Spanish; the map for "sequence" is called *secuencia*; "cause and effect" is called *causa y effecto*; and so on. There is substantial research that emphasizes that ELLs benefit from cognate recognition to comprehend the second language (García & Nagy, 1993). According to Montelongo, Hernández, Herter, and Cuello (2011), "Cognates are words that are orthographically, semantically, and syntactically similar in two languages because of a shared etymology" (p. 429). This is a critical dimension of the use of Thinking Maps with English language learners.

Implementation of the Thinking Maps training began with ESL and dual language teachers participating in a full-day professional development experience supported by systematic, ongoing follow-up over a period of 4 years. The effort *immediately* expanded to all teachers in the school as evidence of success and effectiveness emerged. Teachers awakened interest among their colleagues by having them observe students' work. The principals were supportive and provided numerous opportunities for teachers to develop their expertise with Thinking Maps thus implementing a whole-school model. This design ensured use of common visual tools and a common cognitive language for teachers and students. It was unmistakable that students, especially ELLs, demonstrated significant and meaningful use of academic language in each of the maps. This synergistic approach led to an organic implementation for whole-school capacity building. It proved to create a powerful level of teacher engagement that has endured over the years. The district leadership slowly yet methodically introduced Thinking Maps throughout the schools is the district: one school at a time.

From the beginning, the focus was on the transfer of these visual tools to students for their independent use. Follow-up sessions were designed to support teachers and students in their use of the maps at increasingly sophisticated levels. Other teachers within the buildings began to see the increase of language expression, vocabulary development, and thinking of students, especially by English language learners. The process of building capacity grew through small professional learning communities by training grade-level teachers and then the whole school. Teachers met with their colleagues to share student work and approaches on how they used the Maps. Over time, teachers recognized that *all* students could benefit from these cognitive tools.

English language learners were assumed to need a significant amount of oral language before they could think seriously about a subject. But what about a *visual* language that acted as an external memory for their words from which they could think and see the cognitive connections between ideas? Understanding the depth of words, text, and the knowledge embedded in academic learning is a critical factor in thinking. Helping ELLs to activate their thinking, however, regardless of the level of language proficiency is essential to *making meaning* of learning. This critical concept created a new paradigm for seeing how cognitive models and academic language intersect to support the achievement of ELLs. Cynthia Slotkin (2008), retired principal and who initiated the implementation of Thinking Maps at the Jefferson Elementary School in New Rochelle, described the role of these cognitive tools for the students in this way: "When the children sit down to work the curriculum becomes much clearer and more evident to them because they have a visual representation." Addressing the benefit of Thinking Maps in fostering self-mediated learning, Ms. Slotkin further explained, "(the students) really analyze the topic they are learning and start to think about which maps they are going to use and why . . ."

The implications for the use of Thinking Maps extended beyond the students. Teachers, as well as students, became more focused and intentional in the cognitive dimension of learning. Differentiation became more than creating different tasks. Teachers began to challenge and elicit in students the different ways their students could think and express their thoughts given an academic task.

Reflecting on the impact Thinking Maps had on her teaching, Hildy Martin (personal interview, April 15, 2009) noted that she was now "more conscious of the cognitive processes behind everything I do with my students." As a result, this acute awareness of the cognitive processes, along with the Thinking Maps associated them, transferred to her students. Hildy reported that the students were now spontaneously identifying the cognitive patterns during learning experiences and initiating the use of the appropriate Thinking Maps.

The Impact

In the study *The Effect of a Cognitive Model, Thinking Maps on the Language Development of ELLs* (López, 2011), conducted over two years, Thinking Maps was found to have a positive impact on the academic language development of ELLs. The study's results indicated that the inherent qualities of the Thinking Maps facilitated teachers' abilities to address the academic goals of the curriculum. Several of the qualities described by respondents included the academic language that is intrinsic to Thinking Maps, lending each map a consistency of cognitive purpose and goal. Results of this study also indicated that schoolwide implementation positively contributed to the efficacy of the Thinking Maps. Respondents noted that students were able to recall and use these visual tools from one classroom to the next and one school year to the next. All students, and most especially ELLs, engaged with these tools regularly, and over time, with language and content that was complex.

We know that researchers have repeatedly found that the use of visuals tools is an effective strategy for ELLs. Visual tools have been demonstrated to be especially effective when content-area teachers consistently used them to deliver instruction. The consistency and coherence offered by Thinking Maps were found to be essential characteristics to the successful academic language and learning experience for all students, especially ELLs. In addition, because of their direct association with fundamental thinking patterns, i.e., sequencing, compare/contrast, cause/effect, and so on, Thinking Maps were well designed to address the challenge of providing ELL students and struggling learners with high level, differentiated cognitive tools for constructing meaning. In the 2-year study (López, 2011), a teacher commented the following during a focus group:

> The maps give each thought process a name and a concrete visual to go with it. Something that kids have [that they] can hold onto and can use and refer back to . . . and as the kids go through the grades and [become] more comfortable, more and more flexible with their use of the maps. I think that it can only have a positive impact on achievement. (p. 95)

Educators in the district believed ELLs would demonstrate a different result in language and academic performance if a conscious and intentional decision to focus on the cognitive aspects of learning was consistently implemented, with frequency and fidelity, using the visual models associated with Thinking Maps. The shift, they believed, would be on what the students were able to do as opposed to their perceived deficiencies. Maia Starcevic (personal interview, April 15, 2009), a Dual Language teacher at Jefferson Elementary School, emphasized this point:

> With the eight maps it's always what you can do . . . how you can show your thinking . . . whether you read or you write, there is always a place for you to show your thinking on those maps. It's a powerful message.

Cindy Slotkin (personal interview, April 14, 2008) further noted that the students were able to, " . . . take their thoughts, talk about what their findings are, and then begin to write. . . . We found," she continued, "that the children, all of a sudden, were using language in a deeper and more meaningful way."

This dynamic was also well-documented in the Columbus Elementary School of the City School District of New Rochelle in New York. The principal and teachers reported that the use of these visual tools gave ELLs the opportunity to make visible the organizational patterns in text. Dr. Yigal Joseph (personal interview, April 12, 2008), (now retired) principal of Columbus Elementary School observed that "Thinking Maps brought to our teachers and students a metaphor for understanding deep cortical thought processes so that students are not just passive recipients of knowledge."

Thinking Maps allowed ELLs and all students to concretely sort through text to identify and select critical information and use those same cognitive patterns to reconstruct the text to communicate their understanding of it. This was essential for ELLs' understanding of academic text. Because of the universal nature of the visual language and the cognitive processes associated with Thinking Maps, Dr. Joseph believed that their use supported the school in creating inclusive structures in which their ELLs could be taught in classrooms among all students. As one concrete measure of the impact Thinking Maps had on his students, Dr. Joseph reported that for the first time 80% of his students in the 3rd, 4th, and 5th grades achieved proficiency in English Language Arts on the 2009 New York State standardized assessment. However, Dr. Joseph (personal interview, April 12, 2008) was quick to add, "Always remember, a child is not a test score. A literate citizenry is just a citizenry that can read. It is not a citizenry that can think."

In observing and monitoring how English language learners used multiple Thinking Maps to represent the complexity of their thinking about various topics, it was evident that Thinking Maps served to elevate the *expectations* of academic language development of ELLs and refined the teaching and learning experience with a laser-like cognitive focus and purpose. The examples below are representative of the diverse ways students have been representing their content and concept understanding at all grade levels and throughout the curriculum.

Figure 8.1 is an example from a second grade bilingual classroom. Notice how the map is used in the students' native language (Spanish) where children are comparing and contrasting two versions of the Cinderella story. From this Double-Bubble Map the students were able to produce a highly developed analysis of the two versions of the story. The use of the map in this learning experience facilitated the use of academic vocabulary (same, different, alike, common) and enabled the students to reveal their comprehension of the stories in response to the question of comparison.

Figure 8.1 Student Cinderella Double-Bubble Maps in Spanish

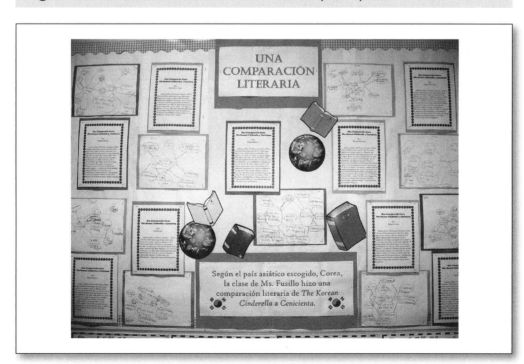

The ability to simultaneously engage students' critical thinking ability with second language development is evident in Figure 8.2. The students are able to describe their thinking as they conduct an analysis comparing two countries. The flexibility of the maps allows students learning English to express their thinking with pictures and words without compromising the critical thinking skill of making comparisons. In addition, so that ELLs can have a grasp of the significance of sequencing, this image has Flow Maps that depict the sequence of events in the life of the students.

So that ELLs can meet the Common Core Literacy Standards it is critical that they develop cohesive writing pieces. In Figure 8.3, the students are able to use the information contained in their Circle Maps to develop short essays. Over

Figure 8.2 Student Use of Multiple Thinking Maps Including Pictures

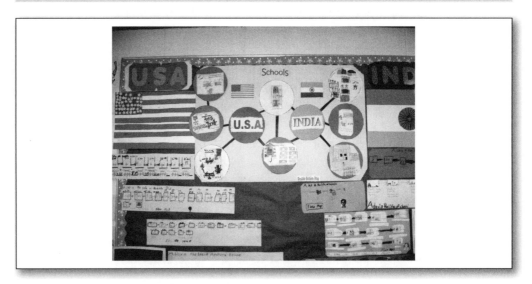

Figure 8.3 Student Writing From Circle Maps

time, students are able to expand their thinking so that they can develop pieces of writing with points of view and evidence as they use the information from the various Thinking Maps.

We know that thinking is not linear, so honoring the multiple ways students think, the Thinking Maps encourage diverse thinking and expression. For example, in Figure 8.4, students use the eight Thinking Maps and eight different cognitive processes to explain their thinking about what they learned after a visit to Museum of Modern Art in New York.

Figure 8.4 Student Use of Multiple Thinking Maps to Represent Thinking About Museum Visit

The work literally shows how the students are thinking about the content, not simply recording it.

Thinking Maps have provided students in the City School District of New Rochelle, especially ELL students, with a cognitive bridge to language and literacy. As their fluency with these tools continues to develop, the students will have a road map, an internal compass, for engaging confidently and competently with increasingly complex information in school and for navigating their lives beyond formal education. This had a positive feedback effect on teachers. The use of Thinking Maps provided a window through which, according to teacher Maia Starcevic (personal interview, April 15, 2009), they could "know the children well through their work and their thinking." As the students' level of confidence and competence rose, so too did the expectations that teachers had for their students' capabilities. This, we believe, is a significant finding, and expressed by a participant in the López (2011) study as follows:

Our expectations for our ELLs, and all students, have really increased . . . and with our expectations being higher, students work to achieve that. Because they know that's what we expect and they start to expect that of themselves, and having these tools like Thinking Maps allows them to get to that level and really express themselves. (p. 106)

Higher expectations by teachers and the shift in dispositions by students as they became more confident also led to transformative results observed over the course of the case study, not only in the form of increased test scores, but also in ways that transcend those measures. Vilma Arizaga (personal interview, April 15, 2009), a bilingual kindergarten teacher at Columbus Elementary School, noted, "Thinking Maps are a great tool we as educators are offering our kids. We're making them feel in control about how they are thinking and to be able to assess their thinking." This is critical to the academic language development of ELLs because students develop a strong sense of confidence.

The study's findings demonstrated that the use of Thinking Maps promoted verbal expression among students. Verbal expression is critical if ELLs are to succeed in American schools (Chard, 2006). As teachers work with ELLs to develop oral language skills, they adjust their own language accordingly. This adjustment allows the teacher to provide comprehensible input (Echevarria, Vogt, & Short, 2008). It appeared that the use of Thinking Maps as a visual-verbal-spatial language propelled students to articulate their thinking regarding a given task. The following comment by a teacher corroborated the literature with regard to verbal expression and highlighted the influence of Thinking Maps in this area:

Years back when I worked in the guided reading group, a lot of times . . . when I sat with a group I'd have to ask them questions and we'd go back and forth about the questions . . . and now, what I can do is that . . . have them write a map, choose a map and then they fill in the map. When they show their thinking on the map and then they show their evidence in the frame, it's not me leading them with questions, it's them picking out the things that are important and I'm not telling them what's important . . . they can pick that out for themselves because they have a way of representing it. (p. 103)

The work undertaken in New Rochelle with Thinking Maps utilized strategies that were initially implemented in this system for English language learners but were appropriate and made available for all learners. Moreover, as the students moved through the grades, the principals in the middle and high school began to prepare their teachers to continue to support students' use of Thinking Maps because the students had internalized these tools for learning and making meaning in response to cognitive and academic demands. Special attention was drawn to students who traditionally tend to get "stuck" at the intermediate level of English proficiency. Although students at this level demonstrated growth in communicative/oral skills, it was evident that they needed to engage in the cognitive demands of text in the areas for reading and writing. For them, Thinking Maps were the bridge to literacy and academic language development, the critical pathway to making meaning and for extending learning beyond the borders of the school.

REFLECTIVE PRACTICE ■

Language development evolves in context and through social interactions. If culture influences the structure and functions of a group's language, the social interaction supports making meaning and clarifies interpretations of what is being learned. The schools in New Rochelle that are using the Thinking Maps systemically understand the great potential of having a shared, common language of visual tools with content and language expression. The use of Thinking Maps in a whole-school approach creates a language that supports a *cognitive-cultural* pattern through questioning, clarifying, semantics, syntax, and naming. Cognitive-cultural patterns are cultivated within a learning environment that is engaging.

Cultivating cognitive cultural patterns does not mean that a singular approach to thinking and learning is advanced. Instead, the use of Thinking Maps promotes a linguistic and cultural style of inquiry that fosters expression of thought and mediation of understanding through dynamic social interaction and engagement supported by a common language. Another participant in the study said, "I've never met a student yet who hasn't felt secure to add something, or contribute something to a map . . . and I've taught at 3rd, and 4th, and 2nd—so it just seems [that the Thinking Maps classroom is] a very secure place for them to take a risk, to talk to someone, to talk to us, to express themselves, and so they always find something to say" (López, 2011, p. 177).

Teachers of English language learners who use Thinking Maps view these students as thinkers. They no longer describe them as limited English proficient. The teachers have become professionals who reflect on their pedagogy and thought processes to mine the knowledge ELLs bring into the learning environment. The teachers of New Rochelle believe that acquisition of language and content will depend on their precise use of teaching strategies and the cognitive visual tools they introduce to their students.

Reframing the way we look at how English language learners are educated could be the single most important goal in American education today. Reframing our discourse about how to support ELLs in meeting the challenges and opportunities of the 21st century is critical. Thinking Maps serve as essential tools that propel ELLs to gain the academic language needed in meeting the new Common Core Standards and the complexities of today's world. Teachers of ELLs using Thinking Maps are dedicated to enhancing the thinking of their students. They are attentive to how students construct knowledge. Rather than breaking down information, these teachers and their students use the maps to powerfully scaffold information, construct deeper understandings, and develop insights that extend beyond the specific content being studied. This visual choreography, guided by the teacher through deliberate instructional actions, including questioning for inquiry, and supported by the skillful use of these cognitive tools, evokes purposeful language for meaningful learning by their students. Jeanne Canon (personal interview, February 12, 2013), an ESL teacher from the Eastchester Public School, a neighboring district to New Rochelle, said,

> Using Thinking Maps with my English language learners has made me
> a better teacher. In order to use the maps effectively, I must consider
> the thinking and the appropriate language required for my students to

complete a learning task. Before Thinking Maps, I would create lessons without truly considering the thinking required by the learners. Now I am more reflective in my practice.

As it has for teachers in the City School District of New Rochelle and other school districts, this approach compels us all in education to reframe our goals and methods of instruction for English language learners. This educational/ social imperative is necessary so that English language learners can succeed in our American schools and become the thinkers and leaders they are capable of being and become the global citizens whom our country and those around the world will rely on in the 21st century.

QUESTIONS FOR ENQUIRY

In the previous chapter, DeSiato and Morgan discussed the significance of shifting their focus from improving learning to improving thinking. While obviously not suggesting that an improvement in learning was undesirable, they clearly contended that it was not enough. In this chapter, the authors argue that a similar shift in education needs to be made for English language learners, this time expanding the emphasis on improving language development to include improvement on thinking, as well. Why is this shift deemed so urgent, and what might be the social, economic, and political benefits this shift represents for this population of students and the broader population, as well?

In this chapter as well as the previous one, Thinking Maps emerged as a universal language that reached and united all members of the school communities in which it was used. Since this chapter was specifically about language and thought, what might be the significance to having a common, visual, cognitive language for thinking that is shared throughout a school? What might the implications be if this language was shared not only within a school or district, but across educational settings around the world?

Imagine if we continued to treat medical conditions today with the medical knowledge from 50 years ago. Teachers' pedagogical knowledge can influence their perceptions of their students and thus have a powerful influence over the opportunities that students are given to develop, reveal, and demonstrate their intelligence. In what ways do the focus on thinking and the access to current, research-based tools and instructional practices to support learners in developing and communicating their thinking help alter perceptions and create new opportunities for all learners?

■ REFERENCES AND FURTHER READINGS

Arizaga, V. (2009, April 15). Interview by E. López & L. Alper [Video recording]. The language of the mind: Cognitive bridge for literacy and academic language development of English language learners. Retrieved from http://www.thinkingfoundation.org/newrochelle/index.html

Armbruster, B. (Ed.). (2002). *Put reading first.* Washington, DC: U.S. Department of Education.

Capps, R., Fix, M., Murray, J., Ost, J., Passel, J., & Herwantoro, S. (2005). *The new demography of America's schools: Immigration and the No Child Left Behind Act.* Washington, DC: The Urban Institute. Retrieved from http://www.urban.org/publications/311230.html

Chamot, A. U. (2004). *Issues in language learning strategy research and teaching. Electronic journal of foreign language teaching.* Retrieved from http://e-flt.nus.edu.sg/v1n12004/chamot.pdf

Chamot, A. U., & O'Malley, J. M. (1987). The cognitive academic language learning approach: A bridge to the mainstream. *TESOL Quarterly, 21*(3), 227–249.

Chard, D. (2006). *The struggling reader: Interventions that work.* New York, NY: Scholastic.

Cummins, J. (1994). Knowledge, power, and identity in teaching English as a second language. In J. Richards (Ed.), *Educating second language children* (pp. 33–55). Boston, MA: Cambridge University Press.

Darling-Hammond, L. (2010), *The flat world and education: How America's commitment to equality will determine our future.* New York, NY: Teachers College Press.

Echevarria, J., & Short, D. (1999). The Sheltered Instruction Observation Protocol: A tool for teacher-researcher collaboration and professional development. *ERIC Digest EDO, 99.* Boston, MA: Cambridge University Press.

Echevarria, J., Vogt. M., & Short, D. (2008). *Making content comprehensible for English learners: The SIOP model* (3rd ed.). Boston, MA: Pearson Allyn and Bacon.

Freire, P. (2009). *The pedagogy of the oppressed. 30th anniversary edition.* New York, NY: Continuum International.

García, G. E., & Nagy, W. E. (1993). Latino students' concept of cognates. In D. J. Leu & C. K. Kinzer (Eds.), *Examining central issues in literacy research, theory, and practice* (pp. 367–373). Chicago, IL: National Reading Conference.

Goldenberg, C. (2008). Teaching English Language Learners: What the research does and does not say. *American Educator, 32*(2).

Jackson, Y. (2011). *The pedagogy of confidence: Inspiring high performance in urban schools.* New York, NY: Teachers College Press.

Jamilah, E. (2000). Research shows lag in Hispanics' bachelor's attainment. *Black Issues in Higher Education, 17*(3), 16.

Joseph, Y. (2008, April 12). Interview by E. López & L. Alper [Video recording]. Retrieved from http://www.thinkingfoundation.org/ell/index.html

López, E. (2011). *The effect of a cognitive model, Thinking Maps, on the academic language development of English language learners.* (Doctoral dissertation). St. John Fisher College, Rochester, NY. Retrieved from http://fisherpub.sjfc.edu/cgi/viewcontent.cgi?article=1056&context=education_etd

MacIntyre, P. D. (2007). Willingness to communicate in the second language: Understanding the decision to speak as a volitional process. *Modern Language Journal, 91*(4), 564–576.

Martin, H. (2009, April 15). Interview by E. López & L. Alper [Video recording]. The language of the mind: Cognitive bridge for literacy and academic language development of English language learners. Retrieved from http://www.thinkingfoundation.org/newrochelle/index.html

Montelongo, J. A., Hernández, A. C., Herter, R. J., & Cuello, J. (2011). Using cognates to scaffold context clue strategies for Latino ELLs. *Reading Teacher, 64*(6), 429–434.

No Child Left Behind. (2001). *Why NCLB is important.* Washington DC: U.S. Department of Education. Retrieved from http://www.ed.gov/nclb/overview/importance/edpicks.jhtml

Norton, B., & Toohey, K. (2001). Changing perspectives on good language learners. *Tesol Quarterly, 35*(2), 307–322. Retrieved from http://search.ebscohost.com.ezproxy.cnr.edu/login.aspx?direct=true&db=ehh&AN=18692432&site=ehost-live

Slotkin, C. (2008, April 14). Interview by E. López & L. Alper [Video recording]. Retrieved from http://www.thinkingfoundation.org/ell/index.html

Starcevic, M. (2009, April 15). Interview by E. López & L. Alper [Video recording]. The language of the mind: Cognitive bridge for literacy and academic language development of English language learners. Retrieved from http://www.thinkingfoundation.org/newrochelle/index.html

Thomas, W. P., & Collier, V. (1997). *School effectiveness for language minority students.* Washington, DC: National Clearinghouse for Bilingual Education/George Washington University, Center for the Study of Language and Education.

Vygotsky, L. (1978). *Mind in society: The development of higher psychological processes.* Cambridge, MA: Harvard University Press.

Whorf, B. L. (1956). *Language, thought and reality* (J. B. Carroll, Ed.). Cambridge, MA: IT Press.

9

Coaching

Editors' Introduction

Consider these questions: What does it mean to become aware of your own thinking, change your own thinking, and then in turn shift your daily actions and patterns of behavior? Given this difficulty, how is it possible with integrity and authentic engagement to "mediate" someone else's thinking—such as a teacher you are coaching—so that they, on their own, may shift how they make decisions in classrooms? And here are some additional, leading questions for the reading of this chapter: Why would we ask teachers to become more reflective about their own practice? How would we coach teachers to become reflective about their own thinking (metacognitive), when, in fact, they themselves may not have had explicit guidance in developing their own thinking?

This chapter engages each of these questions with depth and guidance toward new ways of considering improving teaching, without offering simplistic solutions. What does seem obvious is that if we are concerned about improving the quality of teaching in schools around the world toward developing "thinking" students, we need to have a congruent focus on teachers and our administrators. A common belief is that teaching is second only to air traffic controllers in complexity and stress. Why? Because in both professions people are thinking through and making hundreds of decisions, large and small, every hour and every day. They carry inside them an abiding sense of commitment to those they are serving. Teachers often do feel as if their students' lives do depend on them, especially those working in underresourced schools.

Teachers' decision-making processes, planning, reflection, and continuous improvement—in essence, the effectiveness of their thinking—is instrumental to change in our schools in the 21st century. Teachers most often work in isolation in their classrooms, with minimal coaching, feedback, or facilitation of their patterns of thinking. When a principal, peer coach, or any "outside" visitor enters their classrooms, many teachers may feel defensive, because they think they are in part getting evaluated by people who don't spend enough time within their room to experience the holism of the teaching, learning, and classroom dynamics.

Here is an opportunity to delve into the complex and important area of developing teachers' decision-making, reflectiveness, and improved instruction. Kathy Ernst, a leader in the field of mathematics instruction and coaching, takes us into three case studies revealing how Thinking Maps and reflective questioning enable visible coaching, creating an authentic environment for dialogue and inquiry. After a brief background on coaching, Kathy introduces us to part of a comprehensive case study from St Roberts School in the United Kingdom, showing how this accredited Thinking School explicitly used

(Continued)

(Continued)

Thinking Maps for coaching new teachers. Kathy then paints two detailed portraits of teachers she has coached over several years, sharing their interactions and reflections. You will also see in the most explicitly visible terms how the mediation of thinking may occur when there is that third place—a map—that is a safe haven for discovery away from the complexity of teaching. It is a place where the Habits of Mind of openness, clarity of communication, and interdependent thinking thrive.

IMPROVING THE QUALITY OF TEACHING THROUGH VISUAL COACHING AND SUPERVISION

Kathy Ernst

■ THE ROLE OF ADMINISTRATOR AS COACH

School administrators who supervise teachers share a fundamental role with coaches—to advance student learning by improving the quality of teaching. Since the core of teachers' work is devoted to planning, enacting, and reflecting on lessons, the work of supervisors and coaches is therefore grounded in the cycle of pre-lesson-planning conferences, observations of lessons, and debriefing conferences. During the pre-lesson-planning conference, the coach or supervisor can support the teacher in developing lessons with successful learning outcomes for all students. They may also ask teachers to reflect on their improvement goals, identifying particular aspects of their lesson for focused observation and feedback. During the lesson, supervisors and coaches gather descriptive data about student and teacher behaviors, which serve to guide the postlesson reflection and analysis. In the postlesson conference, skillful supervisors and coaches set a tone of collaborative inquiry and learning as they and teachers reflect on lessons, raise and explore questions about the teaching and student learning, and identify pedagogical processes that advanced and which could advance student learning in the future. They engage the teacher in identifying specific aspects of their practice in need of improvement and coach the teacher in exploring actions that could result in improvement. However, facilitating change to improve the quality of teaching is only possible when effective tools and processes are skillfully used. Several coaching models have proved to be effective, including Cognitive Coaching (Costa & Garmston, 1999), Instructional Coaching (Knight, 2007), and two math-specific models: Content-Focused Coaching (West & Staub, 2003) and Pedagogical Content Coaching (Silicon Valley Mathematics Initiative, 2007). These and other effective coaching models call for respectful, trusting relationships, collaborative learning, and teacher reflection mediated by the coach.

Improving instruction is a complex process that requires teachers to reflect objectively on how their teaching impacts student learning. It also demands that teachers develop and apply the dispositions necessary for productive inquiry into possible changes in their practice that could advance student learning. Embracing these changes with commitment and conviction is often preceded by a reexamination of their assumptions and beliefs about teaching and learning.

The role of the coach or supervisor is to mediate cognitive shifts by facilitating teachers' reflective processes in thinking about how their instruction impacts student learning. Costa and Garmston (1999) state that when teachers take the journey into their own processes " . . . a shift occurs when the focus or operation of the brain moves (usually suddenly) from the processes in which it is engaged to newly selected ones" (p. 33). I relate this phenomenon to an "AHA!" moment. When a teacher *sees* and *believes* in the need to improve their practice, they are more likely to change their behavior to align with their newly altered cognitive maps of reality. Costa and Garmston offer that "all behavior is rationally based on rather simple cognitive maps of reality" (p. 33).

Yet how can they SEE these maps that are webbed across the complex interconnections in the brain that are harbored in the recesses of one's own mind? And then, how does the coach or supervisor mediate cognitive shifts that result in improved instruction and meaningful change *for students?* More precise, how can the coach or supervisor help teachers recognize and loosen the hold their existing schemas have on their thinking without devaluing the important role they play in informing their thinking?

I have asked myself these questions. Over my years as a coach and supervisor in the field of mathematics teaching, I have reflected on the purposes of the major components of the coaching/supervision cycle. I have seen opportunities to facilitate learning and transformation of practice, and I have wondered if the strategies, questions, and tools I use are sufficiently explicit, effective, and efficient for facilitating deeper teacher reflection and growth. I came to question whether the techniques I was using for capturing and representing observations might be one barrier to building trust and productive dialogue between the teachers I was coaching and me. The techniques I have used and that are ubiquitous across the coaching and supervision professions include linear scripted notes of the lesson, checklists, and a variety of idiosyncratic markings on paper along with my spoken memories of the lesson held in my mind. Was my "objective" data, *which I intended to share,* transparent and visible to the teachers? If the intent of the coaching/supervision experience is for teachers to *reflect* on my observations and integrate my notes with their own "cognitive map" of what happened and why during the lesson, I became aware that it is incumbent on me to offer the most visible record of my version of the classroom experience. Maybe I needed to offer my "map" of the experience. How, I wondered, could I make visible the patterns of interactions I observed and invite the teacher to similarly construct, or reconstruct the patterns they experienced as they conducted the lesson? How could I make the reflective process so necessary to transforming and improving practice a productive, interactive one? How, too, could I prepare teachers to be able to conduct the same level of reflection *without me?*

After being introduced to Thinking Maps as tools for students over a decade ago, I came to look even more closely at my role as coach. My experience and success with using Thinking Maps to promote and develop reflective practice—thoughtful engagement before, during, and after the act of teaching by teachers—has offered me a way of representing my "cognitive maps" of the classroom observation as a visual display for teachers to see more fully and reflectively. My experiences, which I share below in detailed studies of two different teachers I have coached and supervised, is parallel in many ways with a particularly rich description of how the coaching of new teachers' thinking was key to changing practice at an accredited Thinking School in England. Let's look at parts of an in-depth case study by St Robert of Newminster Catholic School and Sixth Form College (high school), which will give us a clear picture of how coaching teachers sits within the larger context of also improving student thinking across a whole school.

■ NEW TEACHER COACHING IN A THINKING SCHOOL

Thinking Maps were introduced to all staff at St Robert as a key strategy to support the school-wide commitment to developing thinking as a foundation for learning. As a starting point for the long-term vision, it was believed that teachers' use of Thinking Maps would help shift the focus of the educational experience to student-centered learning, that teachers' collaboration and conversation would become more focused, and that new dispositions and process skills would lead to greater coherence in their beliefs and practices about teaching. The effectiveness of the teaching was also expected to be significantly enhanced for all members of the school community. As the implementation got underway at the school, members of the drive team came to recognize a unique opportunity to integrate the use of Thinking Maps into teacher professional development. This, they believed, would be congruent with their efforts to highlight and elevate thinking as the central goal of their instructional program and to their commitment to develop a Thinking School environment that extended beyond the teacher-to-student relationship.

The indicators of success were seen in shifts in teaching and also in the data gathered through confidential surveys. A comprehensive case study was published by St Robert's (n.d.) drive team led by Kevin Steel with video clips, statistical analysis, and survey documentation. Here is a summary of the preliminary findings:

> After the use of Thinking Maps, it was shown that there was less time by students "gathering" information and more time processing and applying information. Students spent 77% of their time engaging in higher-order thinking skills. It could be surmised that the implementation of Thinking Maps has facilitated this. To substantiate this claim, we also analyzed staff responses to a questionnaire, which compared time spent at each thinking level before the implementation of Thinking Maps. "We decided to test the impact of the implementation of Thinking Maps on learners' academic self perceptions to determine whether or not the maps changed the way in which a group of 11–12 year olds conceive of themselves as learners within educational settings." (p. 15)

We used the "Myself As a Learner Scale" (MALS) developed by Professor Robert Burden. "Using the MALS data on 156 learners on entry (September) produced a mean score of 60.5 and after retesting 6 months later the mean score had risen to 67.2. This demonstrates a 10% rise in students' positive self perceptions as learners and active problem solvers. The key elements, as identified by MALS, are:

- confidence in one's own ability to do well in a variety of academic learning situations
- enjoyment in problem solving
- lack of anxiety
- access to and use of a wide vocabulary

When coupled with the questionnaire on Thinking Maps to the same cohort, our preliminary findings indicate that the introduction of Thinking Maps as a tool for teaching and learning has contributed to the increased learner confidence in their own ability and motivation as learners." (p. 15)

The leaders at St Robert, having begun the implementation of Thinking Maps and acutely focused on thinking process development, also noticed a lack of alignment between their existing coaching practices and their desire to promote the Newly Qualified Teachers' (NQT) reflective thinking. They noticed that because the observers controlled the information and often sat across from the teacher during the coaching sessions, power dynamics were immediately reinforced, making it difficult for these new teachers to remain open-minded and objective about the feedback. The impact of the power dynamics on the quality of the interaction between people is essential in small groups, across whole faculties, and school systems in the following chapter presenting research on Thinking Maps for a range of leadership practices (Alper, Williams, & Hyerle, 2011).

Prior to the introduction of Thinking Maps into the supervision process, the postconference "debriefs" of NQTs' classroom practice followed the traditional methodology for feedback and setting targets for improvement. This usually involved the observer reading from his or her linear notes, attempting to focus in on aspects of the lesson that went well to encourage the new teacher to continue adopting specific strategies that worked, and identifying elements of planning and delivery that did not work so well. A significant barrier within this process appeared to be that the NQT did not have immediate access to the written notes (because the coach was reading from scribbled, handwritten notes). As a consequence, teacher postconferences relied on the accuracy of recall being agreed on by both observer and the NQT, and often a selective account of what had been captured by the observer. The St Roberts drive team recognized that the new teachers often found themselves "regarding comments intended to improve classroom performance in a negative manner," (p. 16) reducing their self-esteem, *inhibiting their thinking,* and creating a barrier for growth through the existing process. When asked to describe the existing process, teachers responded with such adjectives as judgmental, threatening, linear, and passive.

Figure 9.1 Bubble Map of the Traditional Feedback Method

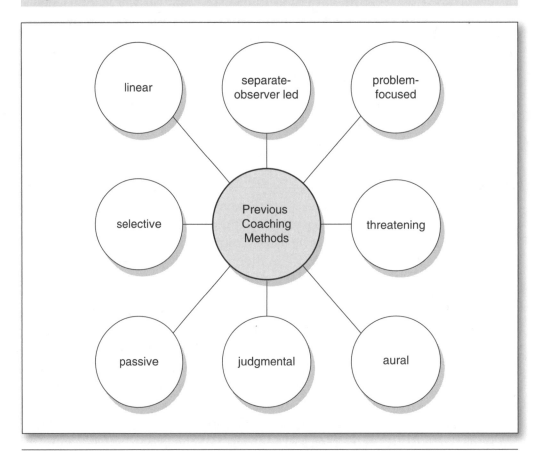

Source: St Roberts of Newminster Catholic School and Sixth Form College (n.d.). *Thinking Maps and school effectiveness: A study of a UK Comprehensive School Report.* Retrieved from http://www.thinkingfoundation .org/research/case_studies/st-roberts/pdf/st_robert_case_study.pdf

Clearly, these responses were not evidence of practices that would promote the development of a school-wide culture conducive to facilitating thinking.

As described by St Roberts' supervisors, the use of Thinking Maps during the conferences signaled a fundamental shift in the power dynamics of the interaction, with *transparency* now a central feature of the experience. Thinking Maps promoted a collaborative process in which the new teachers began reflecting on their instruction, engaging with their own learning, and generating their own decisions about how to improve with the support of the coach. Important to note, these new teachers were already relatively fluent with Thinking Maps because they had been using them in their teaching with an explicit focus on improving thinking and learning of content knowledge. In the context of whole-school shifts, the maps were thus perceived as simply an extension of and deepening the use of a common visual language for learning and leading.

Lesson debriefs began with new teachers being given the opportunity to describe the lesson the coach just observed using the Circle Map for generating ideas about the lesson and Bubble Maps for more discrete, descriptive observations. This process allowed time for the young teachers to reflect on their experiences, and their description set the agenda for the ensuing discussion. It also allowed for the teachers' experiences, perceptions, and thinking to become the central feature of the coaching interaction. From reading the case study, it becomes clear that the coach's use of Thinking Maps in this way communicated to the teachers that the goal was to support the teacher in developing his or her ability *to reflect on and learn from* his or her experience in the classroom. The use of Thinking Maps was also seen as a language teachers could use for externalizing the experience, for seeing it in a way that allowed connections to be made and a critical analysis to form. For the new teachers, as well as for students in their classes, Thinking Maps became tools for mediating their own processes of learning while capturing a visual view of their verbalizations.

In viewing the lesson debrief of the case study, it seems as though the visual storytelling provided by Thinking Maps gave the newly qualified teachers an opportunity to return to the experience, reconstruct it, and add to the narrative. Together, the new teacher and the coach continued the process of collaborative inquiry into the experience.

In specific areas, as we will explore below with examples from my experiences using the maps, the focus on the Flow Map allowed for easy movement into a meaningful discussion, supported by other Thinking Maps used to display and discuss aspects of planning, teacher behavior, learner behavior, and outcomes. One new teacher commented on this benefit: "It is a lot easier to view the lesson if it is presented sequentially. I was surprised how logical it is and it is easier for both of you to see it and discuss it" (St Robert, n.d., p. 21). The coaches and teachers reported that the use of the Tree Map allowed for the target setting to become more focused on the discrete aspects of teaching and learning. These visual representations clearly highlighted those pedagogical processes that were effectively employed and those aspects that needed to be changed for increased effectiveness. Here again, the use of Thinking Maps ensured that the discussion regarding next steps would remain focused and precise.

The anticipated outcomes identified by St Robert, after some practice with the maps, included the hope that " . . . the NQT would more easily understand those micro elements of teaching and learning which were required to be tweaked in order to transform teaching and learning in the classroom" (p. 17). The identified outcomes were three-fold, giving

- the NQT visual access to the observer's thinking (and inevitably judgments) about the lesson being observed;
- the observer visual access to NQT feelings and perceptions about the lesson;
- the NQT and the observer clarity on the areas for development and strategies to be deployed in order to make teaching and learning more effective. (pp. 17–18)

Further analysis emerged from these highlights:

The lesson de-brief began by inviting the NQT to create a bubble map to describe the lesson she had just delivered. This allowed the NQT thinking time for reflection, so she could set the agenda for discussion, and the observer time to focus on how the NQT felt about the lesson and the reasons behind those feelings.

After initial exploration the new map was then "double bubbled." The NQT compared and contrasted her impressions of the lesson with her bubble map of a previous observation. In this sequence the NQT was given a chance to discuss the planned changes made by her prior to delivering the lesson in order to seek improvement.

The observer's flow map was produced which clearly made visible to the NQT the structure of the lesson, key events, planned tasks and transitions between teacher–learner activity.

By allowing the NQT visual access in this way, a discussion occurred about whether or not it represented an accurate record of the sequences which occurred in the lesson. Data captured in each sequence could be seen and thus the focus moved more easily into an effective discussion about aspects of planning, teacher behaviour, learner behaviour and outcomes. (p. 18)

Offering the NQT access to a visual map of the lesson meant the map itself became the object of the discussion about performance. It allowed the fostering of a relationship based on mutual respect for each other's roles. The NQT moved from being merely a recipient of negative feedback (for that is all they seem to hear) toward being an active partner in a coconstructive relationship.

The discussion about teacher performance was summarized by the use of a Tree Map. In the past, traditionally a lesson debrief would have in it some brief targets (bulleted) for improvement and a number of points that went well. The use of the Tree Map clearly allowed for the target setting to become more focused visually on the micro aspects of teaching and learning within a wider array of information visible on it. This characteristic of Thinking Maps is analogous to the use of a city map by a person unfamiliar with the territory: One can see the destination (micro data) within the larger expanse of the wide-angle view of the whole city (macro data) to make sense of the options and decide on the best route. We are now all familiar with this capacity in real time because our smart phones locate us on the map, often through Google Maps, and offer optional routes as we zoom out. This corresponds to what students are also doing as they map content knowledge: They can see, remember, reflect on, and interpret details within the more encompassing conceptual map of knowledge. This brings about confidence, clarity, and a sense of confidence in the capacity to make meaning in context.

As a result of using Thinking Maps, and in one particular interaction between a coach and a new teacher, the action researchers at St Robert reported that the ensuing work with Thinking Maps directly promoted:

- Clarification and negotiation about the validity of statements that each party made
- An opportunity for the NQT to generate his or her own ideas about how the lesson could have been improved

- A valuable discussion about the potential strategies the observer could offer the NQT in the future
- A discussion about shifts in planning that may need to occur to enhance effectiveness of similar lessons in the future (p. 18)

Teachers and school leaders at St Robert of Newminster observed that an added value of using Thinking Maps was that offering the new teachers access to a visual map of the lesson meant that the map itself—and not only their teaching practice in an abstract sense—became the object of discussion about performance. As one new teacher commented, "There was a lot less pressure. We could focus on things that make an effective lesson and for me to concentrate on. The maps can also be kept as a form of reference in my file for me to refer back to" (p. 21). As her comments suggest, each Thinking Map became an instrument of thoughtful engagement. The maps created a dynamic space for shared concern and interest, forming the basis for a dignified exchange of ideas and a collaborative inquiry process, allowing the observer and the new teacher to join together in a common pursuit of learning. Stepping back from the coaching cycle, it is also easy to see that this is the common pursuit a faculty takes on when using Thinking Maps and other pathways toward the development of a Thinking School.

Through a detailed investigation into coach-teacher interactions below, the idea of the Thinking Maps as a third place outside the participants, as a vehicle through which they could explore patterns of thinking rather than a singular performance, begins to emerge. The map may not be the territory in fact, but it is the landscape on which teachers and coaches can journey in the process toward improving teaching in discrete terms, and ultimately, improving reflective practice for long-term growth.

OBSERVATION AND REFLECTION ■

Given the outcomes of the case study presented above focused on new teachers across a Thinking School, now let me take you into an in-depth view of coaching cycles with two more seasoned teachers. You will see how Thinking Maps have made my supervision and coaching in the area of mathematics teaching more explicit, efficient, and effective. The first experience is with Rosa, a third grade teacher, as we made our way from preconference to observation and postconference. The second example is with Sheila, a sixth grade teacher, who offers her reflections on the process using Thinking Maps.

ROSA ■

Prelesson Conference: Lesson Planning

In our prelesson conference, Rosa told me she wanted to introduce her students to the standard subtraction algorithm using base ten blocks as a model. Guiding Rosa through a lesson-planning process, I asked her what math she wanted her students to learn in the lesson. As is typical of most teachers, Rosa had an idea of what she wanted to do but was unclear about what she wanted her students to *learn.* Literally drawing out her thinking, I constructed a Circle Map to help us define learning goals for her students. I wrote LESSON GOALS in the center circle. We then used the metacognitive frame as a mediating tool for Rosa to reflect on the following: What do your students know and understand about subtraction? Place value? What subtractions strategies do they know and apply? What are their misconceptions? What is their prior knowledge and experience with base ten blocks? How does this lesson align with the school's standards? How will the lesson engage students? What difficulties do you anticipate students will have? What extensions or modifications might students need? As we engaged in a conversation around responses to these and other questions that were being visually represented, it became evident that Rosa's students first needed to show that they could connect the model of base

Figure 9.2 Circle Map of Lesson Goals

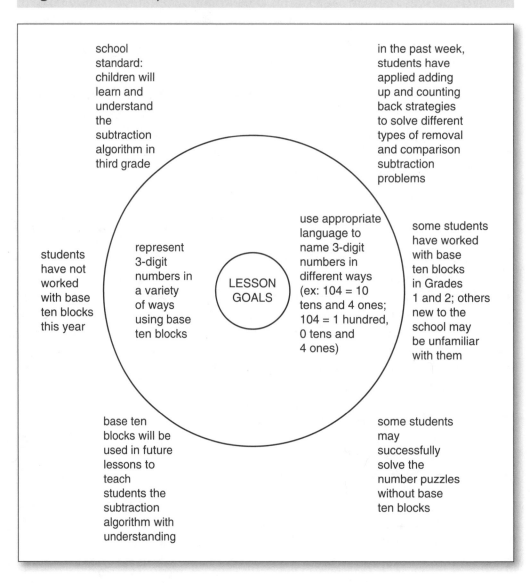

ten blocks to a conceptual understanding of the place-value structure of the number system. This conversation enabled us to more explicitly define what Rosa wanted students to learn in the lesson. It was clear that students needed more experience naming 3-digit numbers in flexible ways before using base ten blocks to explore the standard subtraction algorithm.

Using the learning goals from the Circle Map as a reference, Rosa created tasks that would challenge students to build 3-digit numbers in different ways using base ten blocks. After solving the problems together, we discussed the mathematical challenges they might pose for students and refined the student activity sheet.

The next step in our planning process was to determine how Rosa could assess her students' thinking and problem solving. We decided that the most valid approach was to *observe* her students in the act of solving the problems.

Figure 9.3 Tree Map for Observing Students at Work

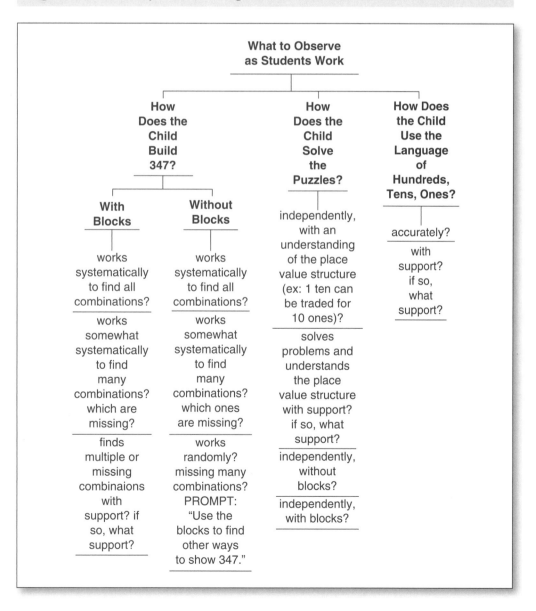

But what was important for us to *observe?* It became clear that we needed to look back at the key learning goals in our Circle Map so that we could then anticipate the range of student responses for each of those goals. The Tree Map, a visual tool for developing categorization, was the cognitive map we could both access. As Rosa quickly scanned the lesson goals from the Circle Map to construct the major categories in our Tree Map, she commented, "It's great to have such a clear, *visual* picture of the goals. I can easily scan it to connect what's important to teach with what to observe as kids solve the problems." We then worked on the number puzzles to anticipate the range of approaches and understandings her students might demonstrate. The outcome of that work is represented on the following Tree Map, which categorizes what was important to observe as children worked.

Next, we used a Flow Map to plan the sequence of events in the lesson. Rosa first constructed a draft Flow Map of the lesson components: the launch (introduction), the work time, and the class discussion (wrap-up). Before teaching the lesson the next day, Rosa revised her Flow Map by refining her questions and prompts. She again noted how the visual explicitness of the Circle Map helped her plan a lesson focused on her "big picture" learning goals: "As I planned the sequence of what to do and say in my lesson Flow Map, I kept going back to my Circle Map to remind myself of the learning goals for students—and to make sure my launch and wrap-up aligned with those goals. Am I getting at the math I want them to learn? I also focused on the language I used in the launch: Was it clear? Will students understand what to do when they work independently?"

Lesson Observation

As I observed Rosa's lesson, I constructed a Flow Map to record the classroom dialogue and actions. In addition to seven pages of Flow Maps of the lesson, the lesson observation data included two pages of an ActiveBoard printout documenting what Rosa charted with students during the launch and class discussion. Following the lesson, Rosa and I brought the lesson artifacts—student work, my Flow Map scripting the lesson, and the ActiveBoard printouts—to our postlesson conference.

◼ POSTLESSON CONFERENCE: EVIDENCE REVIEW, LESSON ANALYSIS, AND ACTION PLANNING

As we sat side by side, I laid out the Flow Map of the lesson in front of us. Enlisting her participation, I said, "I couldn't possibly document everything I saw and heard, so if there is something important that I left out or is in need of revision, we can change the map." Making my complete flow of the lesson transparent and then inviting Rosa to change or add events from her memory were moves intended to establish a tone of openness, equity, collaboration, and trust. It was also intended to return Rosa to the experience so she, too, could reconstruct the events as she remembered them and activate her thinking related to the lesson. I wanted to support her by bringing the same clarity and focus she experienced in the preconference setting to this stage of the coaching process. As we glanced over the pages of the Flow Map in front of us, I asked Rosa, "What part of the lesson would you like to focus on?" Rosa indicated that she wanted to take a close look at her wrap-up class discussion, since this was an aspect of her practice she wanted to improve. But first, she was eager to "read" the lesson story with me—to reflect on and discuss the sequence of events in the lesson.

For the reading of the lesson story to yield rich reflection, dialogue, inquiry, analysis, and action planning, the Flow Map must reflect a descriptive, non-judgmental, and accurate account of the lesson events. As we read the lesson story, events were so visually and sequentially represented that questions about the mathematics and teaching moves naturally emerged in the context of student learning and behaviors. Here's an excerpt of the Flow Map from my observation of the class discussion (wrap-up).

Figure 9.4 Flow Map of Lesson Observation

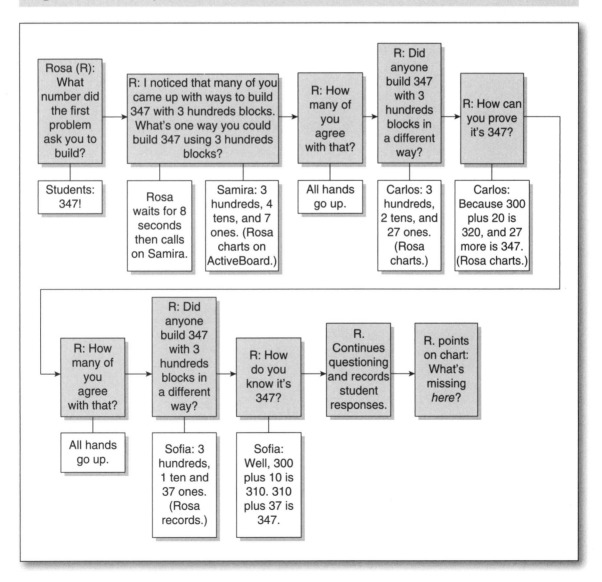

James Stigler (2002) asserts that teachers must learn how to analyze practice: "By *analyze*, I mean that they need to think about the relationship between teaching and learning in a cause-and-effect kind of way. So if a particular student isn't learning, the teacher can generate a hypothesis that links back to the instruction" (p. 7). As Rosa and I read through and discussed the Flow Map of the lesson observation, we used the Multi-Flow Map to examine causes and effects of various teaching moves. In her class discussion, for example, Rosa had recorded students' different ways of representing 347 on the ActiveBoard. Noticing that there were missing combinations, she pointed to her chart and prompted, "What combination of blocks is missing *here?*" and repeated this questioning for other missing combinations, denying the children an opportunity to discover the patterns and reason about them on their own.

I wanted to explore with Rosa the effects of such leading questions, so after we used the Flow Map to revisit her questioning, I asked, "What are the effects of your showing students where something's missing?" We explored this question using a Multi-Flow Map. One of the effects that Rosa noted was that the

Figure 9.5 Teacher Representation of Student Responses to Math Problem

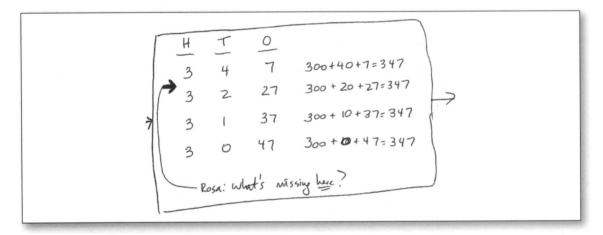

Figure 9.6 Multi-Flow Map of Question Prompts for Deepening Student Thinking

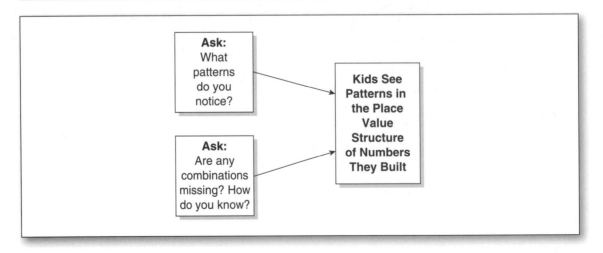

students didn't have an opportunity to find patterns themselves or to use what they knew about patterns to find missing combinations. "If your purpose is to build a deeper understanding of the place-value structure of the number system," I asked, "what questions might cause the *children* to look for patterns and discover *for themselves* if any combinations are missing?" We used another Multi-Flow Map to collaboratively generate questions that could prompt deeper thinking from the students.

Rosa readily appreciated how these simple questions, and others like them, could cause a shift in her teaching—a shift that could activate her student's thinking and more fully engage them in exploring mathematical ideas and connections. The use of the Multi-Flow Map in this way provided her with a visual field to think explicitly and clearly about the connection between her teaching and the students' learning.

Throughout the postlesson conference, as we reviewed the lesson evidence, we continued to analyze student thinking and behaviors that stood out or surprised Rosa. We also analyzed student work, sorting it into piles of varying strategies with which students solved the number puzzles. At the end of our postlesson conference, we used the *Action Planning* framework represented as a

Figure 9.7 Action Planning Tree Map

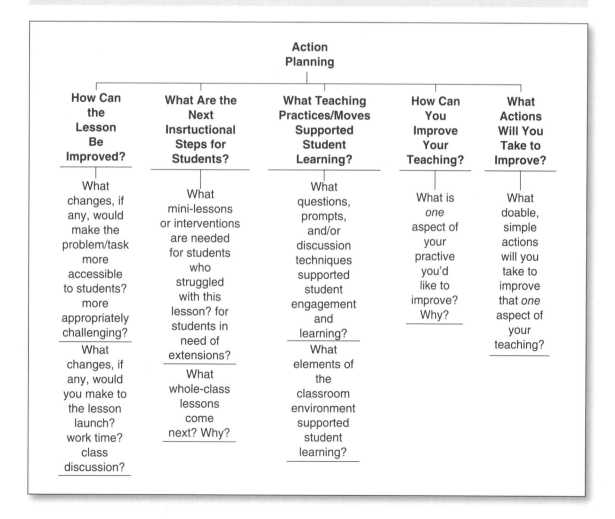

Tree Map to guide our planning for instructional improvement and successful student outcomes in the future.

By this point in the coaching process, Rosa and I had engaged in such rich conversations about the teaching and learning that she quickly identified how the lesson could be improved. She readily determined next instructional steps for students that emerged from our lesson review and analysis. I then asked Rosa to identify moves that advanced student learning because I wanted her to recognize and build on her success.

If a teacher is unaware of a skillful move they made, I'll identify it and use a Multi-Flow Map to engage the teacher in an inquiry about the effects of their move on student learning. Seeing this positive analysis so visually and explicitly represented serves not only to build a teacher's sense of competence and success, but also ensures that they will more intentionally continue the practice. Next, I ask a teacher to generalize from this lesson *one way* they would like to improve their teaching.

In Rosa's case, for example, she said that she didn't know how to structure her class discussions so that students could deepen their understanding of the big ideas of the lesson. "I want to make my class discussions more intentional." Encouraging her to think flexibly, I asked Rosa what *actions* could she take to make them more intentional. At this point, she reflected for a moment.

Rosa proceeded to describe, in a crescendo of enthusiasm, how the construction of the Circle Map defining the lesson goals kept her planning, instruction, and assessment of the children's work and thinking aligned and on track. Rosa realized if she were explicit about what she wanted children to learn and was clear about how to assess their learning during the lesson, she could see what misconceptions, challenges, strategies, or thinking emerged. Her class discussions could be structured to intentionally surface important issues and ideas and to help students make explicit connections about the mathematics in the lesson. Reflecting on the use of the maps during this process, she said, "Thinking about the learning goals kept me focused on what I needed to do to support kids' learning—when I take time to do that, I'm a better teacher." This big idea, which I recorded in the frame of the postconference Tree Map (see Figure 9.8), was a significant insight for Rosa and evidence of the cognitive shift she made as a result of this coaching session.

Rosa and I then constructed another Multi-Flow Map to facilitate our thinking about what *actions* could cause her class discussions to be more intentional.

Finally, we added these actions to the last branch of the *Action Planning* Tree Map. This map, along with the other Thinking Maps, served as an accessible, visible record of the work and thinking constructed throughout the coaching cycle.

Without fail, teachers I've supervised or coached have asked for copies of the Thinking Maps at the end of the postlesson conference because they want to refer to them as they implement changes in their practice. The maps also serve as springboards for future reflection, documenting professional growth over time. During my next coaching cycle with Rosa, for example, I started our prelesson conference with a brief review of her *Action Planning*, discussing her

Figure 9.8 Multi-Flow Map for Improving Intentionality of Classroom Discussions

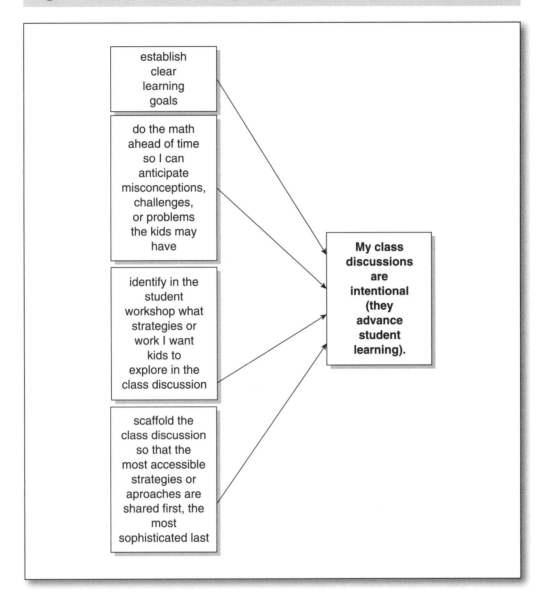

progress in making her class discussions more intentional and the impact her changes have had on student learning.

SHEILA ■

Several years ago I used Thinking Maps in my supervision of Sheila, a sixth grade teacher, and I asked her to reflect on the experience and the implications for using Thinking Maps during the supervision cycle. Her detailed analyses offered below reflect the dynamics and outcomes I perceived through working with Rosa and other teachers as we move from gaining trust, to the collaborative process of lesson inquiry, to the refined focus on her thinking and her students' thinking and learning.

Figure 9.9 Expanded Action Planning Tree Map

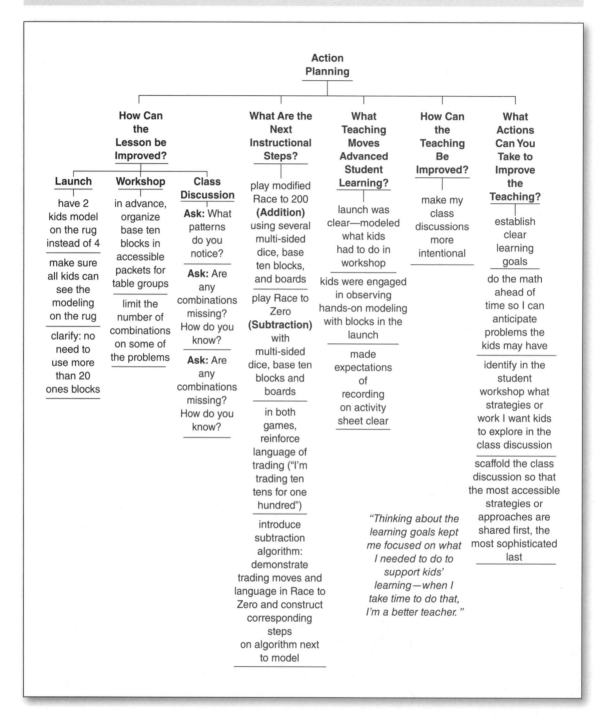

As noted above, setting the tone of collaboration and trust is essential and immediate in the postlesson conference as the Flow Map of the lesson is laid down on the table as a visual display. Suspending judgment of another or of oneself are difficult challenges, but ones that must be achieved if trust, collaboration, and confidence are to be developed. Sheila articulated the impact on her of being invited into a genuine process of inquiry and the significant change this represented from her past experiences:

> To review the lesson, Kathy and I sat at a table, side by side. Kathy laid out the papers, organizing them in the order of the lesson itself. As we began the retelling, Kathy stated that she might have left something out or might not have seen something quite as I had, leaving the maps open for additions or revisions that I felt were important. Kathy's saying that enabled me to feel like the marks on the page . . . were not set in stone. I also felt that my input on the record of the lesson was valued. This disarming technique has been missing from past experiences—especially from those in which I've disagreed with an administrator's interpretation.

Sheila made another crucial observation. Below, she describes the impact of reviewing such a map of her lesson and the power it had to *depersonalize* the experience by visually shifting the focus from the teacher to the teaching:

> The Flow Map approach does more than just offer the opportunity to talk through and collaborate about the lesson . . . The map itself is the most objective record of a lesson I can imagine, short of a film. As an objective record, it is inherently less threatening and harder to write off as "her take on my lesson" or "his interpretation of my teaching." It is easier to tune out the desire to "look good" when I am simply looking at what happened. The map review is not about establishing or defending my intentions—it is foremost a consideration of the real actions and reactions that I took in the lesson, and the discussion of how those actions did or did not meet the overall goals of the lesson lead naturally out of that consideration.

Finally, Sheila reflects on how Thinking Maps are invaluable tools for mediating inquiry and analysis in the postlesson conference through their ability to make patterns of thinking visible:

> Better than a film, the map both isolates each move that teacher and students make and shows those moves as they connect and lead to one another. When we reviewed the maps, I noticed patterns in the frequency of certain types of moves and also saw patterns within series of moves. As we looked at the series of moments, I considered what kinds of questions and prompts I used. Are they open enough? Do the students respond by offering thoughtful answers that show understanding or do they respond with short, simple answers? Do I accept short, simple answers or do I probe for explanations and understanding? Do I accept the right answer too quickly, letting students off the hook without exploring their thinking and bringing the other students along? These kinds of questions are difficult to explore based on the memory of a lesson. However, when you look at the map and you can

see the words that you chose, the reaction(s) you received, and where that series of actions led the class, you really can think about, "What would have happened if I . . ."

■ VISUAL COACHING AND SUPERVISION AND THE USE OF COGNITIVE MAPS

As I look back on my experiences with Sheila, Rosa, and the many other teachers I've supervised or coached, I am struck by the simplicity of how Thinking Maps engage teachers at deep levels of reflection. These educators reflect what Costa and Garmston (1999) say about the impact of reflection, dialogue, and inquiry on teacher cognition:

> When teachers talk about their reasons for their instructional actions and respond to questions about their perceptions and teaching decisions, they often experience a sense of professional excitement and renewed joy and energy related to their work. Talking aloud about their thinking and decisions about teaching energizes teachers and causes them to refine their cognitive maps and hence their instructional choices and behaviors. (p. 33)

When Costa and Garmston use the term *cognitive maps,* they are giving definition to the thinking patterns held in the minds of teachers as they navigate daily classroom experience and as they then, most often, verbally reflect on those experiences through the coaching or supervision cycle. Thinking Maps are concrete, visual representations of these linear and nonlinear cognitive processes and mental maps that are often expressed through talk. As noted above, like any map of a city, country, or world, Thinking Maps simultaneously detail or compress information into rich patterns for interpretation and reflection within a broader context or holism of thinking. We are not getting lost in the conversation and words alone that are feeding the growth of each map. The degree of detail always depends on the purpose at hand.

So it is with Thinking Maps: They make the detailed verbal conversations of coaching, supervision, and cognitive maps *visible* and thus accessible so that teachers can *see* the patterns or experiences and the impact of their actions on students. They can *see* and *look back on* and *look forward to* how changes in their instruction can advance student learning. Seeing, in this case, is believing in themselves as they safely explore their thinking. As explicit and concrete third-point references, the Maps mediate, in powerful and fluid ways, changes in beliefs, thinking patterns, and practice.

■ FROM DEPENDENCY TO INTERDEPENDENCE AND SELF-MEDIATION

Skillfully used after training and practice (these are not simply "graphic organizers" to fill in), Thinking Maps are powerful tools for building and sustaining a culture of collaboration, trust, inquiry, and learning in the coaching and supervision cycles. Because of their generative, visible qualities, collaborative construction of the Maps occurs successfully when the teacher and supervisor or coach sit side by side. This stance sets a tone of mutuality and equity—a place where all ideas are valued and considered. Whether establishing goals for improvement or planning or debriefing a lesson, all eyes are on the data and the maps on the table in front of them. In this way, the maps serve as a third point, visually shifting the focus from the teacher to the teaching. This deceptively simple move depersonalizes the experience for the teacher, creating a climate that invites risk-taking, inquiry, and openness to learning and change. The explicit record of the lesson planning, lesson experience, and lesson review *requires* such a nonthreatening climate; without it a teacher can feel exposed and vulnerable. Reflection and learning can be inhibited. Maps of the lesson observation, if scripted with accurate and descriptive data, provide a concrete, indelible picture of the teaching and learning.

When teacher and supervisor/coach enter a retelling of the lesson story, they can readily access the sequence of actions and dialogue and isolate moments for further inquiry and analysis. They can use the maps to examine cause-and-effect relationships between the teaching and learning and to identify actions that will advance student learning. These analyses can result in deep conversations about the content, student understandings and misconceptions, and effective teaching strategies. The maps mediate cognitive shifts by providing teachers with a visible lens through which the teacher can *see* and *understand* the need to change their practice. Through the use of Thinking Maps in this context, a teacher's pedagogical content knowledge is developed and student learning is advanced.

From a practical perspective, Thinking Maps provide focus and clarity throughout the coaching or supervision cycle, so time is used productively and efficiently. A teacher and supervisor or coach can effortlessly see, from student work and maps of the lesson plan and the lesson observation, whether students learned what the teacher intended them to learn. The maps also serve as an explicit document of the thinking and work that can be readily accessed and reflected on in the future. At a quick glance, a teacher can review the *Action Planning* Tree Map from their last coaching or supervision session to see where they were and how they planned to improve their practice. They can use a Multi-Flow Map to reflect on the causes of subsequent improvement in teaching and the impact, or ripple effect, of these actions on student learning for years to come.

THINKING MAPS SUPPORT SKILLFUL ■ COACHING AND SUPERVISION

There is ample evidence demonstrating the ways in which Thinking Maps can be skillfully used by coaches and supervisors to engage teachers in efficient and effective processes of reflection and improvement. As we have seen, the maps serve as a compelling third party in the supervision or coaching cycle, literally and figuratively drawing out the best of everyone's thinking and dispositions. As visual representations of the cognitive processes, they cue teachers and supervisors or coaches to be mindful of how they are thinking. This metacognitive stance, as well as the maps themselves, activates the use of questions to guide the conversation, inquiry, and analysis. Risk taking and reflection are promoted as all eyes are diverted from the teacher to the teaching, dynamically represented in the maps on the table. Curiosity is piqued when teacher and supervisor or coach wonder about the causes and effects of pedagogical moves on student learning. Flexibility is engaged as they predict possible student responses on tasks or generate actions the teacher can take to advance student learning.

Ultimately, the patterns of thinking and dispositions so essential to reflection for continuous improvement must be practiced and transferred to independent use by the teachers themselves. Supervisors and coaches can play a critical role in developing teacher agency by using Thinking Maps in their prelesson conferences, observations, and postlesson conferences. In doing so, the opportunity for improving the quality of teaching through reflective practice is deeply enhanced.

QUESTIONS FOR ENQUIRY

Reflective practice, as richly illustrated in Ernst's chapter, is considered by many to be foundational to improving teachers' growth and development. One might even consider reflection to be an essential life skill. How, then, might the development of teacher reflectiveness influence shifts in instructional practices and change the actual experiences of students in the classroom?

The visual coaching process that Ernst uses with teachers not only promotes reflection but also, potentially, causes shifts in how teachers perceive themselves as learners. Ernst suggests additional changes that the visual coaching process stimulates "a reexamination of their assumptions and beliefs about teaching and learning." What might some of these shifts be and how might the specific shift in self-perception cause teachers to realign their relationship with their students? What implications might this have for a Thinking School?

In Chapter 5, Hubble shared with us a compelling portrait of the development of a Thinking School and the deliberate, intentional processes used to shift or move the school forward on that journey. What parallels, if any, do you see in the journey of a school in becoming a Thinking School and that of a teacher being coached in the process of becoming a thinking, reflective practitioner?

What is it about the use of visual tools, in this case Thinking Maps, that makes them as effective with adults as they are with children? How might this connection influence the way educators make decisions about other practices they investigate for inclusion in their Thinking School?

■ REFERENCES AND FURTHER READINGS

Alper, L., Williams, K., & Hyerle, D. (2011). *Developing connective leadership using Thinking Maps.* Bloomington, IA: Solution Tree Press.

Costa, A., & Garmston, R. (1999). *Cognitive coaching: A foundation for Renaissance schools.* Highlands Ranch, CO: Center for Cognitive Coaching.

Knight, J. (2007). *Instructional coaching: A partnership approach to improving instruction.* Thousand Oaks, CA: Corwin.

Silicon Valley Mathematics Initiative. (2007). *Pedagogical content coaching.* Retrieved from http://www.noycefdn.org/documents/math/pedagogicalcontentcoaching.pdf

St Robert of Newminster Catholic School and Sixth Form College (n.d.). *Thinking Maps and school effectiveness: A study of a UK Comprehensive School Report.* Retrieved from http://www.thinkingfoundation.org/research/case_studies/st-roberts/pdf/st_robert_case_study.pdf

Stigler, J. (2002). Creating a knowledge base for teaching: A conversation with James Stigler. *Association for Supervision and Curriculum Development, 59*(6), 6–11.

West, L., & Staub, F. C. (2003). *Content-focused coaching: Transforming mathematics lessons.* Portsmouth, NH: Heinemann.

10

Leading

Editors' Introduction

Every year there are hundreds of books written on leadership within and across every field, but especially in the business world, having the additive effect of tens of thousands of texts on leadership lined up in professional libraries over the past few decades. Institutes on leadership abound with many focused on a combination of inspiration, collaboration, and the ambiguous negotiation of leadership roles in society. One of the groundbreaking books that had ripple effects across education, Leadership and the New Sciences, *was written by Meg Wheatley in the early 1990s. She drew from an array of sources and offered that we could draw from our understanding of physics and nonlinear "systems" to shift how we interact with each other and design leadership structures away from the linear mindset. Wheatley (1992) states:*

> Our thinking processes have always yielded riches when we've approached things openly, letting free associations form into new ideas. Many would argue that we've used such a small part of our mental capacity because of our insistence on linear thinking. (p. 116)

Not surprisingly, this focus on linear thinking—nested within the formalities of top-down hierarchical relationships—is conceptual infrastructure for leadership...and learning. Schools that have focused on the development of thinking have drawn on a variety of approaches that engage dynamic collaborative structures and models such as Thinking Maps, Habits of Mind, Six Hats Thinking, and enquiry methods for breaking through the linear mindset, and also linear lines of leadership across their schools.

Additionally, around the world a new and odd phrasing for describing those with new ideas that help shift our thinking are called thought leaders. Ultimately, this term does convey the importance of new ideas developed by key people across fields who challenge conventions, and think different, as the late Steve Jobs promoted for those using Apple products. With smart phones, smart cars, and even "smart chickens," and "smart" popcorn brands popping up in markets, we may be convinced that we should all become smarter, thinking leaders.

The chapter ahead draws us into the field with a rich case study excerpted from research in the book Developing Connective Leadership: Successes With Thinking Maps *(Alper, Williams, & Hyerle, 2011). The setting is a small school district. Thinking Maps have been introduced and implemented across the schools, driven in large part by the superintendent. But what happens when this leader, who wants "thinking" to pervade day-to-day classroom activities as well as leadership and coaching practices, comes up against one the most challenging problems an administrator can have: a grievance by a teacher that is certain to go to union arbitration?*

This detailed story, reflections by all the participants, and analysis in this chapter serve to bring the ideals of Thinking Schools into focus. Systemic organizational change, and a shift in mindsets supported by explicit models and tools for thinking, are essential to bringing about change in classrooms at the most fundamental level. This is because until all educators in a learning community become "thinking leaders," thinking approaches used by teachers will remain the domain of classroom practice. Teachers, administrators, the superintendent, parents, and community members who serve on school boards need to align the practice of decision making and problem solving with classroom practices.

Certainly, the common language of Thinking Maps supports interconnective leadership that is not driven by linear, "top-down" thinking processes. As you see in this case study, the importance of thinking through ideas and recognizing emotional frames helps move people from working from positional power to relational problem solving. We see educators engaging and sharing their rich interdependent patterns of thinking, all surfacing from within the heartfelt interplay of thoughtful people.

LEADING CONNECTIVELY

Larry Alper and David N. Hyerle

TOP-DOWN TO FLAT WORLD ■

The hierarchical structure of leadership in most organizations, including schools, and thus the way roles of authority are traditionally defined and exercised, often impede the development of truly collaborative environments. This top-down design also inhibits thinking in the moment and constrains the explicit development of thinking of all members of schools over time. Networking of ideas and interaction among members of the school community can't develop when lines of communication are rigidly defined and processes are not reciprocal. In schools, this constricted flow of thinking often leads predictably in a particular direction rather than toward the full expression of possibilities for educators and, in real terms, for the students they serve. Such cultures can certainly change, but doing so requires reevaluating beliefs and then introducing new practices and reforming structures to align with the desired change in culture. The development of respectful and sustained conversations in building "equitable partnerships must be accompanied by district and school structures that replace hierarchy with networks and redefine roles, practices, and policies that have historically created and protected uneven power relationships" (Lambert et al., 1995, p. 100). Linda Lambert and colleagues are on target with this assertion: not only does the organizational structure need to change, but also the *practices* and *processes* through which school members communicate between and among the network of people need to be congruent with this change. This is of critical importance for educators committing to make "thinking" as a foundation for the ethos of their schools.

Over the past generation there has been a well-documented shift from top-down to more horizontal, "flattened," or distributed leadership structures across all types of organizational cultures. In the past, the business world has been dominated by top-down management styles, reflecting a command and control mindset, where ambiguity and complexity are met with procedural practices rather than directly engaged. However, that isn't necessarily true in all those settings. When asked what she looked for in the people she hired, Ursula Burns, the CEO of Xerox, answered, "I want them to be confident and uncertain" (Bryant, 2010). In a speech he delivered at a 2005 conference on international education, Michael Eskew, the CEO of UPS, offered a similar statement regarding the qualities he valued in his workforce: "Learning how to learn is a trait we will always value. . . . While information is much richer today, complexity and uncertainty have not abated. In fact, they've increased" (p. 5). What, then, do these two leaders of major corporations recognize about the current realities of the business environment that caused them to respond so similarly and, to some people, so unexpectedly? Both appear to recognize that a major condition of the current environment is change—and rapid change at that—and that agility as a learner will enable one to thrive and continue to contribute to the organization regardless of the changes that occur.

Does shifting to a more flattened leadership structure ensure high-quality thinking, clarity of communication, dynamic and open collaboration, effectiveness and efficient problem solving, and ultimately "better" decisions? In the case of some manufacturing companies, such as in the automobile industry with real-time inventory, a line worker can now literally hit a button and stop the conveyer belt if there is a significant quality control issue. But when dealing with the complexity of schools with students from a range of family configurations and larger communities in an ever more diversifying society (rather than dealing with manufacturing widgets and cars) the thinking and decision-making processes are challenging. There are no "stop" buttons to push in a child's education. And there is no guarantee that positive outcomes will come about by simply distributing power laterally rather than top-down. Hundreds of leadership books are published every year, many in the field of education, as schools attempt to move from centralized decision making behind closed doors to collaborative leadership through which all members of the organization contribute in a significant way to solving highly complex, nonlinear problems each framed by moral dilemmas.

In this chapter, we look closely at how the definition, criteria, and intended outcomes of Thinking Schools explicitly convey that all members of the learning organization, whether teachers in classrooms with students, or teachers in working groups with or without administrators, are consciously practicing and improving their thinking through a range of approaches including the use of visual tools for cognitive and critical thinking, dispositions for mindfulness, and modes of questioning for enquiry. This vision also reflects the bully pulpit outcry from business and political leaders around the world: Schools must become places that are seen as the "training ground" for improving student thinking and learning in this century. We need to take them at their word. Thinking Schools are now serving as incubators for the development and expression of the practices and dispositions associated with thought-filled actions and decision making. If a school is on this journey toward the systematic development of student thinking, then it makes sense to align these very same practices by the educators throughout the school. Congruence is necessary between what is happening in the classroom and what is happening in faculty meetings. Classroom teachers, school administrators, and board and community members may become more proficient at teaching for thinking when they are leading as developing thinkers.

The implication that this new environment has for leadership practices where there can be no *illusion of fixity* is that skillful leadership and skillful participation is required of all members of the school community. Dickmann and Stanford-Blair (2002) state that " . . . it is the leader who acts mindfully, nurturing her or his own intelligence and the intelligence of others, who sets the tone for an organization poised to be successful in the new century" (p. 133). Over time, in a school that has made this kind of commitment, all members of the community are seeing themselves and each other as so-called "thought" leaders and embrace the responsibility and opportunity this statement represents.

In this writing we investigate the use of Thinking Maps as a common visual language for "nurturing intelligence" across Thinking Schools and for facilitating an additional way of communicating, improving dispositions and shifting mindsets, and directly supporting rich questioning for independent and interdependent enquiry across leadership roles and responsibilities. This focus on "thinking leadership" in many ways, as we shall see, resonates with previous chapters showing how Thinking Maps and other approaches blend together to facilitate significant shifts in belief systems and practice: Richard Coe's description of the multiyear journey his school embraced toward becoming a Thinking School (Chapter 6); Donna J. DeSiato's and Judy Morgan's focus on district-wide development of thinking as the central thrust for change at every level of decision making (Chapter 7); and Kathy Ernst's view of improving teacher performance via supervision based on visible coaching (Chapter 9). Each of these chapters is in its own way a case study for how to engender thinking leadership and organizational change.

Below we offer a summary of our 3 years of research on Thinking Maps in a variety of school districts that brought about individual, team, school-wide, and system leadership changes. In summary, our findings clearly show five characteristics of shifts toward deeper thinking emerging from within each context: (1) clarity, (2) efficiency, (3) collaboration, (4) empowerment, and (5) sustainability.

These themes have also been amply represented in the literature on leadership and expressed in a variety of ways. However, as we discovered, leaders in our study reported that using Thinking Maps gave these themes added meaning. These findings, abstracted from case studies, can be further explored in the book *Developing Connective Leadership: Successes With Thinking Maps* (Alper et al., 2011).

After offering some background to our research, we showcase one school system and, in particular, one superintendent, who when faced with a complex, highly charged personnel problem related to a teacher's possible dismissal was

Figure 10.1 Multi-Flow Map of Major Themes

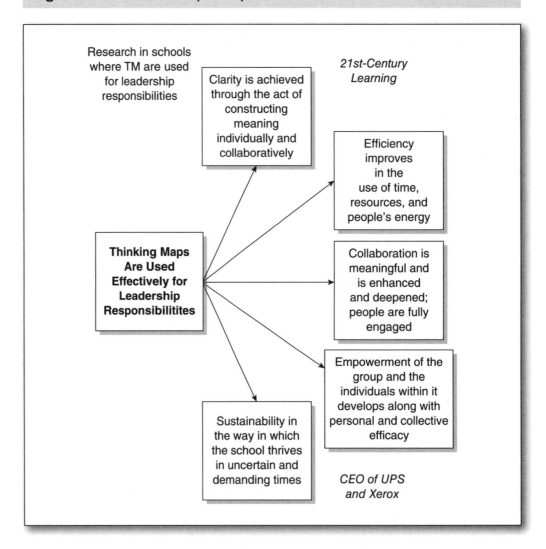

able to draw on Thinking Maps to help resolve the issue. As we shall see, this was possible only because the teacher and everyone else in the district had become fluent with this language for learning, leadership, and dealing with complex problems.

■ GHOSTS IN THE MIND

Over many years of reflective practice in schools and through research in psychology and the cognitive neurosciences, we are now more aware of how people are unconsciously self-deceiving: Our individual, ever-changing brain structures have been wired tight, frozen in some instances by our past experiences and the schemas that frame our thinking. Look into Daniel Goleman's (1985) first book, *Vital Lies, Simple Truths: The Psychology of Self-Deception,* for a full analysis of how our emotions and cognitive states of mind deeply influence our capacities to see ourselves and others with an open mind. "Schemas are the ghost in the machine," (p. 75) Goleman writes, for these connected patterns drawn from experience, substantiated and reinforced in our minds drive our perceptions of the moment and prevent transformational thinking and actions.

How do these "ghosts" influence our work as leaders? As one example, when we sit in or lead a faculty meeting, we already have an invisible, ghost-like frame of reference for what a faculty meeting is about: maybe a mixture of good, bad, and indifferent drawn from our career experiences in faculty meetings. Faculty meetings may also bring up past experiences of *family* meetings. We bring to our concept of *"faculty meeting"* our own mindsets (Dweck, 2006), relationships, and established mental and emotionally connected imprinted patterns that are the perceptual windows through which we see what is happening and what we expect to happen. Our brains actively seek to see what we already know. We are often comforted by replaying the same recording even if the repeating story is negative. A dysfunctional and uncomfortable "normal" often feels better than change to an unknown new place. We have found in our research that the capacity for each of us as individuals and then collectively to identify the existing patterns of experiences, patterns, and "frames" that ground our perceptions and actions is a key to creating participatory, connective leadership in one-on-one conversations, grade-level meetings, and large group sessions such as faculty meetings. We all know that it is often difficult to consciously reframe and repattern our ways of thinking. This may be because we can't easily step back, reflectively, and *see* ourselves and *see* our thinking at work.

As human beings we have primarily depended on the spoken and written word to convey what and how we think. Across districts, schools, and class-rooms, we state what we think in our minds through linear strings of words: We write memos, emails, and reports, and we create long, often inaccessible strategic plans. Words, while powerful, do not adequately represent the rich, diverse, overlapping connected patterns of thinking bound in the deeper structures of spoken language and written texts, concepts, and schemata. These are the ghosts in the background of our minds that stay with us, invisible. Our ideas are born in dynamic, complex, multilayered, and differentiated patterns of thinking, but usually we are forced to articulate them in sound bites and/or data bits on spreadsheets.

So how do we as educators, responsible for conveying high-quality communication every day to students, show other people our own connected patterns while seeking out and seeing others' points of view? If our best thinking comes by making connections and building patterns, then what would these patterns *look like?* Simply, what does thinking look like? This may strike most people as an odd question. Many people are now looking to brain mapping as a visual depiction of thinking, but this is the anatomy of a networking brain, not the actual patterns of thinking our mind is generating. Most often we perceive thinking as hidden in the brain and mind behind the interior monologue of our moment-to-moment thoughts and dreams, the words we use to communicate our thoughts to others, the papers we write, the e-mail we send off, and the mathematical spreadsheet problems we solve. We squeeze our words out in strings of sentences like toothpaste from a tube, but we know deep down that our thoughts and concepts are underrepresented by words alone. Even a picture that "says" a thousand words doesn't do justice to the complexity of our ideas.

As we discovered through the numerous schools we studied, the well-meaning and collaborative participants in a strategic planning processes, for example, could not *see* their thinking or transform their actions accordingly until the principal mapped them out using Thinking Maps. This was deeply expressed in Kathy Ernst's description of Visible Coaching in Chapter 9, because the visual representation of thinking patterns offered both detail and a wide-angle view through which teachers could become more reflective and self-interpretive. In the case study below we see how a teacher and a principal had truly "lost sight" of the important focus of their interaction and were unable to "see" beyond their positions and the history they shared that now distorted their vision. Not only was their vision impaired by their emotional "ghosts," so, too, was their ability to think.

The current context and frame of reference for this transitional point in the history of our educational systems nationally and globally is essential for understanding how Thinking Maps offer a new language for communication and improvement of thinking, learning, and leading. Leaders in the field of education, like parents, businesspeople, and students as future innovators in a global network of technologies and "knowledge workers," are asking for a new way to facilitate learning and the coleadership in the collaborative, fluid work structures of the 21st century. New kinds of tools and models need to drive to the center of complexity, ambiguity, nonlinear patterns, and emotional frames and also be more than quick-fix strategies for an immediate problem, but engage whole professional learning communities in the improvement of their thinking.

■ A CASE STUDY OF LEADING WITH THINKING MAPS

At first blush, the concept of Thinking Maps may look all too simple, and that is good because as it turns out, simplicity is an essential quality of the maps. The capacity to think, reflect, and then transform our thinking into new behaviors and actions is foundational to living in this new century of connective technology, global knowledge creation, and knowledge transfer. Through its seeming simplicity, Thinking Maps can animate high-quality thinking and nurture self-reflection, metacognition, and dynamic reflective leadership within groups of people. The essential and unique human quality of empathy grows ever more present when we have a language for connecting our thoughts together. In this way, the social ecology of our community is supported and enhanced by a language that enriches the interdependent nature of our interactions and, at the same time, facilitates individual thought and expression in a coherent manner.

The ensuing case study involves traditional levels of power within a school system: a teacher, a principal, and grievance chairperson, and the superintendent of schools—and how through the use of Thinking Maps they were able to level the conversation about the quality of teaching and the conflict that arose from this point of change. It is an example, too, of how the key leaders involved—the grievance chair and the superintendent—were united in their desire to restore not only integrity to the process that had devolved between the principal and the teacher, but also to do so in a manner that elevated the nature of the interaction. This was also congruent with their efforts to create a school system with thinking as the foundation.

This story comes from a full array of case studies focused on Thinking Maps as a language for "developing connective leadership." The analysis of these case studies led to the identification of five major conceptual themes, summarized above, about connective leadership in schools that had implemented Thinking Maps for multiple years in their schools. This story provides an opportunity to see Thinking Maps as a foundation for leading Thinking Schools. So often we believe that to make change in schools requires the improvement of teachers—when in fact to make significant change requires that *all* participants be engaged in the process.

Here's a situation school leaders know all too well: Parents and students complain about a teacher, accusations are made, and while people have raised such issues before, nothing documented in past performance evaluations and no concrete evidence in personnel files indicate any problems that needed attention. Immediately, the teacher feels threatened, the principal is under pressure to act, the union responds to ensure an appropriate process is followed, and the superintendent is called on to intervene, while the issue agitates school board members.

In Superintendent Michael Sampson's case (for legal/privacy concerns, names have been changed), however, by the time the issue reached him, communication between the teacher and the principal had broken down completely. Feeling threatened, the teacher had already filed a formal grievance with the union. Emotions were running high, and restoring communication on their own was beyond the reach of the teacher and principal. Fortunately for Michael, he had cultivated trusting relationships throughout the system, and most, if not all, viewed his involvement as a positive and hopeful step. Nonetheless, the conflict seemed intractable, with all parties rooted in their beliefs and emotions, and headed for arbitration.

Although relatively new to this district, Michael had successfully begun the process of establishing a strong reputation as a solid instructional leader. He introduced Thinking Maps throughout the system, something he had done successfully in his previous district as the assistant superintendent for curriculum and instruction. Michael extended the introduction of Thinking Maps beyond the classroom to include members of the district's leadership team. He used the maps in his own practice, facilitating meetings and communicating information to others with these tools. Because each Thinking Map represented a thinking *process* (cause and effect, sequencing, or categorizing), by using them, Michael was prompting his colleagues to both understand new content and actively interact with new ideas. He was leading in a manner that supported and challenged their thinking. In essence, he was also communicating through his actions that the system could not progress without the ability of those within it to think.

Michael knew the work with Thinking Maps well, believed in it, and was respected for his engagement in the implementation process. Others definitely viewed him as someone who "walked the talk." Even so, Michael did not foresee the degree to which the ensuing events would challenge his belief in these tools and, consequently, his own reputation as a district leader.

Because of the delicacy of the situation or his reluctance to introduce something into the dynamic that might be perceived in the wrong way, Michael Sampson did not initially decide to use Thinking Maps to facilitate a resolution in this circumstance. However, the chair of the grievance committee and seventh-grade English teacher, Sharon Henderson, did. Sharon suggested to Michael that they use Thinking Maps to facilitate their meeting with the teacher, two principals, a union representative, and the grievance chair. Sharon described her decision to propose the use of Thinking Maps in this grievance situation:

> The typical interaction was him (the principal) talking at her (the teacher) and her closing down and walking away. I was complaining (to Michael) about the principal's administrative style, and he defended the administrator—we had to find a way for it to work. I was using maps in my classroom, and I realized that when using the maps, I am not standing up here spouting great knowledge—the maps are taking focus off me and putting the focus more on the students' thinking and the tool—the tool is speaking to kids, not me—the tool is generating thinking, not me—takes the focus off me as the expert and allows us all to work together as a team. . . . I had this realization that this was what was needed in this grievance situation. We needed to get visual focus off of us as individuals and onto a neutral focus both people focusing on the same thing—both looking down on this tool—use the tool to solve this problem.

Sharon astutely made the cognitive leap from the classroom to grievance setting. Just as the maps mediated the interaction between teachers, students, and ideas and experiences, Sharon saw the same possibility in a situation in which the constraints of role and emotions prevented communication at the level necessary to resolve this issue. Through the use of this common language, Sharon understood the important role the maps could play in shifting the focus from the people to the behaviors or teaching practices. Attention could be jointly directed to the aspects of the situation that needed to be addressed and to finding solutions rather than to locating blame or defending positions. The externalization of the problem through the use of the maps provided a safe and constructive visual context for all involved to locate their attention. As Sharon notes, the maps create a collaborative space for people to construct ideas together and jointly pursue understanding. They focus attention and promote the *thinking* of those involved on the content of the conflict and the ways to solve it, not on the people involved.

Both Sharon Henderson and Michel Sampson recognized that the need to restore integrity to the interaction between the principal and teacher, and to the grievance process in general, was essential to the creation of a "thinking" school system. Believing it was necessary, however, was not enough. They also understood that the tools to do so were available to all members of the school system and needed to be used in this situation. The use of Thinking Maps in group and interpersonal settings is inevitably collaborative. It begins with simple body language. When leaders begin to map out issues and identify steps to resolve them, they sit down side-by-side with a teacher or others with whom they are engaged in the mapping process. The physical orientation of the participants—focused together on the visual landscape of ideas they are cocreating—signals a power-sharing relationship.

The use of the maps also helps make thinking explicit. In interactions in which participants do not visually represent their ideas or do so in a narrow linear manner, statements may easily go unquestioned or carry weight without further examination. The cognitive patterns used to represent ideas in Thinking Maps, however, invite a level of questioning and precision that helps communication become clear and accountable. This can be critical to the outcome, particularly when emotions run high and the relationship of those involved is perceived as unequal.

Here's how Sharon, the grievance chairperson, described the impact of Thinking Maps in this situation:

> The teachers' union felt the principal was not being event specific [with the teacher]—the principal was using terms like *always* and *never* without specifics, and the teacher was like, "Prove it." The Thinking Map forced both parties to look at a particular incident and not do rabbit trailing—going to change the confrontation and the focal point. . . . It also gave the teacher something to walk away with that included her input. One thing that was important was that the administrator was not always holding the pencil—that she [the teacher] also got to hold the pencil and fill it [the Thinking Map] in. We have a very controlling administrator—tends to enjoy that controlling element. The use of the maps releases some of the administrative control and allows the teacher to take ownership.

This strategy has several advantages. First, the leader and the person being led share the responsibility to identify the problem and come up with a solution. Second, the maps allow both parties to focus more on the issues and less on the emotions. All leaders we interviewed agreed that sitting down with the maps diminished the emotional nature of these difficult situations with challenging teachers—even when the outcome was a firing.

As the meeting approached with his building principal, the teacher, the grievance chair, and the head of the union, Michael remarked, "I had a sleepless night the night before thinking that if the Thinking Maps didn't work in this meeting they'd be dead at Sedgwick (school system name changed)." He went on to say that his credibility as a leader was also at stake. He had invested much of his leadership career in this work and had professed his belief in these tools for student and adult learning and development. He had modeled the use of the maps in a variety of situations, demonstrated his knowledge and facility with them, and was being asked to apply this to a very real, complex, ambiguous, and intensely difficult situation. Could they engage uncertainty with confidence in a hot-button, career-changing context?

In the case of the teacher with the grievance, she was retained, and the teacher improvement plan was dropped. Michael's successful application of the maps in this interaction affirmed his belief in these tools and, more important, allowed him to be faithful to his beliefs about communication and problem solving in school settings. As a leader, Michael is genuinely collaborative and holds an abiding faith in the ability of people to accomplish extraordinary things, even in the most challenging circumstances. Using the maps supported Michael in going forward in this interaction with an uncertain outcome, but with the confidence that clarity and constructive resolution could be achieved with everyone's dignity preserved or, in this case, restored. On reflection, Sharon observed:

> There was a benefit that I never foresaw—not only did we use the maps to diffuse a problem and they were effective and I think will continue to be effective in event-specific issues . . . but what I never foresaw was the benefit from the improvement in the relationship between these two people (the principal and the grieving teacher). For the first time ever, after the meeting, the teacher actually asked for input from the principal— she said it went quite well—this is a complete turn-around . . . we'll have to see if it continues, but so far, so good . . . I credit the maps with diffusing the problem and giving us a plan and a hope for the future.

Not only did the use of the maps help identify strategies for the teacher to improve and a way of resolving the conflict driving the grievance, but in the end, the use of the maps also gave the two parties involved in this substantial conflict a language for talking with each other in the future. The teacher—who prior to the use of Thinking Maps refused to have any more conversations with the principal—now asked to work side-by-side with the principal to improve her classroom performance. A relationship was reclaimed, or perhaps established for the first time, but just as important, the relationship was now built on an appreciation of each person's ability to think and to do so interdependently.

Experiences like this one have a way of empowering people directly and indirectly associated with the event. The successful outcome achieved through Sharon's and Michael's intervention and decision to use Thinking Maps to resolve a complex situation had ripple effects for them and their colleagues. Not surprising, their success in this situation encouraged them and others in the system to deepen and expand their use of this powerful language furthering the development of the organization as a thinking school system.

Michael discussed using the maps with his teachers when engaging in observations. Note the following example.

> With the amount of experience I've had with the maps and my background in Cognitive Coaching (Costa and Garmston, 1999), I find this is

an enormous asset to guide collaborative planning and also do coaching to guide reflection of particular individuals along the way. For example, one of my Thinking Maps trainers is doing a lesson tomorrow and sat down with me to do a pre-observation conference—I'm going to be the observer. She used the circle, frame, and tree maps to outline the lesson for me. As we talked about what she wanted me to observe in the lesson, together we constructed a multi-flow map of the assessment/evidence that would be available of what objectives to look for. We used another map together to plan for that observational assessment. It is in part my own evolution of knowing these Thinking Maps but also the fact that I'm willing to use them and allow teachers to see how much I value them.

As Michael observed, his ongoing use of the Maps contributed to the development of his fluency with these tools. At the same time, his total engagement with them reinforces their use for teachers as well as models his own willingness to take risks and grow in his practice.

Sharon, the grievance chair, discussed how after this experience she started using the maps when teachers came to her with a grievance. First, they would brainstorm all the issues using a Circle Map. Then, because these interactions are so emotionally laden, she would have the person potentially filing the grievance use a Bubble Map to describe all the emotions he or she felt about the event, issue, or experience.

Sharon observed that it was very important to "validate emotions but then move on." The use of other Thinking Maps allowed the person involved to look more closely at the issue, develop a deeper understanding of it, and consider a range of possibilities before choosing a particular path. These experiences are intensely emotional, but by keeping attention on the maps—on the *thinking*—the issues remained in focus, meetings were productive, and tension and negative emotions were minimized.

As stated above, the capacity for each of us as individuals and then collectively to identify the existing "frames" that ground our perceptions and actions—and to consciously reframe and repattern our ways of thinking—is a key to creating participatory, connective leadership in one-on-one conversations, grade-level meetings, and large group sessions such as faculty meetings. In the situation that Superintendent Michael Sampson was asked to intervene in, the principal and teacher were rooted in their roles, unable to cross those boundaries to establish clear, constructive dialogue. The principal's inability to recognize the frames from which the teacher and he were responding and how

Figure 10.2 Sample Flow Map for Grievance Process

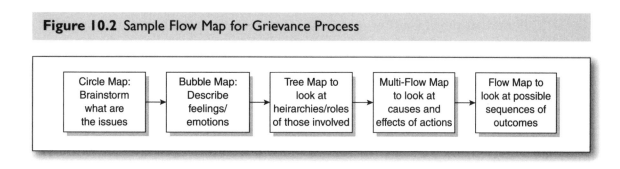

his approach was driving the teacher into a more defensive posture made the situation seemingly intractable.

Connective leading is about fostering the connections between and among people, between and among ideas within patterns of thinking, and across visual and virtual planes, which the diversity of those present and represented inform and enrich. To lead connectively means to invite possibilities into the process with the bold and confident view that, by design, the collective wisdom of the community of learners will emerge, and from this, effective and meaningful solutions will be determined. Connective leading requires skillful facilitation because it is about interconnecting people in the complex dance of both personal and professional conversations. This critical dimension of leadership is expressed in all aspects of the school community—classroom, meeting room, and boardroom. Its need becomes apparent when emotions are heightened and threaten to dominate interactions. However, when exercised from the beginning and with a common, visual language that represents thought in cognitive patterns, connective leadership builds individual and collective confidence within a Thinking School community to address even the most highly charged situations respectfully and effectively. As Superintendent Donna J. DeSiato observed, "With Thinking Maps, it's not about power and position, it's about understanding and being understood."

Connective leading requires a significant leap of faith, a fearlessness, and a confidence in self and others in the face of emerging truths—perhaps even uncomfortable realities. The decision to become open to possibilities and to initiate the dynamic interaction between self and others, mind and experience, can be as unsettling as it is exciting. It can be somewhat akin to walking a tightrope without a net underneath. Thinking Maps, however, provide a conceptual net for capturing and representing ideas dynamically and to see connections. The discomfort that often accompanies uncertainty gives way to the confidence Thinking Maps develop in people in their individual and collective ability to think.

■ OUT OF THE AUDITORY AND INTO THE VISUAL

As we researched the impact the use of Thinking Maps had on school communities when applied to different areas of leadership, five themes emerged and are evident in the case study just discussed: clarity, efficiency, collaboration, empowerment, sustainability. As we look more closely at these themes, consider that these are worthy qualities to develop for Thinking Schools.

Clarity, as we came to understand it through the comments of the leaders we interviewed, is not the presumptive certainty of one's opinions but something that develops from a satisfying process of constructing meaning alone and in concert with others, from suspending judgment and engaging in a process of individual and collective dialogue to allow patterns to emerge. These internal and external conversations were facilitated by a visual language that made evident the content of the ideas, the processes used to arrive at them, and the frames of reference that influenced them. Clarity, too, came from knowing that the actions one decided on aligned with core values and beliefs.

The interaction between the teacher and principal in the aforementioned case study had certainly become cloudy, lacking in both clarity and focus on what was most essential—the improvement of instruction. Superintendent Michael Sampson was able to use Thinking Maps to rebuild communication pathways by ensuring that the dialogue was about teaching, not the teacher or the principal. The Maps provided an external locus of attention and enabled everyone involved to look at, think about, and learn from the patterns rather than judge the people.

Efficiency, we learned from our research, was not to be confused with *expediency.* Certainly, time was an influencing factor in all the scenarios leaders discussed with us. However, the stress occurred not so much from having too little time, but rather from being aware that they could not use their time as effectively as they believed they should. Having more time does not necessarily guarantee that it will be used well. In inefficiently led meetings or in personal processing that gets bogged down, frustration develops not from running out of time but from using that time inefficiently—something more time wouldn't solve. With Thinking Maps, leaders reported that people were more focused and deeply engaged, their attention was more sharply directed, their thinking was attuned, and their ability to do what the brain strives to do—*see and construct patterns*—was supported. The leaders felt the resulting decisions and the actions that developed had integrity and were not simply made to "get it done."

Collaboration was certainly identified in our research as both an essential aspect of learning communities and an area in which the use of Thinking Maps contributed positively in significant ways. However, as Michael Fullan (2001) observes, "Collaborative cultures, which by definition have close relationships, are indeed powerful, but unless they are focusing on the right thing, they may end up being powerfully wrong" (p. 67).The collaboration that school leaders spoke of in our research was not simply the act of bringing people together but of grounding the collaborative process of learning in which participants were engaged at all levels—intellectually, emotionally, morally, politically, and so on.

In the context of collaboration, dispositions such as intellectual curiosity, commitment to understanding, and suspension of judgment—striving for clarity—were essential elements of the process of working together. While Thinking Maps were a vehicle for bringing people together, they also served to focus the attention of the group on the ideas and not each other. The collaborative process, while social in nature, became highly purposeful and insistent on achieving clarity. Michael Sampson's use of Thinking Maps in the grievance setting to literally draw everyone's attention to the practice of teaching and not the teacher herself helped restore trust and safety to the interaction, essential elements for productive and meaningful collaboration.

As is now perhaps becoming apparent, the interplay of these themes is in itself a crucial observation about the influence Thinking Maps had on these school communities. The collaborative processes described and the clarity and efficiency with which people arrived at understandings individually and collectively could not have been achieved at the levels reported to us if people didn't feel empowered to contribute their ideas to these important processes in their school communities.

Empowerment not only was experienced and exercised as a right of those participating in a democratic context, but also emerged from the confidence gained through using the maps in the ability to formulate and communicate one's thinking and clarify one's ideas internally and to others. The internal web of the school community operated at its highest degree of efficiency and effectiveness when all members of the school were fully engaged, affirmed, and able to confidently engage in situations in which answers and solutions were not immediately apparent. Roles define responsibilities. They do not determine the value of people's contributions, nor should they inhibit people's ability to contribute. Leading thinkers across a school meant not only to enable others to feel *empowered*, but also to know better *the power of their own minds.*

As demonstrated in the Visible Coaching chapter by Kathy Ernst, and in the example cited in this chapter, significant and lasting improvement in teaching will come when teachers are engaged, supported, and assisted in developing their ability to reflect on their own practice and mediate their own growth and learning.

It's not surprising that we would reserve *sustainability* for last. We learned the leaders were not simply speaking about maintaining some sort of status quo or holding precious what their schools had become. Instead, the sustainability they referred to and reached for was the dynamic state of learning, the constant process of becoming built on and sustained by a common visual language for thinking. This common language expressed a core value of these schools—that thinking is the foundation for all learning at all levels throughout their school communities. Eleanor Duckworth, educator and author, once wrote that it is virtuous not to know. It's what we do when we don't know that will ultimately determine what we do know (Duckworth, 2006, p. 67). In the 21st century, where change is the norm, Thinking Schools will embrace the opportunities that present themselves, adapt to new circumstances, and create their own futures, as Senge (1990) proposes healthy organizations will do.

Sustainability, then, is about not simply surviving in these dynamic and uncertain times, but thriving with the benefit of the clarity, efficiency, collaboration, and empowerment that leading connectively through the use of Thinking Maps can inspire.

■ THE INSTRUCTIVE/DESTRUCTIVE POWER OF EMOTIONS

Supporting people in being able stay in heated discussions and staff meetings that might otherwise go awry, and transform and *sustain* a conversation about difficult topics without driving down into what often feels like a bottomless well of emotions or a competition of ideas, is, perhaps, the greatest challenge to any leader. Done successfully, confidence (and trust) in self, the group, and the organization as a whole gradually develops and helps create a culture of sustainability over the years.

In the course of human interactions, issues easily become quite complex and murky as emotions inform and influence them. Often people feel challenged to remain dispassionate in these interactions, believing that they must set aside their emotions in order to see and think clearly. Attempts to suppress emotions can, however, have the opposite effect on achieving clarity because emotions can be powerful and useful forces in guiding and informing thinking. However, unconsciously allowing emotions to direct thinking and actions can also lead to what some refer to as an *emotional hijack* in which emotional filters not only inform but also control our actions. Daniel Goleman, Richard Boyatzis, and Annie McKee (2002) write, "The prefrontal area (of the brain) can veto an emotional impulse . . . Without that veto, the result would be an emotional hijack, where the amygdala's impulse is acted upon" (p. 29). Such impulsive actions are often taken defensively and aggressively (fight-or-flight) and can cause irreparable harm in already delicate relationships. Power and authority often expressed in hierarchically defined roles also contribute to situations in which emotions can easily create misunderstandings and result in misguided and unproductive actions. This was especially evident in the conflict Michael Sampson was urged to resolve.

Many of the leaders we spoke with viewed Thinking Maps as the visual and practical extension of the brain's executive functioning. From the routine task of designing and executing a simple plan to the more demanding challenge of responding to the endless stream of information and the intricacies of human dynamics in the workplace, each person worked overtime to lead in a positive, constructive, and sometimes visionary direction. Thinking Maps, as we saw and heard from various school leaders, including Superintendent Michael Sampson, were indispensable in building, supporting, and enhancing the capacity of the brain to activate memory and language, direct attention to achieve both short- and long-term goals, and resolve issues of moral and ethical complexity, with emotions as a guide, not as the determinant.

This highly attuned orchestration of thought and feeling results in what Goleman et al. (2002) call *resonant leadership,* or the ability to skillfully, respectfully, and effectively organize and inspire the feelings and thoughts of others as well as oneself toward shared goals. Superintendent Michael Sampson was not only able to employ Thinking Maps to resolve a difficult conflict, but in doing so he also began the process of restoring trust and confidence in the district's ability to handle extremely sensitive matters effectively and with dignity. As efficacy studies have shown, such confidence in the organization often translates into similar feelings of confidence within the individuals of the organization. In this way, the space is opened for skillful thinking to become the defining feature of the school community.

The use of Thinking Maps helps remove artificial boundaries or separateness that narrow interpretations of role relationships can impose. The maps create a visual landscape that allows individuals to express and contextualize the holism of ideas through multiple thinking processes and frames of reference. The nature of this representation system—its grounding in inherent cognitive skills and intimate alignment with how the brain interacts with ideas and phenomena—sets it apart from other visual models or graphic organizers and allows it to function as a common, visual language across roles as well as ages.

The opportunity to fully represent the holism of their ideas clearly empowered many of those we interviewed. Former Superintendent Veronica McDermott observes, "Since the maps are rooted in the psychology of cognition, they, too, push users to be creative and to propel their thinking beyond the obvious." The maps foster deeper attention to one's own thinking and to the ideas of others in a way that fundamentally changes the nature of the interaction. They enable people to participate in the collective construction of meaning. In doing so, they support a type of listening that literally and figuratively *draws* users into the dialogue and enables them to attend deeply to what is expressed. This type of listening, what Art Costa (2003) refers to in part as *generative listening,* occurs when "you can slow your mind's hearing to your ears' natural speed and hear beneath the words to their meaning"(p. 33). Just as the graphic artist Milton Glaser (2008) describes the act of drawing something as the opportunity to truly know it, literally drawing out ideas *draws* us to them, enabling us to take the time to listen and look deeply for the essence that exists beneath the surface.

■ LEADING CONNECTIVELY

For many of the leaders we spoke with, including Michael Sampson and Sharon Henderson, the use of Thinking Maps altered that internal dialogue and reframed their interactions with others in such a way to allow for greater clarity and reciprocity. As Lambert (2009) asserts, "The brain's capacity to find patterns and make sense of the world is liberated within such relationships that encourage mutual care and equitable engagement" (p. 11). So often, people describe the experience of using Thinking Maps in group settings as literally finding themselves on the same page with others involved. This is not to say that agreement is automatically achieved. Rather, a space is opened in which all involved enter as equal partners in the generation of ideas as they work toward shared meanings and sound decisions. The purposeful, focused interaction that the use of Thinking Maps facilitates can be quite disarming in a positive sense. Thinking Maps suspend the impulse to compartmentalize things or arrive prematurely at clarity.

Instead, drawing out their own and others' thinking allows people to become part of what Jaworski and Flowers (1998) describe as *the unfolding* in which we accept others as "legitimate human beings" and appreciate the ever-changing nature of our world and our constantly evolving understanding of it. In this way, we genuinely engage in the process of meaning making, an act of individual and collective construction that rejects "the illusion of fixity" and embraces the challenge and pleasure of living in "a world of continual possibility" (p. 11).

School leaders, especially principals, have tremendous influence over the degree to which their schools and the individuals within them act intelligently and effectively. Influential leaders understand the fundamental nature of learning not only as it relates to students, but also as an essential dimension of the dynamics of a thinking school community itself. With a vision of what it means for a school to be a thinking community, they work intentionally and skillfully to bring others into this vision and develop their capacities to contribute in positive and constructive ways. Across the reach of this book on Thinking Schools, there may be no more profound change in a school for students than seeing in their teachers as leaders—not just "modeling" thinking processes, dispositions, questioning, and enquiry for classroom purposes—but in the reflective practice of improving their own dynamic processes of thinking as leaders.

QUESTIONS FOR ENQUIRY

In this chapter, Middle School teacher and chair of the grievance committee, Sharon Henderson, challenged Superintendent Michael Sampson to use Thinking Maps in a novel way—to transform a seemingly intractable situation between adults into one that could have a beneficial conclusion for all involved. In essence, she was asking for a realignment of practices across the entire system to reflect the district's commitment to thinking as a foundation for learning for all members. Why was Sharon's insistence on this so urgently necessary, and what purpose or purposes might such an alignment of practice across all roles and responsibilities in a school or district serve in a school's effort to transform itself into a "thinking school"?

Both Sharon Henderson's and Michael Sampson's actions suggest that they were in the process of reconceptualizing their professional identities as leaders, an outcome that was perhaps initially unintended or unconscious but, with experiences such as this, could become more deliberate. What might be some of the implications such shifts in self-perception would have in other aspects of their respective roles?

In what ways might interconnective leadership be similar or different from interactive leadership? How does the use of a common, visual language for thinking, such as Thinking Maps, promote both interactivity and interconnectivity?

In this chapter, a CEO is quoted as saying she wants her employers to be "confident and uncertain." The authors themselves suggest that "fearlessness" might be a critical dimension of successful leaders. If these attributes are indeed worthy of development in leaders, in what ways did the use of Thinking Maps support the leaders in this case study to tap into and perhaps develop these essential qualities? How might this connect to your goals for students?

REFERENCES AND FURTHER READINGS ∎

Alper, L., Williams, K., & Hyerle, D. (2011). *Developing connective leadership: Successes with Thinking Maps.* Bloomington, IN: Solution Tree Press.

Bryant, A. (2010, February 21). Xerox's new chief tries to redefine its culture. *The New York Times*, p. BU1.

Costa, A., & Garmston, R. (1999). *Cognitive coaching: A foundation for Renaissance schools.* Highlands Ranch, CO: Center for Cognitive Coaching.

Costa, A. L. (2003). *The school as a home for the mind: Creating mindful curriculum, instruction, and dialogue* (2nd ed.). Thousand Oaks, CA: Corwin.

Dickmann, M. H., & Stanford-Blair, N. (2002). *Connecting leadership to the brain.* Thousand Oaks, CA: Corwin.

Duckworth, E. (2006). *The having of wonderful ideas and other essays on teaching and learning* (3rd ed.). New York, NY: Teachers College Press.

Dweck, C. (2006). *Mindset: The new psychology of success.* New York, NY: Random House.

Eskew, M. (2005). *Education in an age of globalization.* Speech by Michael Eskew, Chief Executive Officer and Chairman of UPS. Retrieved from http://www.google.com/url?sa=t&rct=j&q=&esrc=s&source=web&cd=10&ved=0CFsQFjAJ&url=http%3A%2F%2Fncssfl.org%2FEskew-Speech.doc&ei=PbbJUqPRGrTTsATIsYDQDQ&usg=AFQjCNGWhCZlhSFRAum2hcn8_LUHOUayeA&bvm=bv.58187178,d.cWc

Fullan, M. (2001). *Leading in a culture of change.* San Francisco, CA: Jossey-Bass.

Glaser, M. (2008). *Drawing is thinking.* New York, NY: Overlook Duckworth, Peter Mayer.

Goleman, D. (1985). *Vital lies, simple truths: The psychology of self-deception.* New York, NY: Simon & Schuster.

Goleman, D., Boyatzis, R., & McKee, A. (2002). *Primal leadership: realizing the power of emotional intelligence.* Boston, MA: Harvard Business School Press.

Jaworski, J., & Flowers, B. (1998). *Synchronicity: The inner path of leadership.* San Francisco, CA: Berrett-Koehler.

Lambert, L. (2009). Reconceptualising the road toward leadership capacity. In A. Blankstein, P. D. Houston, & R. W. Cole (Eds.), *Building sustainable leadership capacity* (pp. 7–28). Thousand Oaks, CA: Corwin.

Lambert, L., Walker, D., Zimmerman, D. P., Cooper, J. E., Lambert, M. D., Gardner, M. E., Szabo, M. (1995). *The constructivist leader.* New York, NY: Teachers College Press.

Senge, P. M. (1990a). *The fifth discipline: The art and practice of the learning organization.* New York, NY: Doubleday.

Wheatley, M. J. (1992). *Leadership and the new science.* San Francisco, CA: Berrett-Koehler.

11

Country

Editors' Introduction

Addis Ababa is the central, capital city in the country of Ethiopia that is itself becoming a crossroads for the African continent. When walking the three-mile road from the small airport to the Hilton hotel that was once the only luxury accommodation in town, you would now see block after block of land and buildings in every phase of construction interspersed with empty lots and tarp-covered homes. Quiet and welcoming coffee houses under shade trees are intermingled with shiny new office buildings and debris-strewn lots. Mules are guided alongside speeding cars and motorcycles. Many people are smiling, working hard, talking on cell phones, because this is a country that did not build a network of telephone poles in its recent phase of development: It built cell phone towers. In the far distance on the outskirts of Addis, a city of 8 million in a country of 88 million, beyond the largest medina in Africa taking up several square miles, the new outsized African Union skyscraper stands as an obelisk alone above the fray, as a symbol of and investment in Ethiopia, known for its coffee export in the present and as an ancient cradle of humankind.

Some years ago, the Ethiopian government, realizing that they needed to move as quickly in improving education as in communication infrastructure, mandated that the traditional structure of teachers lecturing to rows of 60 forward-facing students in each classroom had to change. Immediately. They instituted a policy for reorganizing classrooms into groups of five or six, with a single student in each group being the designated group leader. While this may strike some of us as a radical, undemocratic mandate from above, on reflection, it may be considered a well-advised, reasonable shift reflecting what we know about the impact of collaborative learning, the need for students to articulate their ideas verbally to others, and a necessary awakening to the realities of the demand for guiding students right now into the interdependent networking skill of the 21st-century, global marketplace. Ethiopia and other countries around the world do not have time or the resources to slowly make changes in education over the next several generations. In schools, there is very little paper, few books, minimal professional development for teachers, and in most homes a lack of nutritional support. Many students, in reality, need food for thought, as their brains, minds, and bodies come undernourished into classrooms.

This last chapter of the book may be read as a challenge to our ideals of Thinking Schools against the hard realities of life for children in a proud country with a rich heritage that is now one of the most impoverished places on Earth. Bob Price, a global trainer and a coauthor of Growing Thinking Schools from the Inside Out *(Thinking Schools International, 2011), and his colleague Bereket Aweke, a former teacher and principal in Ethiopia, have a story that they are growing together from grassroots to whole*

(Continued)

(Continued)

thinking schools. The story is unfolding at this writing, because the superintendent for the Addis Public School recently gave his full commitment to growing thinking in all 300 schools in the city.

This effort will only grow from the inside out because the true development of thinking abilities is something that cannot be forced, only facilitated and mediated. Bob and Bereket bring us a moving story, not a static one. From a western perspective, we may consider that "we" are bringing something to share with the people of Ethiopia, or Malaysia, or anywhere else for that matter. But the vision of Thinking Schools is that of a different order of change and global networking: not the first-order change of tinkering with the system, or the second-order change through which new models for teaching and learning are dropped into a system. Third-order change is an engagement through which active participation, learning, sharing, documentation, and research is, as Bob and Bereket suggest, bidirectional between "outsiders" and "insiders." People from within their own school and within their own complex histories—cultures, languages, and individual experiences—think and make change by envisioning and then planning their own journey, creating their own pathways for thinking.

THINKING SCHOOLS ETHIOPIA

Robert Seth Price and Bereket Aweke

Thinking Schools Ethiopia (www.thinkingschoolsethiopia.com) is a growing collaborative project, with the different pathways of Robert Price and Bereket Aweke coming together as common journey. These paths were begun 12,000 kilometers apart, yet now travel close together in ideas and ideals of educational thinking. Our story is unfolding as we write, a story emerging from an ancient, historic land and a country that pushes to consciously shape its own future through progressive, generational change in the beginning years of the 21st century.

There seems no time to lose in Ethiopia and in other rapidly developing countries around the world. This is also a story of educational change happening in an unlikely place (from the western world perspective), yet a powerful historical lesson and model in a time of transformational education change worldwide. Ultimately, as with the vision of Thinking Schools, it is an opportunity for multidirectional change as we have learned from each other and as countries such as the United States can learn from the experiences and exchange of ideas in Ethiopia.

■ THINKING AT A CROSSROADS

Robert Seth Price's Frame of Reference

In 2009, in the United States of America, my life partner Helen and I moved to the self-titled "crossroads" city of Indianapolis. This metaphor of *crossroads* is reflective of my evolution of thinking, learning, and changes with life, with my educational collaborations and evolving frame of reference.

After a very long and meaningful process and shortly after moving to Indianapolis, Helen and I traveled to Ethiopia to meet and bring home our two adopted children. It was meaningful for all the obvious reasons, but because I am an educator who has worked extensively for underserved, under-resourced students in urban schools, the adoption of Ethiopian children from a socioeconomically poor region of the world is itself deeply moving for me. We now have a multiethnic family, a "world" family.

I have always used and experimented with a range of technologies, especially the use by students of photography and video. The final phase of the actual adoption process was of course charged with emotion knowing that the transitional time in Ethiopia of bringing home a sister and brother was as powerful as giving birth. Thankfully then, just as many new parents take photos and video of the arriving child, our chosen adoption agency, Children's Home Academy, required that we stay in the village for a full week as we came to know our new family members and the community from which they came. They also videotaped the interactions during the week, edited the moving pictures, and delivered to us and our children a video record for future reference and reflection. Our children would know the place and time from where they came.

At this time in my life, I had recently decided to build on my wide-ranging and deep experiences collaborating with the National Urban Alliance (NUA), an organization that is based on the practice of a "pedagogy of confidence." As defined by Yvette Jackson (2012), NUA draws from a belief that all children and youth, when provided High Operational Practices, inspire and develop High Intellectual Performance within the frames of cognition, language, and culture. My initial travels to Ethiopia also coincided with my increasing involvement with Thinking Foundation and later Thinking Schools International (TSI), both organizations grounded in research and motivated by a belief that thinking approaches are a central foundation for change and balance in the educational experiences of students.

Bereket Aweke's Frame of Reference

In Ethiopia, during the first decade of the 21st century, I was a recent graduate of Addis Ababa University. I was born into a family of six to parents who had minimal education but were understanding and progressive about the importance of being responsible, open minded, and respectful. Above all, they conveyed a belief in a freedom to pursue one's passion. A sixth-grade teacher of mine sparked the ideal of intelligence and motivation that led to my success with the high school exit exams, opening the way to the university. After graduating from Addis Ababa University with a degree in biology, I discovered the available jobs were mostly in teaching. My second job was with Children's Home Academy school and adoption agency in 2009. This coincided with Robert Price's second trip to Ethiopia to facilitate a week-long professional development with 80 educators on thinking methodologies. It was at this week-long hands-on workshop we first met.

The initial meeting of Robert, Bereket, and Asnake Amanuel (director of Children's Home Society and Family Services Ethiopia) was the seed of change for both personal and collaborative growth, our own individual stories and backgrounds being a sum greater than the parts. I thought to myself that perhaps a revolution of educational practices with "growing thinking schools from the inside out" would be a catalyst that would be transformational in design, elevating the capacity of the people of Ethiopia.

■ ETHIOPIA'S HISTORICAL FRAME OF REFERENCE

It is important to have a context for Ethiopia to understand the potential that is before us and the people across the country.

We share this brief history as a frame of reference for the grassroots element of our learning, and for further understanding the highly collaborative relationship we have been developing as friends and colleagues.

Ethiopia has been an independent nation since ancient times, being one of the oldest countries in the world, while most African nations in their modern form are less than a century old. A monarchy for most of its history, the Ethiopian dynasty traces its roots to the 10th century BCE. Besides being an ancient country, Ethiopia is one of the oldest sites of human existence known to scientists today. Having yielded some of humanity's oldest traces, it is most likely the place from where *Homo sapiens* first set out for the Middle East and points beyond.

Ethiopia is now the 2nd most populous nation in Africa (and 13th largest in the world) with over 90 million people and the 10th largest by area. The capital is Addis Ababa. Ethiopia is bordered by Eritrea to the north,

| **Figure 11.1** Map of Africa |

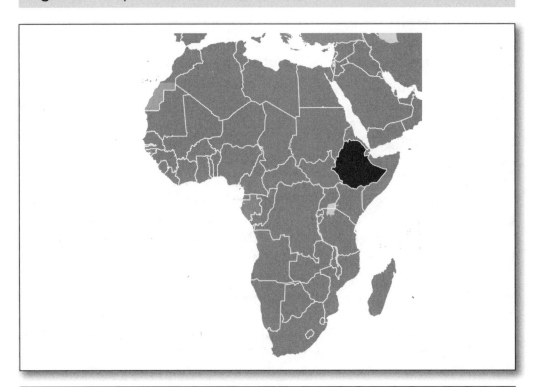

Source: Cartographic Division of the United Nations.

Figure 11.2 Map of Ethiopia

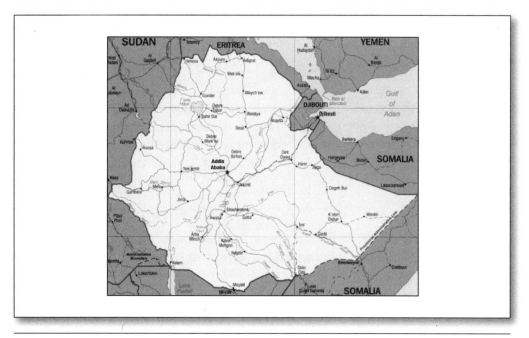

Source: Cartographic Division of the United Nations.

South Sudan to the west, Djibouti and Somalia to the east, and Kenya to the south.

Ethiopia is one of a few African countries to have its own alphabet, in addition to its own time system and unique calendar, 7 to 8 years separating it from the Gregorian calendar. It has the largest number of UNESCO World Heritage Sites in Africa, with high-quality coffee beans being one of its top exports.

When Africa was divided up by European powers at the Berlin Conference, Ethiopia was one of only two countries that retained its independence. It was one of only four African members of the League of Nations. After a brief period of Italian occupation, Ethiopia became a charter member of the United Nations. When other African nations received their independence following World War II, many of them adopted the three bold colors of Ethiopia's flag. Green recalls the land and hope for the future, yellow stands for peace and love, and red is symbolic of strength. The capital Addis Ababa has become the location of several international organizations focused on Africa. Ethiopia is one of the founding members of the Non-Aligned Movement (NAM), G-77 and the Organization of African Unity (OAU). Today, Addis Ababa is still the headquarters of the African Union, the Nile Basin Commission, and UNECA.

Education in Ethiopia had been dominated by the Ethiopian Orthodox Church for many centuries until secular education was adopted in the early 1900s. Prior to 1974, Ethiopia had an estimated illiteracy rate well above 90% and compared poorly with the rest of Africa in the funding of schools and universities. After the 1974 revolution, emphasis was placed on increasing literacy in rural areas. Practical subjects were stressed, as was the teaching of socialism. Education received roughly 13% of the national budget in 1992. By 1995, the rate of illiteracy had dropped substantially to 64.5%. Projected adult illiteracy rates for the year 2000 stood even lower at 61.3% (males, 56.1%; females, 66.6%). As of 1999, public expenditure on education was estimated at 4.3% of GDP (Teferra & Altbach, 2003).

The current system follows very similar school expansion schemes to the rural areas as the previous 1980s system with an addition of deeper renationalization providing rural education in their own languages starting at the elementary level. The sequence of general education in Ethiopia is 6 years of primary school, 4 years of lower secondary school, and 2 years of higher secondary school, yet Ethiopia has the seventh lowest literacy rate in the world in global country rankings.

The first Growing Thinking Schools Ethiopia workshops Robert led coincided with a phase of development by the Ethiopian government's dramatically increased focus on improving access to education. Approximately three million pupils were in primary school in the 1994–1995 school year. By 2008–2009, primary enrollment had risen to 15.5 million—an increase of over 500%. Progress had been enabled through a sustained government-led effort to reduce poverty and expand the public education system equitably. This had been backed by substantial increases in national education expenditure and aid to the sector, as well as improved planning and implementation capacity at all levels. Increased regional and local autonomy and community participation have also had a key role in expanding access to education across the country. Further development included a focus on creating a learner-centered environment. The latter often prompted participants to ask me: What does a learner-centered environment "look like"? They had mostly experienced a lecture (chalk and talk) structure that had been their norm. From the perception of UNESCO Program Director for Ethiopia, Dr. Awol Endris, the first workshops on Thinking Schools were not about incrementally improving skill development, but a change in mindsets:

> I would like to see this continue in some form . . . this was a complete success . . . to have on an ongoing basis . . . for public school teachers . . . that would assist the whole education system in the country because this was a workshop about changing minds . . . acquiring a new set of beliefs about what education is all about. (http://blog.thinking-schoolsethiopia.com/?p=658)

The excitement and positive embrace of the initial six starting points for the Thinking Schools approach as described in Chapter 1 (e.g., reflective questioning, collaborative learning, visual mapping, structuring environment, collegial coaching, community building, etc.) were identified outcomes of fully participating in methods that participants were certainly aware of, but few had exposure to these strategies in practice. Also, these methods were being offered within a whole-school vision of Thinking Schools, grounded as it is in transformational, dialogical, participatory approaches that were the center of our workshops.

MULTIDIRECTIONAL DEVELOPMENT ■

Some of the early results of the Thinking Schools Ethiopia approach offers an "outside-the-box" view of change that might catalyze change with other nations caught "inside the box" of educational traditions that have become calcified. This is because the design is framed by the idea of collaborative development. What does this mean? International development conventionally involves first-world "developed" countries extending various forms of support to third-world countries in a unilateral relationship. Aid in the way of financial funding, scientific, and intellectual innovations often flow in one direction only, as if peoples with different cultures and who simply have less industrial and/or scientific development do not have insights into human development. Resources and capacity in development are understood within existing structures as being only in the hands of industrialized nations. Human capacity for innovation and other human resources are often overlooked or devalued.

A model of "multidirectional collaborative development" shifts this assumption and belief system to one where all participants recognize their own capacity for aiding others. Expertise is surfaced, shared, translated, and adapted to other contexts for each partner to use as they determine what is appropriate. Examples might be in environmental protection, education, agricultural sustainability, nutrition, and leadership. If the "world is flat" as Thomas Friedman (2005) has proposed, perhaps the potential of real systems change and innovation might evolve in a seemingly unlikely place (or in reality, likely) as Ethiopia if there is a two-way, leveled collaboration.

An essential dimension of the Thinking Schools approach in Ethiopia and in projects in other parts of the world, such as the country-wide implementation in Malaysia as described in Chapter 1 by David N. Hyerle, is the effort to network different projects and thus gain not only multidirectional development but also multidirectional knowledge creation and development. Given its history of independence and successful commitment to raising literacy levels, perhaps Ethiopia is an ideal place to begin such an ambitious effort. (UNESCO IICBA, 2012)

2009: FIRST SEEDS ■

The multiple years of collaborative development from 2009 to 2013 that we summarize here show how first seeds grew toward maturity. The very first visit to Ethiopia by Robert, during his trip for adopting his children, included a visit back to a school and medical facility started by Children's Home Society and Family Services adoption organization in Ethiopia. After leaving Ethiopia, e-mails and sporadic phone calls were exchanged and Skype connections were made, which led to arranging professional development for the school's entire staff at their school. Beyond that, no information had been provided regarding the expected number of participants. Bereket Aweke was one of the newly hired school staff, along with Atsede Tsehaye who now continues her role with the Thinking Schools Ethiopia team.

Robert's Frame of Reference

Over 80 Ethiopian educators worked in a highly collaborative way with me during this 5-day training in Addis Ababa, Ethiopia in August, 2009. Attendees included educators from five different schools, a local government official, several parents, and the UNESCO program director whom I met on his previous visit. It was as much an education about potential as it was a growth of ideas and ideals for the participants. The initial elements of the workshop on Monday morning set the stage for our collaboration and me being drawn to and embracing the high interest by participants. The training began with community building exercises (e.g., commonalities) for us to learn about one another while concurrently building a collaborative spirit. Commonalities processes has the group in a circle, then one person shares a personal interest or experience followed by all those who have a similar interest or experience crossing the circle.

The participants quickly internalized the process and purpose (intentionality) with the whole group. We then divided into four smaller groups to practice and expand on the different community building exercises I had modeled for them, which they did with ease. I have led many extensive professional development initiatives, including here in Indianapolis and urban school districts across the United States, yet there was an unprecedented level of interest and engagement when practicing collaboratively. The participants were serious and collaborative while having a delightful time. Over time, I came to feel this cultural distinction: Ethiopians, by and large, seemed attuned to collaboration, unlike my experiences with the same activities in United States schools. This was my first inkling in this situation of the power of learning while sharing within another cultural context. This continued with hands-on use of Thinking Maps as they began to learn and share one another's frames of reference, about themselves and about education.

The Circle Map and Frame supported them in exploring and sharing their personal history and perspectives. The participants better understood their own frame of references, realizing the importance and influence of prior knowledge, and the power of pedagogy driven by intentionality. This developed further throughout the week as we explored together through dialogue a learner-centered approach using reflective questioning (inquiry), visual mapping, collaborative learning methods, thinking skills, creative use of physical space (structuring the environment), and other foundational methods of pedagogy. The week-long training encompassed the elements that form the basic starting points for Thinking Schools as they begin to investigate broad areas of development. The six starting points of thinking that I modeled in an integrative and dialogical mode of inquiry were:

1. **Reflective Questioning** *high-quality questioning and listening skills*

2. **Thinking Skills** *explicit use of cognitive processes*

3. **Visual Mapping** *the use of visual tools to map out ideas*

4. **Collaborative Networking** *between us in pairs, groups, schools, and global networks that includes collaborative learning; collegial coaching; and regional and global collaborations*

5. **Developing Dispositions** *characteristics, dispositions, and habits of mind are engaged*

6. **Structuring Environment** *considering how the physical space is organized and resources used*

Each day's reflections by the participants, and the final thoughts by everyone in the circle, really left me considering what I had experienced and reassessing the implications of the work we were beginning *together*. While I had brought something from afar in the sense of starting points for Thinking Schools, the commonalities of these entry points resonated with participants across the week as if they were culturally relevant to begin with. We seemed to be sharing universal foundations for developing thinking in support of learning, and with the deepest respect, from different points of view.

With the belief that ideas and innovation happen everywhere, I found myself considering the stagnation of education in the United States sometimes bound by often rigid testing requirements and static quality of "remediated" students, many of whom drop out of school as they languish in remedial classrooms. I reflected on the potential—seemingly against equitable odds monetarily—of change happening in a country now moving my heart. Perhaps the "pedagogy of confidence" defined by Yvette Jackson can be framed in a historical context—figuratively and literally.

Bereket's Frame of Reference

A little before the start of the academic year, I was informed of a 1-week training by a professional from the United States. I clearly remember my first impression at the training: I thought, *It is a different type of training!* The training was full of activity, reflection, and demonstration. This pattern was new to a majority of the participants, and we all were dazzled. It did not take long before a few other teachers and I started to reflect and take the lead.

The training ended as it started, full of energy and excitement. For me, however, it was more than training, it was *a revelation*. I had been searching for a way to make my class interesting, active, and practical, and there I found it: Thinking Maps, community-building exercises, and powerful questioning techniques, were all great practical tools I could implement immediately in my classrooms with room for growth along each pathway toward a larger journey that was just coming into sight.

As trainer, Robert is an exceptional facilitator and educator. His passion for teaching and improved delivery has inspired me from that moment on. Everything he does on the training has meaning and application to my experience. He also did something foundational, instead of just leaving after the training, he tried to "seed" for sustainability (as he always does). He contacted me and all the trainees, searching for teachers to carry on his dream of improving quality education through the Thinking Schools approach.

I am a pragmatic person. The first thing I did was to try to see the background of the training and the research behind it. Luckily, there were a number of quality books Robert had brought with him for the school library, some donated, thankfully, by Thinking Maps, Inc. and Corwin Press in the United States. I was impressed to see that the training areas were all research-based and there were a number of successful Thinking Schools already in other parts of the world. The second question I had was "Is it viable to Ethiopia's context?"

It was!

The training had nothing to do with economic status or to a greater extent the resource availability. All it required was a paradigm shift in our thinking to use our minds and existing resources to deliver active, collaborative, and visually represented lessons. We didn't require a new computer, a new building, or a new high-priced curriculum program (though those are welcomed and needed).

Since all my preliminary questions were answered, I was motivated to apply the training to my lessons and saw an exponential improvement in students' activity, excitement, and creativity, all in a short period of time. My students enjoyed my class because of the collaboration among them. Applying the Thinking Maps decreased their note-taking time and created more time for reflection and discussions. The powerful questioning techniques helped increased participation and enthusiasm to learn. All in all, the 5-day training made me closer to what I had always been dreaming of—becoming an impactful teacher to my students.

■ 2010: THE SECOND PROFESSIONAL DEVELOPMENT VISIT—A GRASSROOTS VISION

The next training included two sets of multiple-day sessions: professional development training for whole schools and leadership training for both educator groups and NGOs in Addis Ababa. Bringing forth 21st-century thinking skills continued to be the main goal in addition to developing an understanding Thinking Schools within the context of the Ethiopian culture.

Robert's Frame of Reference

The more I collaborated with educators in Ethiopia and learned from my readings, the more I realized that often a focus is put on a physical building, statistical data, and even technologies, and less on the actual thinking methods that elevate our brain's abilities. However, the lack of "resources" in Ethiopia—at least in the context of material possessions—leads one to develop a "guided discovery" using the best tools available. This ultimately brings the "brain" and the "human element" into the realm of focus as the best tools available for thinking. This human element is an area that may bring a wealth of understanding out of Ethiopia and to other countries through our multidirectional efforts.

This visit also included a trip to Hossana, a rural part of Ethiopia, for a 2-day training with educators. The professional development sessions included demonstration lessons with "regular" class sizes of over 50 students. As in urban Addis Ababa, the participating educators embraced the Thinking Schools Ethiopia methods with excitement and commitment within the workshops. The students and educators readily and eagerly embraced the various methods of Thinking Schools as observed and practiced during the workshops and through their reflections during and at the conclusion of our collaborations. On my ride back to Addis Ababa, I reflected on how this could in fact be sustainable. I was not interested in merely "sprinkling" some good ideas and heading back to Indianapolis. I knew I was learning so much from these interactions. Going from the enthusiastic interest into deeply embedding educational change through practice, collaboration, and mastery takes commitment over time. And ultimately the workshops would best to be conducted in Amharic, especially regarding the participants' collaborations and reflections with each other. While many participants spoke English as their second language competently, it was clear from my observations that the limited materials and the deeper discussions would be best in their first language. This was especially true with educators from rural parts of Ethiopia.

Several teachers from Children's Home Academy continued to be part of all the sessions in both Addis Ababa and the trip to Hossana. While Thinking Schools Ethiopia had not yet developed a clear road map for the initiative, in hindsight the roots of an initiative were forming. Several key teachers from Children's Home Academy who would become instrumental in taking Thinking Schools Ethiopia forward as a thoughtful, sustainable initiative stepped forward. Bereket Aweke, Atsede Tsehaye, and Dagim Melese were some of the talented educators who inspired me with their youthful, idealistic spirits that sense the potential of an educational revolution. Their depth of thinking, their ability to work interdependently, and their openness as presenters, participants, and models of practice to share collaboratively enhanced the trainings. Every time they were requested to conduct a demonstration lesson at the workshop location or their classroom, be part of a collegial coaching model, and/or discuss their thoughts at coffee shop, they were superb collaborators in the true spirit of that word.

The collaborative spirit grassroots growth of Thinking Schools Ethiopia is also representative in Masresha Amanuel, the school chef who continues to be instrumental in workshop participants being fed well. His deep interest in the success of professional development goes beyond physical nourishment. His keen observations and assistance with his education colleagues in observations and reflective questions seem to model mindful and physical nourishment, which are equally important human nutrients.

2010: PROFESSIONAL DEVELOPMENT VISITS ■ THREE AND FOUR—ORGANICALLY GROWING

The Thinking Schools Ethiopia workshops continued, this time with participants predominantly from private schools during my next visits, as we were attempting to find starting points across different school communities. Concurrently we were seeking insights and inroads into collaborating with government public schools. This had been a primary goal from the beginning. The multiple-day workshops included more whole schools as well as leadership teams representing schools.

The project was unfolding naturally and seeming without end. Additionally, nongovernmental organizations (NGOs) with different purposes and processes became involved in the project. A professional team from an HIV/AIDS training organization signed up for and participated in five days of training after recognizing the thinking skills and methods training as effective for the organization's work with people in the field. One revelation that these community trainers realized is that while just "giving" information on HIV/AIDS or other health services is important in the short term, the long-term development of the thinking abilities inherent in the people with whom they worked was beneficial in the long run. This would lead toward a society based not on the quick fix, but the transformation of teaching and learning across every element of society. Ultimately, people make decisions every day about their actions and behaviors, so the idea of Thinking Schools is that citizens are reflecting on their decision-making process whether it is in the field of health, education, work, or financial literacy, and for starting entrepreneurial enterprises across any field.

What was becoming very clear was the high interest in the workshops, and the identified need by educators for a more systemic implementation of a Thinking Schools approach that was adaptable by the participants rather than disconnected workshops. Over time, school teams came to the workshops, but there was minimal follow-up. At this point, there was no formal infrastructure as well as minimal methods of efficient communication. Two Ministry of Education experts attended all three different sessions. Their participation and insights from an interview conducted in 2011, shared, in part, below, were additional, instrumental elements in the growth of Thinking Schools Ethiopia.

> This thinking process is a day to day activity with each individual [in all classrooms]. When applied in a government school, the people that come from different backgrounds will learn more. This training is very important to be practiced at all levels in government schools across the grades and all subjects. I suggest it is better to select a model school in different regions. In time these techniques will duplicate to all schools in the country.
>
> —Tilahun Teshome, Ethiopia Ministry of Education Expert Daniel Abebe, Ethiopia Ministry of Education Curriculum Designer

Several of the inspiring Children's Home Academy teachers, Bereket Aweke, Atsede Tsehaye, and Dagim Melese, then became more directly involved with the training. They took the lead in conducting demonstration lessons for teachers participating in the multiple-day professional development sessions, made presentations at the workshops, and began collegial coaching with other educators in classrooms. Near the end of the fourth visit, Bereket and Masresha Amanuel were able to secure a very important "formal paper" from a local government official for inviting local government schools. The formal paper was provided and delivered to government school officials near Children's Home Academy on a Friday. On the very next day, through grass-roots lines of communication rather than official announcements, *over 400 Ethiopian educators came to the workshop!*

We set it up into a "theater in the round" to provide a hands-on view and highly interactive demonstrations. This brought the total of Ethiopian educators who had participated in Thinking Schools workshops to well over 2,000 people. And this was not including any of the independent "renegade" workshops presented by previous attendees that were presented out of an immediate desire to share and transfer valuable insights and techniques. We only learned about these workshops after the fact. It was apparent that quality control regarding high-quality delivery and understanding of the content was quickly becoming very important, but what we also learned was that these ideas were not "foreign" to Ethiopian educators since they were so easily transferred and instrumental to those who felt need for new ways of engaging the minds of students.

Robert's Frame of Reference

The ideal of creating a sustainable change in practice continued to grow through the visits. A key element included appreciating and accessing "materials" that were naturally available. I often believe that in the United States we rely extensively on expensive "products" instead of a "guided practice" of using materials that are part of our lives. An example of modeling that practice was one session where the participants were provided handfuls of *dirt* to use in the development of an appropriate lesson (for different grades and disciplines) using thinking methods (e.g., visual mapping, reflective questioning, etc.) that were part of the training. The results were robust and varied—as much as the participants were—in a group that included pre-K teachers through university professors.

Parent involvement and interest also came into focus on these third and fourth visits when I held parent sessions to share more about Thinking Schools Ethiopia. Two of the hands-on sessions attracted approximately 40 parents each, and an additional session had over 100 parents in attendance. As the workshops began to expand, I invited Elizabeth Kesling, a very talented young educator from the United States, to work with me. Her background included collaboration in Senegal, the teaching of children with special needs, and experience with the Reggio Emilia approach to early childhood education. These two areas required deep mediation of thinking and a strong background in alternative, formative assessments. Additionally, I felt it was important to bring into the experience a current youth vision that corresponded with the evolving leadership of Thinking Schools Ethiopia—both to expand my frame of reference and, potentially, as a key role should Thinking Schools Ethiopia grow further.

The fourth visit also found Bereket quickly shifting into the new role as the principal of one of the schools, stepping into the role of leader and liaison in Ethiopia. His involvement in this project had the potential of becoming his main focus. This also filled the growing need for better communication, because the project blossomed to a point where e-mail and occasional phone calls were not enough. Bereket was provided ongoing funding (by Thinking Foundation and myself) for a wireless card Internet connection, at a high cost compared to places like the United States. We have found Skype and other new forms of communication to be essential tools playing an instrumental role in the current development of Thinking Schools Ethiopia.

Bereket's Frame of Reference

My involvement with Robert grew even deeper when I became a coordinator at Children's Home Academy. My new position also gave me the leverage of facilitating upcoming trainings within the school. We used Skype and e-mailed each other once or twice a week to discuss the developments and future plans. The new round of trainings were more significant to me because it involved more teachers and expanding to include neighboring private schools, NGO representatives, and local education officers. At the training, three teachers including myself took leading roles assisting Robert by demonstrating lessons in classrooms to the trainees. The feedback was great, and the motivation created through the demonstration carried me even further on the journey of cofounding Thinking Schools Ethiopia Program.

Here is what I found: *Change is difficult!* Even though the training was gaining a good reputation and regular trainings were carried out on an annual basis, the impact was minimal and fragmented because it was not systematically integrated into school systems. Moreover, focusing on fewer, mainly private schools would not bring the change we aspired for. At this point, I had deep thoughts on what my role should be on this endeavor and how this could grow to impact the many government public schools and private schools nationwide. Finally, I decided to propose to Robert and Thinking Foundation to set up the program "Thinking Schools Ethiopia" to independently work with private and government schools. My proposal got accepted, and I was granted money to start a blog, acquire Internet access, and obtain other equipment for documentation. We drew inspiration from feedback from participants, such as this selection that is representative of the positive response, especially the need to "scale up":

> The training is very good because it goes with the context of our country which has large class sizes . . .
>
> —Dade Girma, Addis Ababa Education Bureau Expert

> The training was so exceptional. Training is a means to do something so it can be scaled up. This implementation needs great commitment. The Minister of Education has already taken steps. The student grouping one to five (already in place) is the best way to coin this Thinking Schools approach. We have an opportunity . . . The teachers are the main actors of implementation.
>
> —Sheferaw Tgiorsis, Addis Ababa Education Bureau Expert

> Thinking School training's methodology is related to the teaching and learning process which helps students to understand things easily . . .
>
> —Fesehaye Nigusie, Addis Ababa Education Bureau Expert

We are being trained on methods to let the students exploit their potentials.

—Dade Girma, Addis Ababa Education Bureau Expert

With the groundswell rising and the obvious need for bringing a coherent plan together for scaling up and creating a sustainable impact on schools, teachers, students, and their parents, I knew I would have to shift to the next level of commitment.

2011: VISITS FIVE AND SIX—SHAPING THE VISION ■

What had started out through an organic beginning now was taking shape with a larger view. The idea of truly "growing thinking schools from the inside out" was now the focus. Constructing actual school buildings is important, but the transformative design of pedagogy within a building is key to transformational change. The timing also was apparent. A USAID report (funded by many international agencies) that had been recently published pointed toward the goal of a learner-centered environment as a mechanism of change with the Ethiopian education system (Asgedom, Desta, Dufera, & Leka, 2006).

Visit five included a 2-day training that included systematically using the *Growing Thinking Schools from the Inside Out* (www.thinkingschoolsinternational.com) facilitator's guide written by David N. Hyerle and Robert Price in collaboration with five other TSI global trainers from the United States and United Kingdom. This guide, as described in the first chapter of this book, is designed to create a formal structure for engaging participants in creating *their own design for change* in the context with leadership teams whether in government or private schools.

The more systematic experience and minimal materials provided the participants with a hands-on application of many Thinking Schools strategies within the context of them developing a systems approach plan for their school. By every measure, it was a success. Instead of being provided a prescribed method—one size fits all—the participants were using 21st-century thinking tools simultaneously to develop an understanding of these methods and to create the vision for their school as a team.

This is key: Participants used Thinking Maps, other visual tools, reflective questioning, collaborative structures, and enquiry methods for generating and organizing their ideas for defining a Thinking School. This was explicitly articulated to participants as the workshops began. We stated that one of our expectations was that they would evaluate many of the approaches as they were using them and begin thinking about which models and microstrategies would be best for their students. They were using the *Growing Thinking Schools* guide as a "travel guide" for their journey on educational change and success. While the plan was only the first step, it was significant in providing them with a "map" of where they could envision going.

During the week, we worked in government public schools, which included conducting demonstration lessons with students. The average class size in these schools is approximately 50 students who were structured in cooperative groupings. It is interesting to note that in 2008 the Ministry of Education had determined that, given the research, it was no longer a viable model for individual teachers to stand in front of rows of students and lecture. A radical, nationwide, comprehensive shift was mandated: Teachers would change the structure of the classroom environment from rows of children facing the teachers into cooperative groups of students facing each other. Each group was required to have a "clever" student to lead their group and respond to teachers for their respective group—most likely structured with "crowd control" in mind.

These formalized new structures for shifting from traditional straight rows of classrooms to table groups, of course, did not ensure that higher-level thinking skills happening in the groupings, or even that even rudimentary cooperative learning techniques were employed. At the same time, it was exciting for many to consider the next step: the potential of the students being physically in position for learning to occur at much higher levels of collaboration and thinking.

Our work offered an array of approaches that could elevate groups of student thinking together with common tools and strategies. Teachers in our workshops began modeling this brilliantly during lessons that included reflective questioning, collaborative learning methods, and visual mapping. The reflections of students and teachers after the lessons on the learning process, the "tools" used for learning, and their personal outcomes confirmed our observations of their interest and the effectiveness of scaffolding the thinking-skills approaches within a group structure. It was becoming apparent to us that the challenge would be to concurrently train the educators to "collaboratively learn" through collegial coaching that supported their development of insights while the students were quickly embracing thinking processes from their hands-on experiences.

By this point, with workshops growing in number and quality, several serendipitous occurrences opened the groundwork to working on a larger scale. Asnake Amanuel, the director of Children's Home Society and Family Services Ethiopia, decided to leave the organization he started to found a new organization to further realize his visions—creating the social entrepreneur organization, Eminence Social Entrepreneurs, in Addis Ababa. It was agreed on that Thinking Schools Ethiopia would become a part of Eminence, providing potential logistical support. (For a clear definition and process for developing and supporting "social entrepreneurs," visit www.ashoka.org.)

Concurrently, we arranged a visit with the Head of Addis Ababa Bureau of Education (AABE). Meetings in Ethiopia often happen at the moment of availability, and this was no different. We met with Dr. Dilamo Otore Ferenje, the Head (superintendent) of the AABE during Robert's fifth visit. It was clear from our discussions that Dilamo was attracted to the Thinking Schools approach and the potential for it to be integrated within Addis Ababa government schools. He requested a proposal. The proposal threaded the next step—both a revision and a presentation by Bereket to several experts from the AABE who had been selected by Dilamo. This presentation led to a request for government experts to be part of a training and to fully evaluate the approach. Below are some of the reflections and understanding of the implications of this work that continued to propel us forward toward a wider expansion of Thinking Schools Ethiopia:

> If we start this thinking skills from early childhood when they are really expert in those skills . . . we'll have a different kind of generation, a generation—a generation who really takes and solves problems . . .
>
> —Ermias Sebsibe, School of Nations Executive Team

> Growing Thinking Schools is concerned in transforming schools from traditional methodology to a methodology which involves the thinking process . . . In your implementation design you have collaborative networks where we should meet, talk and share.
>
> —Atsede Tsehaye, Thinking Schools Ethiopia

These experiences and feedback led to an agreement with the Bureau of Education of Government Schools of Addis Ababa to begin a formal pilot for 30 schools, with the expectations and announcement of scaling up to the whole-school system of 300+ schools within a year. Additionally, a small number of rural government schools in close proximity to Addis Ababa were in the plan to become part of the Thinking Schools Ethiopia initiative. Dilamo Otore Ferenje, the superintendent of all Addis Ababa public schools, announced the short-term plan and the long-term vision:

> This training is a pilot project (late 2012 training with AAEB expert team), next we'll go to schools (2013). We will train teachers and principals. Gradually the program will be at a national level. Let alone your job or other businesses, the Thinking Schools approach and methods helps even in our day to day life . . .

Essential to this design is the collaborative training of additional master Ethiopian facilitators to build the capacity of Thinking Schools Ethiopia/Eminence with a goal to achieve and sustain the scale it has envisioned for this project.

2013: THE FUTURE UNFOLDING ■

In addition to regular professional development for whole schools with Thinking Schools, there are a number of concurrent developments that are the epicenter for large-scale change:

- the Addis Ababa Education Bureau, which governs over 300 large government schools in the Ethiopian capital, recently had its expert team trained by Robert Price and the Thinking Schools Ethiopia team. The next step in implementing "Growing Thinking Schools" is with all 300 Addis Ababa Education Bureau schools. Initially the leadership teams will participate in the same *Growing Thinking Schools from the Inside Out* training, then implementing the approach with their whole school collaborating with Thinking Schools Ethiopia.

- regular ongoing professional development with private schools
- collaborations with NGOs who have a keen interest in education, multiple region-wide rural projects, and a variety of education organizations
- continuing translation of training guides into local native dialects
- continuing use of video for documentation, reflection, and blended training
- UNESCO's written endorsement of Thinking Schools Ethiopia as progressive modern education practices
- revision and a second edition translation of the guides into Amharic

Of course, too often professional development in most places around the world becomes reduced to a dry presentation of a plethora of strategies to teachers—like seeds thrown in the wind—that are then "tried out" without being aligned with an articulated foundation of core values and beliefs—and a vision. With this project growing from the ground up, we have been planting the seeds together. All too often, many programs are started without an integrative approach, with many of the participants never attaining a mastery level of any of the elements—a mile wide and an inch deep. A goal of TSI is to assist schools in explicitly surfacing the background beliefs held by participants and then codesigning a thinking school environment reflecting the needs of their school. Additionally, important components of the initiative include documentation, action research, assessment, and sharing across the global network of Thinking Schools as part of multidirectional development cross culturally.

During the past year, Thinking Schools Ethiopia continues to build capacity and structure toward a vision of a significant educational evolution, if not revolution in thinking. It is change that builds on evolutionary, historical roots of humankind in Ethiopia. What separates humans from other forms of life is our evolved capacities to not just think and respond, but to *think about our thinking* and problem solve at very high levels of sophistication. So it is the ideal of Thinking Schools to focus on the development and enrichment of our reflective, collaborative abilities for the betterment of our world.

The ideals of the Thinking Schools initiatives having begun in different places around the world, based on these broad areas of belief, focusing our forward vision toward the immediate academic needs and long-term sustainability of a process of growing thinking in a new generation of students and educators. This vision has been confidently embodied by many educators across Ethiopia and well represented by Dagim Melese, an educator in Addis Ababa:

The most fundamental cultural shift is acknowledging the importance of Ethiopian minds in terms of creating knowledge, habits and practices of airing views and ideas as regards academic contents by students. The recognition of the actual values are among the important things that are conceived, at least by me, for sustainable change to be established in Ethiopian schools to embrace the most powerful ideals of the Thinking Schools Ethiopia projects.

Thinking Schools Ethiopia is evolving, growing, and unfolding as we write these words. An example of the impact of Thinking Schools while transitioning to a larger scale is the current collaboration with Bikolos Nur Academy, a school in Addis Ababa with 700 students and 54 teachers. Recently, in March 2013, the whole staff of Bikolos Nur participated in 4 days of Thinking Schools training including the use of Thinking Maps and Reflective Questioning. The following student and teacher reflections provide an insight to the immediate and potential impact of the Thinking Schools Ethiopia approach. These reflections, 1 month into implementing Thinking Schools approach including Thinking Maps with the whole school, are similar to reflections heard since the first workshops. But the reflections reveal a more evolved manner of understanding consistent with the Thinking Schools Ethiopia initiative as it continues to evolve, grow, and unfold itself.

> I really think that Thinking maps make a big difference in my life because before I really didn't read my books much because it takes too much time to understand. Now I am interested to open my exercise books making Thinking Maps to actually study and know what I am reading. We can be independent and learn by ourselves, because Thinking Maps are our teachers. They make everything easy so that we can read and remember—it makes you visualize things. Thinking Maps capture our thinking in our mind.
>
> —Hannan Abdulfetah, Grade 9 Student

> Thinking Maps have helped me a lot in studying. Next year I am taking [the] national exam. I am preparing my summaries using Thinking Maps because it is taking a shorter time with Thinking Maps. It is more effective because by looking at the circles and the other maps, I can remember what is inside and that makes it easier for me to study.
>
> —Abdurahemen Kassim, Grade 9 Student

> We are using the maps very effectively and the class is now more student centered with everybody participating. The eight Thinking Maps are so helpful because we can do our work easily—for example our book is a huge book so it is tiresome and consumes much time. But you can use a piece of paper and draw maps and easily analyze the things about the subject in few minutes. When we do Thinking Maps in group work everybody is participating, so it is going to be fun and interesting.
>
> —Hussien Abdulnessir, Grade 9 Student

> Thinking Maps are very easy to use and to remember. Before when we work in groups there was not much argument but now we can easily visualize things and remember what you see in pictures in the mind.

These maps are like pictures and have different designs and [are] very easy to remember.

—Sabontu Ali, Grade 9 Student

I really want to thank the thinkers who give us Thinking Maps and make us think to ourselves and for our students. Thinking Maps are very helpful. I have spent many years teaching chemistry and I have been trying many methods to visualize chemistry to students. The Thinking Maps made everything clear in these first 2–3 weeks after the training.

—Adefres Zerihun, Vice Director and Chemistry Teacher

Thinking Maps makes our life easier and help us impart lessons which were difficult to comprehend. The students have accepted Thinking Maps in a very special way and related to the maps. I hope the Thinking Maps will go on so that we can give them what they deserve and we can get from you what we deserve.

—Huda Seid, Vice Director and English Teacher

Starting with the Thinking Schools training, I understood that the training and the Thinking Maps is participatory. We were at the training on a Friday and started implementing Thinking Maps on Monday. The training has helped me a lot because before I had hard time delivering my subject to my students. But after learning the Thinking Maps and introducing the eight Thinking Maps to my students, my subject is understood more easily. We are always told about student centered teaching but it is with Thinking Maps I could involve all types of learners in my class. This is also the policy of our country and if we regularly implement them and get reference materials, we can even do better. Both the staff and the students have loved it and we thank you.

—Mohammed Awol, Social sciences Teacher

I have used all the Thinking Maps except the Bridge Map in my grade 3 lessons. I am very excited. My students love the Thinking Maps and are internalizing the maps. The Thinking Maps are helping us to identify the level of the students. For example, some students remain in the circle map and others apply the other maps achieving higher order thinking in Blooms Taxonomy. So generally I am very happy as the Thinking Maps assist us in effective teaching methodology and students. Recent result have shown slight increment of growth from last quarter over a period of three weeks.

—Usman Mohammed, Grade 3 Science Teacher

Thinking Schools Ethiopia is very interesting starting from the training. The Thinking Maps make our minds visualize information. In this short time students are referring to and using the Thinking Maps more than the previous methods. All students are more active than the previously because they can easily understand the topics and remember what they are learning.

—Zewdu Hailu, Vice Director and Physics Teacher

As good friends and colleagues who have grown together, we are now on a journey together with others on the team and continuing to build the potential toward a common vision, in the context at hand, and with collaborative processes. It is a journey that keenly sharpens our dispositions, expanding insightful collaborations, literally and figuratively mapping paths (sometimes inside and sometimes outside the box) while continually looking forward to the next steps. It is a story of growing together as educators with a common passion for nurturing the capacities within every child.

Helen and I continue to learn from the two young Ethiopian children we adopted, who are now growing up and going to public school in Indianapolis. They have adapted as they dance and swim and learn in a new culture, propelled by the common human capacities to think, question, and inquire deeply, while reflecting and engaging in the world around them with open minds and hearts.

QUESTIONS FOR ENQUIRY

In support of the project Price and Bereket led in Addis Ababa, UNESCO Program Director Dr. Awol Endris was quoted in this chapter as crediting its impact to the idea that "this was a workshop about changing minds...acquiring a new set of beliefs about what education is all about." Coauthor Bereket himself stated that "all it required was a paradigm shift in our thinking..." Ernst made similar observations in Chapter 9, as did Dellamora in Chapter 2 and Hyerle in Chapter 1. Changing individual or collective mindsets is not an easy thing to accomplish. Having read other chapters in this book about developing "thinking schools," what are some of the key approaches that were used that made it possible for such fundamental and necessary shifts in beliefs about teaching and learning, teachers and learners, to occur? What other approaches would you recommend?

One of Bereket's key insights regarding how to maximize the impact of the work being conducted in Ethiopia was the need for systemic change. In the early stages of this process, he observed that, despite several trainings in which people were highly engaged, "... the impact was minimal and fragmented as it was not systematically integrated into school systems." As you reflect back on the chapters in this book, including the one you just completed, what were some effective strategies for whole-school change that might be applicable to your setting?

How did the designs of the various training sessions influence how participants viewed the work and the challenges and/or opportunities before them? As you think back over the multiple sessions that were conducted in this project, how might you characterize the central purpose of each stage in the process?

During the "Open Education" movement in the United States, many school districts built new school buildings without internal walls dividing classrooms. Many of those efforts failed or were as ineffective as the Ethiopian government's belief that simply requiring teachers to no

(Continued)

(Continued)

longer "stand and deliver" would automatically ensure a change in pedagogy and result in improved learning for students. And yet existing structures, unless changed or simply challenged, can remain impediments to the change that is truly needed. What are some of the other conventions related to education today that would be worthwhile calling into question and why? To borrow from Maxine Greene, how might you imagine education, "as if it could be otherwise," to better serve our students and world today?

■ REFERENCES AND FURTHER READINGS

Asgedom, A., Desta, D., Dufera, D., & Leka, W. (2006, August). *Ethiopia pilot study of teacher professional development. Quality in education, teaching, and learning: Perceptions and practice.* Retrieved from http://pdf.usaid.gov/pdf_docs/PNADH771.pdf

Friedman, T. (2005). *The world is flat. A brief history of the twenty-first century.* New York, NY: Farrar, Straus & Giroux.

Jackson, Y. (2011). *The Pedagogy of confidence: Inspiring high performance in urban schools.* New York, NY: Teachers College Press.

Teferra, D., & Altbach, P. G. (Eds.). (2003). *African higher education: An international reference handbook.* Bloomington: Indiana University Press. Retrieved from http://en.wikipedia.org/wiki/Education_in_Ethiopia

Thinking Schools International. (2011). *Growing Thinking Schools from the inside out.* Retrieved from www.thinkingschoolsinternational.com

UNESCO IICBA—Ethiopia statistics: World Fact Book 2012 and Ethiopia online Wiki. www.unesco-iicba.org

UNESCO. (n.d.). In *Wikipedia.* Retrieved 2013 from http://en.wikipedia.org/wiki/UNESCO

Appendix

Report on the Evaluation of the Impact of the Thinking School Approach

A report carried out by Thinking Schools International and the University of Exeter evaluating the impact of the Thinking School Approach

Produced by Martin Bell, September 2012

Background: The "Thinking School Approach" is defined by Emeritus Professor Bob Burden as *"an educational community in which all members share a common commitment to giving regular careful thought to everything that takes place. This will involve both students and staff learning how to think reflectively, critically and creatively, and to employing these skills and techniques in the co-construction of a meaningful curriculum and associated activities. Successful outcomes will be reflected in students across a wide range of abilities demonstrating independent and co-operative learning skills, high levels of achievement and both enjoyment and satisfaction in learning...."* (Burden, 2006). Since 2005, 55 schools in the UK have gained Thinking School accreditation from the University of Exeter by adopting a **whole school approach** to the teaching of thinking, embedding thinking in the heart of the school and its curriculum. A further hundred-plus schools in the UK have joined the Thinking Schools network, often facilitated and trained by consultants from Thinking Schools International. In most cases, the journey to accreditation has taken at least three years to achieve. In September 2012, the University of Exeter and Thinking Schools International jointly funded a survey to evaluate the impact of the Thinking School approach, as adopted by these Thinking Schools. This is a preliminary survey, identifying areas for further research and evaluation.

The survey focused on five key areas:

- Satisfaction with the Thinking School approach (whole school) by accredited schools
- Attainment
- Thinking Schools International Strategies adopted by Thinking Schools (i.e., Thinking Maps, Habits of Mind, Philosophy for Children)
- Evaluation Methods of the Thinking School approach
- Major benefit and issues of the Thinking School approach

Summary of Key Findings:

- 100% of primary and 87.5% of secondary accredited schools are satisfied with the whole school Thinking School approach; none are dissatisfied.
- 90% of all accredited schools reported an improvement in the quality of lessons; none have seen lesson quality adversely affected.
- 89% state that the Thinking School approach raises attainment; Only one school stated attainment wasn't raised, but neither did it drop.
- All five major Thinking School International programmes are reported to be highly effective.
- 82% of accredited schools would welcome more support with their evaluation methods.
- Benefits greatly outweigh issues

229

2

Report on the Evaluation of the Impact of the Thinking School Approach

Introduction

Initially there will be an outline of the following:

1. The purposes of the evaluation project
2. The leaders invited to participate
3. The focus of the report

Then the main findings of the report will be summarised before expanding on each of the survey areas, supported by data and leader feedback.

1. Purposes of the evaluation project

The evaluation project was jointly funded by the University of Exeter and Thinking Schools International. The purposes of the project were to:

- Report on the impact of the Thinking School approach as defined by Professor Burden and outlined on the TSI website
- To consider the benefits and weaknesses of the approach and to recommend further exploration of ways forward to make improvements
- To consider the effectiveness of the various thinking and learning strategies
- To gather feedback and make recommendations regarding the evaluation and measurement of the impact of cognitive education
- To specifically look at the use and the impact of MALS (Myself as a Learner Scale) on Thinking Schools

2. The leaders invited to participate

The main focus of the project was an online survey. The schools invited to participate and their response is as follows:

➢ Schools accredited by the University of Exeter as a Thinking School or an Advanced Thinking School: 49 were sent the survey; 27 replies were received.

➢ Non-accredited schools that had received at least one full training session from Thinking Schools International: 105 were sent the survey; 35 replies were received.

➢ Additionally, 5 of the thinking leaders at accredited schools were interviewed for further feedback. Quotations are from interviews and comments made on the survey.

3. The focus of the report

This preliminary report focuses on the information gathered from the schools accredited by the University of Exeter. These schools have shown a commitment to the Thinking School approach over time, and their practice has been positively evaluated by the assessors from the University of Exeter. A total of 26 surveys were submitted by accredited schools, though 4 did not answer all the questions. The survey was

Report on the Evaluation of the Impact of the Thinking School Approach, September 2013

3

completed anonymously, and the survey brief suggested that thinking leaders should consult colleagues regarding answers. The minimum time to complete the survey would have been 30 minutes but with consultation would have take considerably longer.

Summary of Key Findings

- 100% of primary and 87.5% of secondary accredited schools are satisfied with the Thinking School approach; none are dissatisfied.
- 90% of all accredited schools reported an improvement in the quality of lessons; none have seen lesson quality adversely affected.
- 89% state that the Thinking School approach raises attainment; 3.5% state that it does not raise attainment.
- 96% used lesson observations as one of the factors when making their judgement on attainment.
- All five major Thinking School International programmes are reported to be highly effective.
- 82% of accredited schools would welcome more support with their evaluation methods.
- Benefits greatly outweigh issues:
    - ○ Common major benefits include the whole school approach, independence and learner ownership, lesson quality
    - ○ There are some sustainability issues for some, for example the training of new staff.

The Survey – Key Areas

A. Satisfaction with the Thinking School approach

The first table shows the levels of satisfaction of accredited schools with the Thinking School approach. Each school was asked to give a score from 1 being very high, to 5 being very low.

Table 1: Levels of satisfaction with the Thinking School Approach

High   Low

	1	2	3	4	5
Accredited primary	64%	35%	0	0	0
Accredited secondary	75%	12.5%	12.5% (1 school)	0	0
All accredited schools	68%	27%	4.5% (1 school)	0	0

22 accredited schools completed this question: 15 were highly satisfied and 6 reported good levels of satisfaction. This very positive endorsement is reflected in the long-term commitment these schools have made to the Thinking School approach. Only one school, a secondary, was neither satisfied nor dissatisfied and no reason was given. All of the accredited schools declared they had adopted a whole school approach to the teaching of thinking.

"You've got to jump in with two feet, it's got to be a whole school approach, otherwise it won't work," Patrick Affley, Headteacher, Christ the King Primary, Cardiff.

In Table 2 schools were asked to elaborate on their decision regarding levels of satisfaction in Table 1, by giving a score from 1 to 5 on given aspects of the school that had been positively affected by the Thinking

4

School approach. A score of 1 can be considered very good and 2 good. The separate primary and secondary figures show the number of schools at each level. The figures on the right for all accredited schools are in percentages. The results here explain why there is such a high level of satisfaction with the approach.

Certain of the aspects in table 2 relate to the "Six Starting Points" of the TSI programme "Growing Thinking Schools Guide." For example, consider the following positive results: Pupil Involvement 96.5% and Collaborative Learning 81.5% - Collaborative Learning starting point; Questioning Skills of Teacher 86.5%, Questioning Skills of Learners 86%, Reflection on Learning 90.5% - Reflective Questioning starting point. All of these eleven aspects are very positively endorsed.

Table 2: To What Extent Have the Following Aspects Been Positively Affected by the Thinking School Approach in Accredited Schools?

1 High to 5 Low	Prim High				Low	Sec High				Low	All High %	%	%	%	Low %
	1	2	3	4	5	1	2	3	4	5	1	2	3	4	5
Pupil Self-confidence	5	7	1	0	0	3	3	2	0	0	38	47.6	14	0	0
Pupil involvement	8	6	0	0	0	1	6	1	0	0	41	54.5	4.5	0	0
Behaviour and respect	3	4	4	3	0	1	3	1	2	0	19	33	20	24	0
Quality of lessons	4	8	1	0	0	4	3	1	0	0	38	52	9.5	0	0
Teacher morale and motivation	2	10	2	0	0	0	6	1	1	0	9	73	13.6	4.5	0
Teacher initiative	4	8	2	0	0	0	6	1	1	0	18	63.5	13.6	4.5	0
Collaborative learning	9	3	2	0	0	1	5	2	0	0	45.5	36	18	0	0
Creative thinking/ learning	4	5	1	0	0	3	4	1	0	0	39	50	11	0	0
Questioning skills - teacher	8	4	2	0	0	4	3	0	1	0	54.5	32	9	4.5	0
Questioning skills - learner	5	8	1	0	0	1	5	1	1	0	27	59	9	4.5	0
Reflection on Learning	7	7	0	0	0	1	5	2	0	0	36	54.5	9	0	0

Clearly in order to interpret individual school results, more information is needed. However, having the results from over 20 school communities does give credence to general trends across a range of schools. In Table 2 we see very positive results affecting the quality of teaching and learning for both pupils and teachers. The one exception is "Behaviour and Respect", with 42% positive and 24% negative in this aspect this is an area for further investigation. One school experiencing positive benefits on behaviour is Monnow Primary near Newport in South Wales.

5

"Behaviour and attitudes to learning have improved considerably," reported Meryl Echeverry, Headteacher.

What is happening at Monnow and in the 42% of schools that others can learn from? This result for "Behaviour and Respect" also does not equate with the high levels of satisfaction with Habits of Mind, Thinking Schools International major programme supporting dispositions development (see Table 11).

One may also identify from Table 2 the one secondary school that is currently struggling with the approach, hence the negative 4.5% score on several aspects.

Of particular note and significance are the very high scores for the positive effect on the following:

- Quality of Lessons - 90%
- Pupil Involvement - 95.5%
- Reflection on Learning - 90.5%
- Creative Learning & Thinking 89%

It is also noteworthy to see high scores in other aspects which indicate improvements and a shift in classroom practice such as Questioning (both for Teachers and Pupils), Collaborative Learning and Teacher Initiative.

"Teachers have increased their capacity and have become better equipped to provide lessons which challenge and stimulate children. They are constantly striving to improve their own practice and this has led to greater collaboration and shared practice," Carol Lawrenson, Headteacher, Spinney Avenue Primary, Widnes.

B. Attainment

The question of attainment and whether the Thinking School approach positively affects standards is extremely important for all stakeholders. The question is not an easy one to answer as many leaders pointed out: the Thinking School approach is just one of a range of strategies schools adopt to improve classroom learning standards. However, of the 26 accredited schools who answered this question, 23 were confident enough to say that the approach does raise standards. The full results are:

1) Yes, Thinking School raises attainment : 89%
2) No, Thinking School dos not raise attainment : 3.5%
3) Unable to answer : 7.5%

"It is incredibly difficult to link the development of thinking skills with the results achieved by students, having said that, GCSE results, A2 and IB results have all shown an upward trend over the five years we have been involved with the programme," Richard Coe, Assistant Headteacher, The Rochester Grammar School.

Paul Fleming, Thinking School leader at Sedgefield Community College in County Durham, reported the following improvements in his school which was accredited in 2012. *"School achieved 64% A*- C in summer 2010. School achieved 66% A*- C in summer 2011. School achieved 81% A*-C in summer 2012. We hope to ensure another increase in results in summer 2013."*

S.K. Tamber of Wood Green Academy in Wednesbury found a similar impact, *"Summer 2012 public examination results were our best ever. 83% of all Year 11 students achieved 5 or more GCSEs grades A*-C, 71% of Year 11 students achieved 5 or more GCSEs A*-C including English and Maths. (Last year's results 2011: 59% of all Year 11 students achieved 5 or more GCSEs A*-C including English and Maths.) In our*

6

recent Ofsted inspection 2012 we sustained our "Outstanding" status, achieving a Grade 1 in Teaching and Learning and all other categories."

A further anonymous survey submission had seen a sustained improvement over a longer period:
"Sept 2005 73% 5 A*-C GCSEs , 67% 5 A*-C including English and Maths. In the top 50% value added. Sept 2012 99% 5 A*-C GCSEs, 89% 5 A*-C including English and Maths. In the top 5% value added."

Primary school leaders also report a positive impact on SATs results: *"Attainment in SATs at the end of KS1 and KS2 has improved,"* Sarah Evans, Thinking Leader, Penn Wood Primary, Slough.

"Higher % of children achieving above national expectation in both key stages, " Rose Cope, Thinking School leader, Kingsdown and Ringwould Primary, Kent.

 Only one school reported that the approach did not raise attainment. It could be queried whether there were other additional factors influencing the issue with standards in this school, but further investigation would be needed to substantiate any such claim.

The schools were asked what evidence they had considered in making their decision regarding attainment in a range of areas. The table below (Table 3) records 87% of all accredited schools used feedback from pupil consultations and an even higher 93% in accredited primaries. This confirms that one key feature of a Thinking School is in place, i.e., schools in which pupil views are highly valued. It is also of significance that the schools have almost unanimously (100% in secondary schools and 93% in primary schools) made their decision in light of the quality of lessons. The approach clearly positively impacts teaching and learning.

There are also some interesting questions raised regarding the contrasts between primary and secondary practice. For example, 87% of primaries have considered pupil work when measuring attainment but only 40% of secondary. It would also appear that from our sample of accredited schools that teacher assessment and teacher tests carry more weight in primary schools when making decisions on attainment.

Table 3: Evidence considered to prove affect on attainment

	Public exams / SATs	Teacher tests	Teacher assess-ments	Pupil interview & cons.	Teacher research & feedback	Lesson obser-vation	Pupil work	Other
Primary (14)	78%	57%	87%	93%	57%	93%	87%	Atten-dance 14%
Secondary (10)	70%	30%	60%	80%	50%	100%	40%	
All accredited schools (24)	75%	46%	75%	87%	54%	96%	66.5%	Atten-dance 8%

Thinking Leaders were asked to comment on their findings regarding attainment and they are recorded in Table 4. The number recorded next to the comment denotes the number of leaders making this comment, for example, 5 primary leaders commented upon improved pupil independence as an impact of the Thinking School approach and this had supported raised attainment.

7

Table 4: Leaders' comments regarding attainment:

	Comments
Accredited Primary	Hard to be sure (3)
	Literacy-Writing exceptional (4)
	Pupils independent (5)
	Reflective (2)
	Teachers say yes
	Teaching improved
	Some outstanding
	Thinking & Learning ability
	Growth mindset
	Resilience
	Attitude
	Collaborative
	Steady improvement in exams over time
	Consistent results; Good effects
	Tools, transferrable skills
	KS1,2 result steadily improving
	Lower ability KS1 more engaged
	Higher % above expectations
	Positive on all types of assessment
	18% rise in T assessments
	Greater depth
Accredited Secondary	Hard to be sure (3)
	KS4 T Leaders performed better than peers in exams
	From 64% A-C 2010 to 81% a-c 2012
	Results improve with ability to use tools
	Write from Beginning
	Particularly IB
	Presentation skills improved
	Confidence
	Transferrable skills
	Problem solving
	Good indicators
	Special – Speaking & Listening

It is interesting to emphasise that schools have noted attainment improvements in specific areas. Wellington Primary in Hounslow saw a dramatic improvement in boys' reading, for example, *"We found a 37% increase in the boys' scores in the reading paper: it was phenomenal,"* Kuldip Kahlon, Deputy Head.

Lynne Finn, Headteacher at Beechwood Primary in Runcorn, also noted improvements in Literacy and more specifically in writing, *"By the end of Key Stage 2, although outcomes reveal a spiky profile due to our small numbers, we always exceed our target and many children achieve their challenge target in SATs. Ofsted recently described our achievement in Literacy as exceptional. We perceive one of the biggest impacts to be on writing standards. Data available should you require it."*

Rose Cope, Kingsdown and Ringwould Primary, states that raised standards are, *"Particularly noticeable in written work, with the use of thinking maps to build high quality pieces of writing. Structure and text*

Report on the Evaluation of the Impact of the Thinking School Approach, September 2013

8

organisation has improved at both key stages. In Numeracy the ability to "Use and Apply" has been improved through the introduction of Building Learning Power and Habits of Mind. Children are dramatically more resilient in their learning and keen to take risks, which has ensured the use of language has improved. In KS1 lower ability academic children have been more engaged in their learning and as such there has been an increase in them achieving 2Cs in Writing and Maths."

A large number of schools commented upon increased learner independence and changes in classroom culture not only impacting standards but also the way in which results are achieved.

"Our results in statutory examinations were always very good, so I don't feel that the Thinking for Learning programme has affected these. However, we used to achieve these results much more through a coaching approach, and felt students' independence was quite limited. Our T4L programme is slowly shifting the balance of responsibility from teacher to student and helping students to become more self-aware, independent learners. We introduced it from a qualitative rather than a quantitative perspective," Anna Jordan, Thinking Leader, Derby High School.

In Table 5 we see recorded responses to the question whether specific groups of pupils have been more noticeably affected in terms of attainment. The figures do not indicate, for example, that only 46% of accredited primaries thought that higher ability learners were helped by the Thinking School approach, but that 46% of these schools felt that higher ability learners were especially benefiting.

Table 5: Specific Groups especially supported by Thinking School approach

	Higher Ability	Lower Ability	Male	Female	Specific Age Group	Pupil Premium	Other
Accredited Primary 13 schools	46%	54%	54%	15%		15%	SEN 15%
Accredited Secondary 9 schools	44%	67%	33%	22%	44%		Visual Learners 11%
All Accredited 22 schools	45%	59%	45%	18%	18%	9%	SEN 9% Vis Ls 4.5%

One group commonly reported to be supported in improving their learning through the support of Thinking School strategies are lower ability pupils and pupils with special educational needs. Judith Stephenson, Thinking Leader from Barbara Priestman Academy, an accredited special school in Sunderland made the following comments:

"It is difficult to prove that the Thinking School approach has had effects on our results, but the external moderator for the Speaking and Listening part of English GCSE was extremely impressed with our students and how articulate they were and how they were able to reason and justify. Also in terms of students with Autistic Spectrum Disorder our students tend to be quite rigid in their way of thinking but the strategies we have put in place, especially the visual ones have helped them to see the curriculum as a whole and have helped them transfer skills from one area to another. The maps are very structured and they like that. As well as the tools from Thinking Schools we have also implemented Dramatic Enquiry across the school and the students really enjoy this. This has helped them with flexibility of thought and has helped them argue

 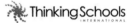

and debate in a structured but relevant way and they are beginning to see things from different people's perspectives, again something that the students with ASD find very difficult. Students have been interviewed about the various thinking tools and the impact they think they have had upon their learning."

An interesting project at Oakwood Park Grammar in Maidstone has also impacted on a specific group of pupils. The boy's school, with the support of Professor Burden from the University of Exeter, has developed a pilot qualification in Thinking Skills. Boys who took this qualification are now involved in activities around school as 'Student Thinking Leaders'.

Lynn Western, the Thinking Skills Co-ordinator at Oakwood Park, explains: *"The thinking skills qualification required the boys to research thinking skills, research the impact of thinking skills on their own learning, research the impact of thinking skills on others' learning and go into primary schools and teach. They had a lot of input into how the course developed which really built their confidence."*

Lynn Western also notes the impact on GCSE performance when these students, who were of mixed ability and from one particular form, sat their examinations last summer... *"When we analysed their GCSE results it looks like that particular cohort who took the thinking skills qualification actually have got much improved results over the rest of the year group."*

Evidence suggests that the depth of understanding of the Thinking School approach, their commitment, new responsibility and opportunity to teach others has had a significant impact on their attainment. Some of this group are now involved in supporting a new group working towards the qualification.

C. Thinking Schools International Strategies

The purpose of a further section of the survey was to gain feedback on the success of the programmes taught to schools by Thinking Schools International. The next tables detail the order that schools introduced the programmes. We can see from the data in Table 6 that the most popular starting point for accredited primaries has been Edward de Bono's Six Hats/CoRT skills. However, in secondary school the almost universal starting point has been David Hyerle's Thinking Maps. What this information doesn't include is whether these programmes were introduced by an external trainer, such as Thinking Schools International or whether the school put together their own training. Some schools will consider they have sufficient expertise or try to cut costs by leading their own training. The impact of the quality of training on successful classroom practice is another potential area for further research.

Tables 6, 7, 8: Order of Introduction

Primary Accredited Schools

Table 6	1st	2nd	3rd	4th	5th	Not used
Thinking Maps	4	11	1	0	0	1
Habits of Mind	4	1	4	3	3	2
P4C/C of E	1	2	3	3	4	3
6 Hats/CoRT	6	2	4	5	0	0
Questioning	1	1	4	5	3	1

Secondary Accredited Schools

Table 7	1st	2nd	3rd	4th	5th	Not used
Thinking Maps	9	0	0	0	0	1
Habits of Mind	1	3	0	2	0	4

10

P4C/ C of E	0	1	2	2	3	2
6 Hats/CoRT	0	2	4	3	0	1
Questioning	1	2	3	1	1	2

All Accredited Schools

Table 8	1st	2nd	3rd	4th	5th	Not used
Thinking Maps	13	11	1	0	0	2
Habits of Mind	5	4	4	5	3	6
P4C/ C of E	1	3	5	5	7	5
6 Hats/ Cort	6	4	8	8	0	1
Questioning	2	3	7	6	4	3

The order of introduction question was also included to examine the relationship of order to the satisfaction with the programmes and perceived importance of the programmes, which are recorded in Tables 9, 10 and 11. Although feedback is very positive on all programmes it appears that Philosophy for Children & Community of Enquiry are relatively lower in terms of satisfaction and importance. However, Table 8 reveals this area has tended to be introduced more recently, thus it could be an indication that the reason for a lower score in Tables 9, 10 and 11 is that these strategies are less embedded than others.

Tables 9, 10, 11: Average satisfaction and importance scores. 1 high / 5 low

Table 9: All 15 accredited primary schools	Satisfaction	Importance
Thinking Maps	1.2	1.3
Habits of Mind	1.8	1.5
Philosophy for Children / C of Enquiry	2.0	1.8
6 Hats / CoRT	1.6	1.6
Questioning	1.3	1.3

Table 10: All 10 accredited secondary schools	Satisfaction	Importance
Thinking Maps	1.25	1.8
Habits of Mind	1.6	1.7
Philosophy for Children / C of Enquiry	1.8	2.4
6 Hats / CoRT	1.4	1.7
Questioning	1.2	1.25

Table 11: All 25 accredited schools	Satisfaction	Importance
Thinking Maps	1.2	1.2
Habits of Mind	1.7	1.5
Philosophy for Children / C of Enquiry	1.9	2.0
6 Hats / CoRT	1.5	1.65
Questioning	1.25	1.2

The above tables reveal an overwhelming endorsement of all of these Thinking Schools International strategies by accredited schools who have been using many of them over a sustained period. A further investigation and study, not covered by the survey, could be made into how these strategies integrate effectively in the classroom.

11

D Evaluation Methods

School leaders were also asked for feedback on their use of evaluation strategies of the Thinking School approach and specifically on the use of Professor Burden's "Myself As A Learner Scale" or MALS.

Of the 22 accredited schools, 8 said they had used MALS and 3 non-accredited schools also reported that they used it. Of this total of 11 schools 8 were primary and 3 secondary schools. The 3 non-accredited schools have used MALS at the start of their journey and will look to use the scale again at a later point to identify change. At this point, then, they have no feedback to offer. The following findings were made by the 8 accredited schools: 1 school found a significant improvement in learner self-perception; 2 schools found a general improvement in learner self-perception; 3 schools found an increased self-awareness in learners.

But this indicates perhaps an issue with how to use the scale. Professor Burden points out that the scale is not intended as a simplistic measure of progress in terms of increased scores in self-perception as a learner through the completion of questionnaires by individuals sitting alone unaided. As one school discovered, the completion of the scale and its impact is improved greatly by discussion with an adult. Another school found MALS helpful in identifying issues of a lack of self-confidence with a significantly low scoring child and through a carefully considered support programme in partnership with the parents were able to address the causes of the issues. MALS used in discussion with an adult would be most suited to a school with an embedded coaching practice. Another school found a similar impact to the Maidstone project outlined previously, i.e., that the highest scorers on MALS had a lead role in the school: responsibility boosts self-confidence.

There is clearly a need for better understanding in how to use the scale. One secondary school abandoned the use of MALS, for example, as the starting results were too positive. One leader felt that the notes provided with MALS were too "academic" for teachers to access. Perhaps this identifies a need for the inclusion of the use of MALS and other methods of evaluation in initial Thinking School training. MALS would be more effectively used if the staff implementing the tool were properly trained. However, this would have time and cost implications. To aid progress Richard Coe at The Rochester Grammar has agreed to carry out extensive and systematic use of MALS.

Table 12: Levels of Satisfaction with Own Evaluation Methods

High   Low

	1	2	3	4	5
All accredited primary	14%	29%	43%	14%	0
All accredited secondary	25%	12.5%	50%	12.5%	0
All accredited schools	18%	23%	45.4%	13.6%	0

The point regarding training and support in evaluation methods is confirmed by the findings in Table 12 which reports on school satisfaction with their own evaluation methods. The results here are much less positive than any other part of the survey. A similar picture was found in non-accredited schools. 82% of the accredited schools, experienced in the Thinking School approach stated that they would welcome

12

support with evaluation strategies. Schools need to have a range of clear evaluation strategies in place when they embark on their learning journey.

E Major Benefits and Issues

The final section of this report will highlight the benefits and issues of the Thinking School approach highlighted by Thinking Leaders in the survey. Schools have not included *all* of their benefits or issues, but only those they perceive as "major". Table 13, below, reveals that the benefits schools have experienced far outweigh the issues. The number next to the benefit or issue indicates the number of schools making this comment.

Table 13: Major Benefits & Issues of Thinking School Approach

	Major Benefits	**Major Issues**
All accredited Schools 14 primary 8 secondary	-Whole school approach - Common language - Cohesion 10 - Independence 7 - Classroom improvements 5 - Curriculum delivery 5 - Parent support 4 - Ownership 5 - Links to other schools/ university 4 -Teacher motivation/ training / innovation 4 - Collaboration 4 - Creativity 4 - Confidence 4 - Enabling skills 3 - Enjoyment 2 - Attendance 2	- Training new staff/students 6 - Engaging all teachers 5 - Time 4 - Cost 3

A common problem for Thinking Schools is sustainability, hence the issue of the training of new staff. Larger schools are more likely to have accredited in-house trainers and the capacity to work alongside new colleagues. Unless new staff and students receive quality training, the whole school practice will be affected. One possible solution may be the development of a mutually supportive network of Thinking Schools who are willing and able to meet the training needs of the group, such as the existing group led by the Rochester Grammar. Alternatively it may be productive for Thinking Schools International to explore the demand for regional training courses for new staff. Maintaining the momentum of practice and the engagement of all staff is also part of the sustainability problem. Again schools in networks can support each other, sharing good practice. Some schools have had success in this area by offering fresh learning challenges to their staff and by providing opportunities for further study, qualifications and career development.

 An emphasis early in this report was on the impacts of the Thinking School approach on attainment, particularly reflected in public examinations. This is because exam results are a key factor in how school performance is judged, particularly in England. This will be a major influence on decisions schools make

13

regarding which teaching and learning strategies to employ, including thinking strategies. However, although public exams are limited in their demands on students to use higher-order thinking strategies, the evidence from the vast majority of accredited schools in the survey, 89%, points to the Thinking School approach supporting exam results.

In addition to attainment, Table 13 again demonstrates the wide ranging benefits of the Thinking School approach. It shows, for example, the massive endorsement of the whole school approach which introduces a common language for learners and cohesion to the work of the school. Sarah Evans, Penn Wood Primary, Slough notes the difference made to confidence and independence: *"Results are more evident in pupils becoming: more confident; being able to think outside the box; asking more questions; making connections in their learning; being able to reflect on their own learning more confidently; starting to know what their next steps should be; becoming more independent learners."*

Carolyn Evans, Headteacher at Rhydyppenau Primary in Cardiff, records the impact on attendance and collaboration, *"Specific benefits include a 50% reduction in absenteeism, also, children are definitely more confident in their learning, more autonomous and more creative in their approach to their work. As a result the school is in a stronger position to implement the Foundation phase, the Skills Framework and a more active curriculum within Key Stage 2. We have also noted improved transition as a result of collaborative work with the high school which implements the same thinking tools."*

Monnow Primary has also noted the effect on attendance and additionally on attitude. Meryl Echeverry writes, *"Attitudes to learning have changed, which has had a direct impact on pupils' attendance and behaviour. "*

Carol Lawrenson, Headteacher at Spinney Avenue, Widnes, also identifies independence as a benefit. Furthermore, she points to the benefits for governors and support of parents, *"Pupils are becoming very independent and interdependent. Their confidence has grown and they are very keen to make contributions to school life. They find learning fun and stimulating and like the way in which the curriculum offers opportunities for them to explore and demonstrate their learning in a variety of ways. Governors can see the benefits of the way in which we approach teaching and learning when they look at data and end of year results. Parents have commented that their children love coming to school and are excited about their learning."*

Rose Cope of Kingsdown and Ringwould Primary has also seen a positive response from parents, *"The parents have been pleased with the impact this has had on independence and a loss of the de-motivation that many of them saw! The children are keen learners who see everything as an obstacle worth engaging with or tackling."*

The last point made by Rose Cope is one that many leaders have made when interviewed, that a significant strength of the Thinking School approach is that learners' thinking, both staff and students, is purposeful and likely to lead to active improvements in the school.

Index

CORWIN

A SAGE Company

The Corwin logo—a raven striding across an open book—represents the union of courage and learning. Corwin is committed to improving education for all learners by publishing books and other professional development resources for those serving the field of PreK–12 education. By providing practical, hands-on materials, Corwin continues to carry out the promise of its motto: **"Helping Educators Do Their Work Better."**